HANDEL'S

MESSIAH

A CELEBRATION

Frontispiece: George Frideric Handel by Thomas Hudson, 1747
(*Staats-und Universitätsbibliothek, Hamburg*)

HANDEL'S
MESSIAH

A CELEBRATION

RICHARD LUCKETT

A HELEN AND KURT WOLFF BOOK

HARCOURT BRACE & COMPANY

New York   San Diego   London

Copyright © 1992 by Richard Luckett
First published in Great Britain 1992 by Victor Gollancz, Ltd.

All rights reserved. No part of this publication may
be reproduced or transmitted in any form or by any means,
electronic or mechanical, including photocopy, recording, or
any information storage and retrieval system, without
permission in writing from the publisher.

Requests for permission to make copies
of any part of the work should be mailed to:
Permissions Department,
Harcourt Brace & Company, 8th Floor,
Orlando, Florida 32887.

Library of Congress Cataloging-in-Publication Data
Luckett, Richard, 1945–
Handel's Messiah: a celebration/Richard Luckett.
p. cm.
Originally published: V. Gollancz, 1992.
"A Helen and Kurt Wolff book"
Includes bibliographical references and index.
ISBN 0-15-138437-1
1. Handel, George Frideric, 1685–1759. Messiah. I. Title.
ML410.H13L8   1993
782.23 — dc20   93-22069

Printed in the United States of America
First United States edition
A B C D E

Contents

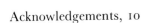

List of Illustrations

Acknowledgements

Since this book is a use of rather than a contribution to scholarship I have abstained from source-notes; those with more than a lay interest will be able to work out my authorities from the bibliography. But this cannot adequately express my indebtedness to the publications of the Handel scholars Robert Manson Myers, Otto Erich Deutsch, Jens Peter Larsen, H. Watkins Shaw, Winton Dean and Donald Burrows, or to those of the historian of music in eighteenth-century Ireland, Professor Brian Boydell, and the architectural and social historian of Dublin, Dr Maurice Craig. I regret that Donald Burrows's monograph on *Messiah* (Cambridge University Press) appeared when this book was too far advanced for me to be able to take account of it.

I am grateful to the late Gerald Coke for permission to quote from the Jennens-Holdsworth correspondence, and particular thanks are due to Kevin Barry for an invitation to Dublin which concentrated my interest in the background to the first performance, to Mary Coleman for practical help of all kinds, to Christopher Hogwood for the loan of materials and some useful leads, to Gerry Bye for handling a great deal of photography very quickly, to Margaret Jones, to Alec Cobbe for the portrait of his ancestor, to John Ward, RA, for kind permission to use his drawings from the 1966 Stour Music programme and to Richard Wigmore for his editorial patience.

Illustrations are reproduced by kind permission of the following owners: frontispiece, Staats-und Universitätsbibliothek, Hamburg; page 19, The Master and Fellows, Magdalene College, Cambridge; page 72, the Gerald Coke Collection; pages 75, 91, 98, 99, 103, 155, 177, 199, 211 and 234, Cambridge University Library; page 116, Alec Cobbe, Esq. (photo, Christopher Hurst); page 237, John Ward, RA; page 48, The National Gallery of Ireland. The reproductions of the *Messiah* autograph are from the Chrysander facsimile.

Introduction

THIS BOOK CELEBRATES THE 250TH ANNIVERSARY OF THE first performance of *Messiah*, which took place in the Fishamble Street Musick Hall, Dublin, at twelve noon on 13 April 1742. It had two performances. The next year it was given three performances in London; in the year after that, 1744, there was no London performance but it was given in both Dublin and Cork – but all of this is told in more detail later. The point is that there has never been a year since 1742 in which *Messiah* has not been performed, and after 1749 its popularity was to become unprecedented. Not only is it the cornerstone of the repertoire of classical music in the concert hall, but it played a vital part in establishing the concept of such a repertoire. Yet at no point has it been kept alive for historical reasons; indeed, as we shall see, almost the opposite has been the case.

Handel has had bad luck with anniversaries. The year of his birth was wrongly given on his memorial in Westminster Abbey. So also was the date of his death – not on the monument itself, but on the engraving of it in Charles Burney's *An Account of the Musical Performances . . . in Commemoration of Handel.* This is a record of the concerts given in Westminster Abbey and in the Pantheon, Oxford Street, to mark what was erroneously supposed to be the centenary of Handel's birth in 1784. Compounding the error, Burney believed that Handel had in fact died, not, as was the case, on 14 April 1759, but on the 13th. This would have been Good Friday, and Burney incorporated the supposition in his revised inscription for the memorial. It would also have been the anniversary of the first performance of *Messiah*.

As it happens, in his *Account*, Burney had painstakingly and correctly established the date of the first performance, which was wrongly given – by a year and a day – in John Mainwaring's *Life* of Handel, published a year after the composer's death. What was more, he firmly believed that Handel had died on Good Friday, having been told so by Dr Richard Warren, who had attended Handel on his deathbed. Warren had probably misremembered because Handel had expressed the *hope* that he might die on Good Friday; his parting was sufficiently protracted for the London press to anticipate the event and announce it on Maundy Thursday. But if Burney's supposition had been correct, we would have had one of those neat chronological echoes or, as they were known at the time, 'day-fatalities', that put Shakespeare's birth on the day (23 April) of his death, and Charles II's birth and restoration both on 29 May – as indeed they were.

If this is confusing, it at least serves as testimony to the natural human instinct to memorialise dates and the equally natural instinct to make neater patterns out of them – and much else besides – than strict accuracy will allow. No one seems to have paid much attention to 1842, perhaps because of the muddle which has been described, and in 1942 there was world-wide preoccupation with a state of affairs that can have done little to gladden the Prince of Peace. This did not prevent a scholar in Denmark from recalling the anniversary and, in marking it for his students, to set out on a course of discovery that would greatly assist future generations to establish exactly what metamorphoses *Messiah*, first played on a Tuesday in Holy Week in Dublin, had subsequently undergone.

Two hundred and fifty years is a quarter of a millennium and an eighth of the Christian epoch – a sufficient milestone. Anniversaries are a good occasion to tell stories about events and, as what has been recounted demonstrates, for improving the record. This can obviously mean one of two things; a recent bias has been in favour of getting the record right. That Handel made memorable observations in broken English is obviously true, but which of those attributed to him are genuine is another matter. But, whilst the passage of time has made this clearer than it once was, if only because of the example of artists such as Henry James, around whom similarly vivid anecdotes have gathered but whose lives are sufficiently well documented to enable us to sort out what they actually said from what we might have liked them to say, it is also the case that evidence of all kinds has been accreted and sifted. So the labours of Horatio Townsend in collecting information about Handel's stay in Dublin can now be supplemented and put into perspective not only by those of Otto Erich Deutsch but also of Brian Boydell; and our knowledge of each successive stage of *Messiah* as it was modified in Handel's lifetime, so strikingly clarified by Watkins Shaw, has now been carried further by Donald Burrows.

My aim has been to collect and digest this material as it relates to *Messiah*. So far as I know I have uncovered no new facts; at best I have put some things in a new conjunction. I have tried to avoid speculation. It is always hard to know the limits of reasonable inference, and there are points at which any student of both Handel and of the oratorio has to make deductions from imperfect evidence. Over the past twenty years the position in respect of *Messiah* has been transformed by the emergence of the correspondence between Edward Holdsworth and Charles Jennens, whose genius in assembling the words has always been obscured by his personal foibles. A sense of these is not diminished by the closer acquaintance to which this correspondence of Jennens with his most intimate friend affords us. It does, incidentally, give us an opportunity to admire the character of Holdsworth and to see why he was beloved by many besides Jennens. But I do not think that this is the end to all accessions of fact about *Messiah*; it seems inconceivable that something will not be discovered to cast light on the relationship between Handel and the 3rd Duke of Devonshire. This might enable us to establish for certain whether or not *Messiah* was specifically conceived for Dublin. I have dealt with this matter as best I can. My reading of what is known is that it was; if this is wrong, we have to postulate a combination of circumstances that was providential – a word which demonstrates how arguments about *Messiah* are constantly in danger of slipping into a metaphysical mode.

My endeavour has been to restrict myself to the concrete and particular, which is why buildings play a larger part in this account than they might ordinarily be expected to; it is comforting to have as a point of reference physical survivals from the time when *Messiah* was first conceived and performed; they make claims on our imagination which are both more assertive and less susceptible of misinterpretation than documentary evidence. Above all they provide a palpable presentation of the record of decay, restoration and re-creation. The buildings where *Messiah* was given its first performances in Oxford, Cambridge and New York still stand; only the Senate House in Cambridge is contemporaneous with Handel, but its architect, James Gibbs, was influenced by the Sheldonian Theatre in Oxford, and in turn had a strong influence on St Paul's Chapel in New York. Those who venture to Fishamble Street, Dublin, can see what remains of Neal's Musick Hall. That anything of it survives is amazing, and no doubt when the last trace of it has disappeared endeavours to preserve what ought to be a place of pilgrimage will come to fruition.

A speculation, which is as ghostly and as haunting as the Musick Hall, should be recorded here, though I cannot have been the first person to whom it has occurred. As the extraordinary character of Jennens comes more into focus (in particular I am referring to events in his later life which are outside the scope of this book), it begins to seem a bizarre possibility that he himself had a hand in fomenting the opposition to the performance of *Messiah* in London in 1743. At least, I do not think that anyone who has grappled with the tortuous workings of his mind would put it past him, and many of 'Philalethes' ' sentiments, in other circumstances, would have come naturally to Jennens.

I am an unrepentant admirer of the attempts that have been made, over the past forty years, to reinterpret *Messiah* musically in such a way that it will resemble, as closely as possible, something that Handel's audiences might have heard. That is why (apart from the intrinsic interest of the story) this book concentrates on what has now become apparent about the performances given in Handel's lifetime. We are not left with one *Messiah*, but with a plurality of *Messiahs*, which seem to me an entirely welcome thing, just as does the fact that there is often considerable and even radical disagreement as to what constitutes a proper manner of performance. But I have not dealt with the tendentious question of performance practice, because it would be absurd to try to do so, and because the most tendentious matter of the whole business is the fanaticism which has characterised debate about it. I have my prejudices, the principal one being that it is no longer helpful for an editor of *Messiah* to include a scintilla of interpretative 'assistance', except in the decent obscurity of notes. A minor prejudice, or perhaps a failure to comprehend, has to do with interpreters who believe that because a piece is written in a recognisable dance form it has to be played as though it were a dance. For all that, I have not the least objection to a *Messiah* that dances.

Perhaps all of this points to the danger of being solemn about *Messiah*. The really damaging things that have happened to it have been the sneers that in the twentieth century have prevented people from approaching it with an open mind. The cheapest is that it is 'bourgeois'. The cure for this is to contemplate the figure of the Earl of Sandwich, one of the moving spirits in the 1784 Commemoration of Handel, which had its climax in a notable *Messiah*. It is definitely not bourgeois to give jobs in a major department of state to friends whose chief qualification is that they are useful musicians, to keep not one mistress, but several, or, indeed, to play the kettle-drums. Nor is it bourgeois to make the major conceptual break-through in the field of fast food. As for the other, more damaging sneer, that *Messiah* is not religious, I can only say what I have said in my last chapter, and observe that I do not suppose that this is a matter that anybody for whom it signifies can possibly resolve except for themselves.

HANDEL'S

MESSIAH

A CELEBRATION

1: A Novel Entertainment

ON 22 AUGUST 1741 GEORGE FREDERIC HANDEL WAS IN HIS fifty-sixth year. For the last seventeen of these he had lived in London at no. 25 Brook Street; for the last fourteen he had been a naturalised citizen of Great Britain, and he had made England his home since 1713. His English was heavily accented, readily imitable, but, as much as German, the language of his first thoughts. His home was modest for the fashionable part of London in which it stood, convenient both for walking in the park and worship at St George's, Hanover Square. It accommodated his servant Peter Le Blond, a cook and one or two maids, and there was a room big enough to rehearse in. The better furniture, mostly walnut, was not in the latest taste; there were some good pictures. Such entertaining as he did was chiefly of colleagues in the musical profession; the little gossip that there was about his private life suggests that any liaisons he may have had were with singers, and were firmly in the past. In April 1737 he had suffered a stroke which had partially paralysed his right hand and left him less than clear-headed at a time when the circumstances of his career were particularly taxing. But he had made a remarkable recovery in the baths at Aix-la-Chapelle and his playing was quite unaffected.

His professional difficulties, however, had not become less. In 1738 he had had the unusual distinction of a statue erected to him (in Vauxhall Gardens) in his own lifetime. He received a Court pension and held the position of Composer of Musick for the Chapel Royal. His activities were a matter of considerable interest on the Continent; they had been recorded in brief in the first German dictionary of music, by Johann Gottfried Walther (1732), in the Stössel concise musical dictionary (1737), and, at length, by Handel's erstwhile friend, the Hamburg composer Johann Mattheson, in the *Ehrenpforte* (1740), a biographical roll of 148 eminent musicians. J. S. Bach is omitted from this because he had failed to reply to Mattheson's request not just for information, but for a detailed and well-planned essay, and in it Handel is grossly misrepresented for the same reasons. He had written over forty operas, five English oratorios, an Italian oratorio, two German passions, numerous sacred and secular choral works, four Te Deums and the dramatic masque *Acis and Galatea*, many cantatas and so much by way of 'hautbois concertos, sonatas, lessons and organ fugues', wrote Dr Burney, speaking of a brief period of his life only, 'that if he had never composed an opera, oratorio, Te Deum, duet, cantata or any other species of vocal music, his name would have been had in reverence by true Musicians, as long as the characters in which they are written, should continue to be legible'. Within the last eighteen months his Twelve Grand Concerti opus VI had appeared, a deliberate emulation of Corelli's great set bearing the same opus number, and proved so successful in rising to this challenge that they became the staple fare of concert rooms and pleasure gardens until the end of the century. No other composer in Europe had even half as much music in print as Handel, and though he received no royalties his copyright was secured to John Walsh junior for the next twelve years.

Yet Handel's position was precarious; it was certainly not as dire as some of his biographers, beginning with Burney, have claimed, but he lacked the security enjoyed by Bach at Leipzig or Telemann at Hamburg, though it is improbable that he could have tolerated the bureaucracy and constant interference by city and parochial councils to which they were subject, and even less likely that he could have endured the servitude, however grand, of Scarlatti in the Court at Madrid, or the restraints experienced by Rameau in the household of the Parisian tax farmer La Pouplinière. It is perhaps most instructive to compare Handel's situation with that of the architect James Gibbs – three years his senior, also a bachelor, and who lived a quarter of a mile away in Henrietta Street – whose buildings and their imitations shaped aspects of Georgian England visually as much as Handel's works did musically. Their paths had often crossed; when Handel was in Rome, much in demand as a composer and performer, in 1707 and 1708, Gibbs was studying architecture there under Fontana and Garroli, and acting as a guide and drawing master to the 'British nobility and gentry who came there to see the Antiquitys'. One of these was the future Earl of Egmont, and enthusiast for Handel, Sir John Percival. While Handel was in the employment of James Brydges (subsequently Duke of Chandos) at Cannons near Edgeware, Gibbs was working on the mansion and the church; in 1720 both men subscribed for copies of John Gay's *Poems on Several Occasions*; they both frequented Lord Oxford's home in Dover Street; and it seems in the nature of things that Gibbs later became as much a benefactor of Bart's as Handel was of the Foundling Hospital, and that Handel's

Gravelot inv.
The Words by Mr Lockman.

G.Bickham jun. Sc.
The Musick by Mr Gladwin.

Handel's statue in Vauxhall Gardens. Engraving by George Bickham after Hubert Gravelot, 1738. Handel's music was nationally popular as no other composer's was, even when his fortunes were at their lowest ebb.

Esther was performed at Oxford to celebrate the opening of Gibbs'
greatest building, the Radcliffe Camera. The essential difference i
that in 1741 Gibbs was able, in effect, to retire. Some of his projects
including much of the Radcliffe, were still in progress, his patter
books were in demand and he still undertook commissions, but h
does not seem actively to have sought them. He owned six house
bringing in £525 a year, and had an annual pension of £150. Hi
household was much the same as Handel's, and just as Handel ha
obligations to his principal amanuensis, John Christopher Smith, Gibb
had them to his draughtsman, John Birlach. When they died the tw
men left comparable sums of money (Gibbs about £17,500, Hande
about £20,000). But in 1741 Handel, although far from bankrupt, lacke
Gibbs's financial security; he had also, and this may have been th
decisive factor in his conduct, his *amour propre* to recover. Even so, his re
action to the long series of reverses which had culminated in the disma
1740–1 season at the Theatre Royal in Lincoln's Inn Fields was, a
reported by his friends, to go abroad, or, as he told Charles Jennens
who plays a vital part in this story, 'to do nothing next winter'.

The natural question is: how can Handel be simultaneously repre
sented as the most successful composer of his time and, as from 1728
the victim of a dwindling popularity? It has always been recognise
that Italian opera was at the root of this, and there has been muc
discussion of the finances of the opera, of the political allegiance
involved, of the cult of the castrato and the prima donna, and o
the advantages and disadvantages of Italian and English words. Th
problem was that all these matters were intertwined: London coul
readily support one Italian opera company, but never two; if the issu
had not become political the sensible arrangement might have pre
vailed, but once it was a matter of faction it was not a question jus
of rival companies but of rival composers and rival singers; singer
could never be bound to companies and might command audience
irrespective of politics, thus further confusing a complex situation; th
debate about Italian and English words might be political, or critical
or both. *The Beggar's Opera* was not so much a satire on Italian oper
as on its content; it was also a satire on the Prime Minister, Walpole
it was watched, apparently with pleasure, by royalty; it was widel
imitated and its imitations undoubtedly took away business from th
lyric stage. Two comments on the situation in the mid-1730s throw
further light. Lord Hervey, aptly described by Horace Walpole a
George II's 'Closet Secretary', reporting a political matter, the enmity

of Frederick, Prince of Wales, for his sister, the Princess Royal, on her
marriage to the Prince of Orange in 1734, says that it was because the
Princess supported Handel, who had frequently taught her singing,
that Frederick 'set himself at the head of the other opera to irritate
her' and continues:

> What I have related may seem a trifle, but though the cause was
> indeed such, the effects of it were no trifles. The King and Queen
> were as much in earnest upon this subject as their son and daughter,
> though they had the prudence to disguise it; or to endeavour to
> disguise it, a little more. They were both Handelists, and sat freezing
> constantly at his empty Haymarket Opera, whilst the Prince with
> all the chief of the nobility went as constantly to that of Lincoln's
> Inn Fields. The affair grew as serious as that of the Greens and the
> Blues under Justinian at Constantinople.

The following year we find Mrs Pendarves, a neighbour of Handel in
Brook Street, who had known and admired him since his first visit to
London, when she was ten, writing to another friend, Jonathan Swift,
the Dean of St Patrick's, Dublin, about the artistic side of things:

> Our Operas have given much cause of dissension; men and women
> have been deeply engaged; and no debate in the House of Commons
> has been urged with more warmth. The dispute of the composers
> and singers is carried to so great a height that it is much feared by
> all true lovers of music that the operas will be quite overturned. I
> own I think we make a very silly figure about it.

With this last sentiment Dr Swift would certainly have agreed, and
Mrs Pendarves was proved quite right: the opera was overthrown.
Lord Hervey, in an eyewitness account of Handel's behaviour in the
audience at an opera of Veracini's, *Adriano*, where he 'seemed in silent
triumph to insult this poor dying Opera in its agonies', summed matters up with an unsympathetic but revealing succinctness:

> That fellow having more sense, more skill, more judgement, and
> more expression in music than anybody, and being a greater fool
> in common articulation and in every action than Mrs. P——t or
> Bishop H——s, is what has astonished me a thousand times. . . .
> His fortune in music is not unlike Lord Bolingbroke's in politics.
> The one has tried both theatres as the other has tried both Courts.
> They have shone in both, and been ruined in both; whilst everyone

owns their genius and sees their faults, though nobody either pities their fortune or takes their part.

Modern writers, naturally enough, have sided with Handel, and he had friends at the time who felt that the public had been ungrateful, while even those who believed that he had brought many of his troubles on himself could be justly shocked, towards the end of his 1740–1 Lincoln's Inn Fields season, at 'the cruel persecution of those little vermin, who, taking Advantage of their displeasure, pull down even his Bills as fast as he has them pasted up; and use a thousand other little Arts to injure and distress him'. Nevertheless, there is a good deal to be said for Hervey's view, and a good deal to explain Handel's obstinacy. From his reported self-criticisms it is evident that he had that unusual gift, a just estimation of his own work. When he asked the Reverend Mr Fountayne for his opinion of a new piece while the band was playing in Marylebone Gardens, and his friend, oblivious of its authorship, turned to him and said, 'It is not worth listening to – it is very poor stuff', Handel replied, 'You are right, Mr Fountayne, it is very poor stuff; I thought so myself when I had finished it', and later in life he was as confident in preferring 'He saw the lovely youth' from *Theodora* to the Hallelujah chorus from *Messiah*. This firmness of judgement is not at all at odds with his willingness to alter, adapt and borrow, as circumstances required, things he could do the more readily because he had the ability to distance himself from his work. He knew, therefore, precisely what he had achieved in the field of Italian opera; whether *we* can do so at the end of the twentieth century is questionable. In one sense we know more about Handel's operas than any of his contemporaries except himself – we can refer to the scores and the sources in a way that they never could, and we have, despite the lacunae, a far fuller record of what was done than even Charles Burney, who knew the man, did – but knowledge is not necessarily understanding, and the cultural relativism and eclecticism which underlie many modern assumptions about time and place encourage us to regard as familiar something that is inherently alien. Contemporary admirers of *opera seria* were too busy enjoying it to explain themselves, so that most of what we learn about it in a critical way comes from those whose aim was either to reform, or laugh, it out of existence.

Its allies could be its worst enemies; in his *General History of Music* Burney has no hesitation in giving Handel's operas more detailed attention than he does to the work of any other composer in any

other category, yet he barely mentions the substance of a libretto, and
appears to regard the dramatic structure as no more than a kind of
manège within which the singers may curvet and arabesque. In so far as
his imagination is fired it is not to re-create the action or the *mise en scène*,
but the performance of those 'wonderful engines' Faustina and Cuzzoni.
Modern accounts of *opera seria* have by and large been apologetic, or
they have preferred minute analysis of matters of text or influence to an
approach which revealed anything in the way of *gusto*.

For that we must go to Stendhal, who hardly heard a note of Handel
in his life, who wrote eighty years after the composition of Handel's last
opera, and whose criticism is almost invariably as wrong in matters of
fact as it is right in questions of feeling. It is cast in the form of lives
of Rossini, Mozart, Haydn and the poet Metastasio, and the only
conceivable point of contact with Handel is that Handel did set three
libretti, by Metastasio, though probably without knowing the identity
of the author. But Stendhal's whole method was avowedly general; he
refused to refute sarcasm by increasing what he had to say on a subject
'which is in all probability *quite* dull enough already, by fifty pages of
parenthetical and explanatory clauses'. He wrote when his hero, Rossini, seemed to be abandoning what could be called the Metastasian
principle, in defence of that principle. He is not in the least abashed
to write of the librettist:

He banishes, as far as possible, everything which would remind us
of the melancholy reality of life. He employs the passions only so
far as they are necessary to interest us: nothing is stern or harsh;
his very dignity is voluptuous. Music, in which he delighted, and
for which he always wrote, though so powerful in expressing the
passions, is incapable of delineating character. Accordingly, in the
verses of Metastasio, the Roman and the Persian, touched by
the same passion, speak the same language, because they will do so
in the music of Cimarosa. In like manner, the virtues of patriotism,
devoted friendship, filial love, chivalrous honour, which are all to
be found in history or society, acquire with him an additional
charm. . . . Metastasio, in transporting us, for our gratification, so
far from real life, was under the necessity, in order that his characters might be interesting from their resemblances to ourselves, of
observing nature scrupulously in the details. In this respect he has
rivalled Shakespeare and Virgil, and has surpassed Racine and
every other poet.

Stendhal's fusillade of paradox and irony, deployed in defence of a noble anachronism which, for all its absurdity, attained to intensity, is the necessary disorientation for access to the world of Handel's operas. Stendhal's Metastasio is an idea rather than a historical figure, a personification of the ideology of *opera seria*. Technically, most of Handel's librettos are pre-Metastasian; even Stendhal's conception does not fully prepare one for the sheer vigour of the best of them, and though he stresses the significance of pride in the genre, Handel's depictions of hatred and envy may come as a surprise. The greatest – *Rinaldo* (1711), *Radamisto* (1720), *Giulio Cesare* (1724), *Rodelinda* (1725), *Ricardo Primo* (1727) and *Serse* (1738) – though they all have a clear (too clear, the enemies of *opera seria* would say) structural unity, are distinguished above all for the line of musical argument that runs through them. If they are properly and confidently performed, without cuts, without the interpretative intrusions of directors and designers more interested in their own imaginations than Handel's, with voices at their intended pitch, with – that most difficult thing – convincingly rendered recitative, we are as far from the traditional 'pearls on a string' conception of a sequence of *da capo* arias as can be.

Handel's perseverance with opera, in the face of the political difficulties and the vindictive squabbling within the companies, is, up to a point, comprehensible. *Opera seria* was the most prestigious, as well as by far the most risky, musical arena. It was prevalent throughout all Europe, with the exception of France, and commanded the attention of courts and kings. The great singers were paid fabulous sums. The great castrati had sacrificed their manhood (or their relatives had decided it should be sacrificed) for the remote chance of glory and riches. Just what that might imply is apparent from the career of Farinelli (Carlo Broschi), atypical in being of noble birth, as he was also in the benevolence of his character, but destined to become, by virtue of the beauty of his voice, the favourite of, and effectively the chief minister to Philip V, and then to Ferdinand VI, of Spain. Yet even he, in the internecine London operatic wars, had been reduced, according to Colley Cibber, to singing 'to an audience of five-and-thirty pounds'. The incalculable factor, of course, to which kings were as much subject as ambitious musicians and footmen in the gallery, was the irrational element, the pull of opera for its own ephemeral sake, the love affair that persists despite and because of the sweat and greasepaint, the squalls and squalor, the cliques and cabals, for the sake of that one shudder of the realised dream. The career of Vivaldi,

for example, can only be explained in these terms. Despite his inter-
national fame as a composer of instrumental music and violin virtuoso,
he refused to recognise, in Tartini's words, that 'a throat is no finger-
board' and devoted most of his energies, between 1713 and 1789, to
the composition and staging of forty-eight operas. Though they are
full of fine music, amongst the nineteen that survive there is no masterpiece to compare with those of Handel, but much evidence of self-
borrowing and little evidence of real integration of music and drama.
Vivaldi's surviving oratorio (he wrote two), *Juditha Triumphans*, to a
Latin text, is far more satisfactory than his operas. But he spurned the
safe though distinguished position of maestro at an *ospedale* and, seeking glory elsewhere, died destitute. It is also instructive to remember
that Telemann, who in 1722 took over the musical direction of the
Goose Market Opera at Hamburg, where, besides his own works, he
successfully produced a number of Handel's, abandoned the enterprise
after fifteen years, and that Rossini – admittedly working at a different
time and in other circumstances – found that thirty-nine operas were
enough.

Telemann could fall back on his civic and Church appointments,
and think of his operatic venture as a side-line; Handel had to find an
alternative field of activity. It is easy, in retrospect, to think of the
oratorio as a more radical departure than it in fact was. Of course, as
soon as Handel turned to oratorio as an alternative, the old polarity
of the rival operas could be restated as opera versus oratorio; and
oratorio was eventually to acquire an audience and atmosphere that
re-established the antithesis in different terms, moral rather than political. But in the 1730s Handel's change of course probably seemed
more natural to his well-wishers than it did to him. There was certainly
nothing strange about the concept of oratorio itself, although it was
Handel who had transformed it from being the term used for something familiar but foreign (something Evelyn had heard at Rome, or
that Samuel Pepys had acquired for his library) to a word that earned
its place in the 1738 edition of Chambers' *Cyclopaedia* and James
Grassineau's pioneering *Musical Dictionary* of 1740, dedicated to one of
Handel's royal pupils, as 'a sort of spiritual opera full of dialogues,
recitatives, duettos, trios, ritornellos, choruses, &c., the subject thereof
is usually taken from the scripture, or is the life and actions of some
saint, &c. The music for the *Oratorio* should be in the finest state, and
most chosen strains. The words hereof are often in *Latin*, sometimes
in *French* and *Italian*, and among us even in *English*. These *Oratorios* are

greatly used at *Rome* in time of *Lent*; here indeed they are used in no other season'.

Dictionary writing is an occupation that demands intelligence while simultaneously denying it, and Grassineau's 'even in *English*' is a touch of licensed irony: Grassineau was amanuensis to Johann Christoph Pepusch, who, despite his German birth, antiquarian knowledge and prejudices and the proficiency of his wife in Italian opera, had always supposed that the music theatre of his adopted country should employ its native tongue. As it happened, Pepusch had been in at the birth of English oratorio, since it was while he was Kapellmeister at Cannons that Handel composed for Brydges a masque on a sacred subject, *Haman and Mordechai*. It was performed (whether staged or not is unknown) probably some time in 1718. As in the case of its secular counterpart, *Acis and Galatea*, several writers are likely to have had a hand in the libretto, Alexander Pope being one of them. We do not hear of the work again until 1727 when 'favorite songs . . . in an Oratoria of Mr Handell's' were performed in a St Cecilia's Day concert at Bristol, and oddly the misspelling of the composer's name reappears in the diary of James Gibbs's friend, Viscount Percival, who was in the audience when Bernard Gates, a bass who had sung in Handel's 1713 *Birthday Ode* for Queen Anne and was now Master of the Children of the Chapel Royal, put on three performances at the Crown and Anchor tavern in the Strand, where a music club had met for many years. One performance was on 23 February, which was Handel's birthday, and Percival reported that 'this oratoria or religious opera is exceeding fine, and the company were highly pleased, some of the parts being well performed'. Gates's boys acted on a stage, while the non-acting chorus was placed between this and the orchestra, which consisted mostly of gentlemen amateurs. Its success prompted an unauthorised performance at what was then London's oldest concert room in York Buildings, Villiers Street, on 20 April. Handel responded by mounting the work himself at the King's Theatre in the Haymarket on Tuesday, 2 May, describing it as 'Esther, an Oratorio, In English. Formerly composed by Mr. *Handel*, and now revived by him, with several Additions, and to be performed by a great Number of the best Voices and Instruments'. The additions included items from *La Resurrezione*, Handel's only other attempt at oratorio, performed in Rome on Easter Sunday 1708.

Oratorio was native to Rome, with its origins in the musical entertainments which, in the sixteenth century, had formed an important

Vanloo pinx.^t   J. Faber fecit 1749

John James Heidegger Esqr

Sold by Faber at ye Golden Head in Bloomsbury Square

John James Heidegger. Mezzotint by Faber after Vanloo. The impresario whose masquerades (masked balls) at the King's Theatre in the Haymarket provoked the wrath of the Bishop of London. He let the theatre to Handel for oratorio in 1738.

part of Filippo Neri's unconventional evangelisation of Renaissance Rome, and taking its name from the community, the Oratory, which gathered around him. But the success of *Esther* showed that there was nothing alien about it in London. Its performance at the Haymarket had been requested by Princess Anne, and the King and Queen, the Prince of Wales and the three eldest princesses attended the first night. If Burney is to be believed, Handel had originally intended his *Esther* at the Haymarket to be acted, but Dr Gibson, Bishop of London, 'would not grant permission for its being represented on that stage, even with books in the children's hands'. Since Gibson was also Dean of the Chapel Royal he was doubly implicated, and Jonathan Swift's scruples about the involvement of his choristers in Handel's Dublin season of 1741–2 indicate that there was nothing extraordinary about the Bishop's concern. As it was, the absence of action would have been unlikely to disturb Englishmen, who were already thoroughly accustomed to long unstaged choral works, since these had for many years been a central feature of the annual celebrations for St Cecilia's Day, 22 November.

These had begun in London in 1683, were organised by a committee of professional musicians and gentlemen amateurs, and, at their most elaborate, consisted of a church service with much music and a sermon in its defence, a dinner (accompanied by music) and the performance of a specially written ode. All the major composers and poets of the day contributed, including Purcell, Blow, Dryden and Congreve. The celebrations were imitated in the provinces, and there were notable meetings at Oxford, Winchester, Wells, Salisbury, Bristol, Devizes, Lichfield, Lincoln, Stamford and elsewhere, including Dublin and Edinburgh. Although the London celebrations appear to have been interrupted around 1703 and the incidence of new odes is less frequent thereafter, this is partly because a repository had been created, and existing odes, such as Purcell's 1692 *Hail Bright Cecilia*, were revived. The occasion itself, a vital stage in the evolution of public concerts in England, continued to be observed; the Crown and Anchor Music Club, with whom Gates had given *Esther*, held an annual concert on 22 November at which, contrary to its regular practice, ladies and professional musicians were admitted, and, as we have seen, it was on that day that arias from the oratorio were given at Bristol. Over the years the odes had become increasingly long and called for more and more elaborate musical forces and effects; *Alexander's Feast*, Dryden's masterpiece, written for 1697 and set (the music is lost) by Jeremiah

Clarke, extended the scope of the ode form by recounting a story, but this innovation, though admired, was hard to imitate and the praise of music through illustration of its characteristic effects remained the standard pattern. The model was popular not merely for the specific occasion: when James Gibbs's magnificent new Senate House at Cambridge was opened on 6 July 1730 the music performed to mark the event was Maurice Greene's setting of Alexander Pope's *Ode on St Cecilia's Day*, originally written in 1708 and now adapted by the poet. The last section, in praise of Cecilia, is omitted, but otherwise the poem (with a certain amount of touching up – it is not Pope at his best) served very well. As it happened, a Cambridge man, John Taylor, a fellow of St John's College, had the duty of making the so-called Music Speech on that occasion, and had very reasonably supposed that his tasks included providing an ode also. His poem is not only better than Pope's, but in addition addresses itself directly to the memorable and important occasion. But the odd fact is that, such was the strength of the Cecilian tradition, it includes exactly what Pope took out, an allusion to the patroness of music:

> By holy Streams that deep-mouthed Organs blow,
> To whom the pious Use is giv'n
> To wing the silent glowing Voice,
> And waft the baptiz'd Saint to Heav'n.

A public so saturated with the cult of the ode to music was ripe for oratorio; indeed, the only person who seems not to have been was Handel himself. After the success of *Esther* at the Crown and Anchor a new member of the club, Brydges, now Duke of Chandos, was proposing that it put on another, newly composed by a protégé of his, William Defesch, who had recently been dismissed as Kapellmeister of Antwerp Cathedral after one of those rows which have been immutable for as long as artists have had to consort with clerics, and had come to seek his fortune in England. His *Judith* proved a success, in due course receiving public performances at Lincoln's Inn Fields, and being immortalised in a cartoon by Hogarth. Hogarth was a friend of the librettist William Higgins who, since he was involved with Gates in *Esther*, may have been behind Chandos's initiative with Defesch as well. It was presumably also the Crown and Anchor *Esther* that prompted Maurice Greene to compose a short but accomplished oratorio, *The Song of Deborah and Barak*, for his rival Society of Apollo that met at the Devil's Tavern near Temple Bar. So it is not surprising that on 6 May 1732, we find Viscount Percival jotting in his diary: 'In the evening went to Hendel's oratorio'. Not only was the royal family there and the house crowded, but since the Viscount had contrived to spell oratorio correctly it might reasonably be said to have arrived.

Nevertheless, for Handel it was a recourse, something he was driven into by operatic failures, but which he failed to take seriously. In March and April 1733 he presented a new work, *Deborah*, and revised *Esther*. *Deborah* used nearly a hundred performers and a great deal of Handel's earlier choral music; the libretto was indifferent. Mr Winton Dean believes that Greene's *Deborah and Barak* of the previous year is 'words and music together . . . a better work'. Even so, Handel's was more liked by most of its hearers than by Lady Irwin who considered ''tis excessive noisy, a vast number of instruments and voices, who all perform at a time, and is in music what I fancy a French ordinary in conversation'. But Handel overplayed his hand, apparently influenced by the Princess Royal's enthusiasm, and doubled his prices for the first night, which was put outside the normal subscription. Though this practice subsequently became standard, it caused great offence, particularly to the subscribers, whose good will was of obvious importance. He did not make the same mistake when in July he went to Oxford and, in the Sheldonian, where a Latin poem in praise of Handel and oratorio was read, 'shew'd away with his *Esther*, an Oratorio, or sacred Drama, to a very numerous audience, at 5 shillings a ticket' and, a few days later, offered 'a spick and span new Oratorio called *Athalia*', concluding the season with *Deborah*. Undergraduates were alleged to have pawned their furniture to attend, and Handel certainly left Oxford much better off than he had entered it. News of his success travelled as far as Paris, reported by the Abbé Prévost, author of *Manon Lescaut*, who was at that time taking refuge in England from his enemies and creditors; he explains what an oratorio is, notes Handel's part in introducing it, and remarks that 'Although the subject is taken from Scripture, the audiences are no smaller than at the Opera'. A gentleman of Cambridge, inflamed by the oratorio, addressed a poem to Mr Handel in the conviction that 'I raise my Voice, but you can raise it higher.' Moreover, it was at Oxford, if not earlier in the year in London, that Handel introduced the practice of performing his organ concerti between the acts of an oratorio.

1733 was thus something of an *annus mirabilis* for English oratorio, even though the conflict between the opera and the oratorio, and the way in which oratorio could be seen as conveniently masking the

As e Soldi pinxit.   F. Morellon le Cave Sculpsit.1751.

Wm Defesch.

William Defesch. Engraving by le Cave after Andrea Soldi. Defesch's oratorio *Judith*, performed in 1733, was an immediate and popular attempt to
imitate the success of *Esther*.

pleasurable with a gauze of piety, were gifts to the satirists – and they did not lose their opportunity. Indeed, the only person who did was Handel himself, who for a further seven years continued to pick at the form. His heart was still apparently in opera (and opera in increasingly desperate straits), while the half-way house of masque, entertainments embellished with scenes but not action, remained another possibility. But Handel's creative processes cannot be accounted for in a cut-and-dried way. He had great surges of inspired activity, during which he seems to have had no difficulty in working on two or more projects simultaneously; there were periods when apparently he had no occasion or motivation to compose at all, and periods when, it seems, original composition was impossible and borrowing, whether from himself or others, the only means of meeting his obligations. The borrowings, naturally enough, have caused a great deal of comment and speculation, not often constructive and seldom generous enough to admit how frequently he took other men's bricks and left them marble. What is incontrovertible is the information they give us about Handel's mental habits, an extension almost *ad infinitum* of his capacity to keep several things in his mind and in progress at once, and to annihilate ordinary concepts of time. His whole life's experience of music appears to have been constantly available to him, there to be summoned to his aid as required. This is particularly evident in the composition of the Twelve Grand Concerti, completed in a month during 1739, and, as has been noted, achieving an immediate and lasting popularity. Handel had written numerous concerti during his career, and they had always been successful, yet he had only published them in a haphazard way. However excellent individually, they do not approach the concentrated vigour of the Twelve, which are, in the sense of the word as Dr Johnson applied it in criticism, perspicuous: they can be seen as a completed whole. Why did Handel not compose them a decade or so earlier? He had written other concerti individually as good as those of opus VI; though some of the borrowings in the concerti (notably from Scarlatti) are very recent, some are from music Handel had known for years. It seems to have been a combination of external circumstances that finally prompted him to gather up his resources and give expression to them in this way – flagging support for his other ventures, the success of his organ concerti, a month free before rehearsals had to start for the opening of the winter season.

Tardy opportunism is not an easy thing to dignify, though Dryden had a good try when he wrote (of a political, not artistic event):

'Twas not the hasty product of a day,
But the well ripened fruit of wise delay.

In 1734 Handel contented himself with revising *Deborah*. In 1735 he once more ran his whole stable, *Esther*, *Deborah* and *Athalia* and embellished them with organ concerti. Seated at the instrument which provided continuo support for the choruses in the oratorios, he supplied, through his meditative preludes that, says Hawkins, 'stole on the ear in a slow and solemn progression: the harmony close wrought, and as full as could possibly be expressed; the passages concatenated with stupendous art, the whole at the same time being perfectly intelligible, and carrying the appearance of great simplicity' and then sprang into 'the concerto itself, which he executed with a degree of spirit and firmness that no one ever pretended to equal', the element of spontaneous virtuosity that, though it was never entirely absent from oratorio in Handel's lifetime, could not compare, when a singer was restricted by the necessity to hold a score and stand in a set place, with the heady freedom of the operatic stage. The most important creative initiative of 1735, however, was not that of Handel, but of Charles Jennens, who sent the composer a package which he acknowledged from London on 28 July:

Sr/
    I received your very agreeable Letter with the inclosed Oratorio. I am just going to Tunbridge, yet what I could read of it in haste, gave me a great deal of Satisfaction. I shall have more leisure time there to read it with all the Attention it deserves. There is no certainty of any Scheme for next Season, but it is probable that some thing or other may be done, of which I shall take the Liberty to give you notice, being extreamly obliged to you for the generous Concern you show upon this account. The Opera of Alcina is a writing out and shall be sent according to your Direktion, it is allways a great Pleasure to me if I have an opportunity to show the sincere Respect with which I have the Honour to be
    Sir
    Your
    Most obedient humble
    Servant
    George Frederic Handel

'Tunbridge' was Tunbridge Wells, where the curative properties of the spring had been renowned for eighty years; the 'Oratorio' was presumably that of *Saul*. In this case it would not engage Handel's attentions for another three years, but, even if it was (which seems most improbable) a text subsequently ignored by Handel and consigned to oblivion by Jennens, it was nevertheless the voice in the wilderness which heralded *Messiah*.

1736 saw a new composition, but to an old text. Dryden's *Alexander's Feast* had been, in poetic terms, the climax of the English Cecilian tradition, but neither its original setting, by Jeremiah Clarke, nor the second, by Thomas Clayton, in 1711, had been published, and neither survives today. The Clarke would have been competent, but this is hardly likely to have been true of the Clayton. Dryden's poem was 'adapted' for music by Newburgh Hamilton, who, like Jennens, progressed from being a subscriber to Handel's publications to becoming a personal friend. Like Jennens, also, he was firmly of the opinion that he had a clearer view of the composer's best interests than Handel himself, remarking in his preface that not only could his compositions 'conquer even the most obstinate Partiality' but also 'inspire Life into the most senseless Words'. Percival, now Earl of Egmont, recorded in his diary on 19 February that he 'went to Mr Hendel's entertainment, who has set Dryden's famous Ode on the Cecilia's Feast to very fine music'; he was right in designating it an ode but, as has been suggested, *Alexander's Feast* is where the ode comes nearest to oratorio, and it can be said to mark the point at which the tradition of the Cecilian celebrations and their offspring, and the tradition of English oratorio, declared their common kinship.

Alexander's Feast is not a true oratorio, for two reasons. An ode conventionally deals in abstractions or allegories (in this case of the passions), coming to a didactic conclusion which is the sum of its parts (in this case the power of music in its most elevated, sacred form); an oratorio tells a sacred story, and though its conclusions may be secularised, the story is its own point. The distinction is particularly evident in the case of the function of the chorus, which in an ode serves essentially as a refrain, a restating of the burden of what has gone before, but in an oratorio is either an extension of the action (where the chorus is a collective personage in its own right, for example, the Israelites in *Saul*) or a commentary on it, though even so in a collective character. The choruses in *Alexander's Feast*, for all their dramatic power, confirm it as an ode. But it should be noted that while it is absurd to call *Messiah* anything other than an oratorio – and Handel was quite clear as to its designation – its choruses have, more than in any other work of its kind, an affinity with what we would expect in an ode. The performance attended by Egmont moved the *London Daily Post* to euphoria:

> Last Night his Royal Highness the Duke and her Royal Highness the Princess Amelia were at the Theatre Royal in Covent Garden, to hear Mr. Dryden's Ode, set to musick by Mr. Handel. Never was upon the like Occasion so numerous and splendid an Audience at any Theatre in London, there being at least 1300 Persons present; and it is judg'd that the Receipt of the House could not amount to less than 450l.

The soprano part was sung by Signora Strada, one of the greatest of Handel's opera singers, soon to leave England; the tenor by John Beard, a new name, destined to become one of Handel's greatest oratorio singers. There was, however, a feeling that the performers were too far from the audience, a defect that was remedied on the 28th by flooring in the pit so that the stage and the first tier of boxes were on a level, and the orchestra 'play'd in a Manner more commodious to the Audience'. The new forms were suggesting a new arrangement adjusted to them; and when *Acis and Galatea* was given on 24 March, the announcement that 'There will be no Action on the stage, but the scene will represent a Rural Prospect of Rocks, Grottos, &c. amongst which will be dispos'd a Chorus of Nymphs and Shepherds' seems unnecessary now, unless we are to understand *Acis* as a piece that had lost its footing, once thought too undramatic to be an opera, now considered too operatic to be an oratorio or ode.

Whatever its long-term causes, there can be no doubt that the stroke Handel suffered in April 1737 was brought on by the stresses of an oratorio season which he had never intended to give and was the consequence of a ban on operas in Lent, which Handel had evidently not anticipated. As a result he was forced to revise his Roman oratorio of c. 1707, *Il Trionfo del Tempo e della Verità*, a performance of which (as of *Alexander's Feast* and *Esther*) was allowed during Passion Week by special licence – an accidentally ecumenical gesture since the words were by Cardinal Pamfili. It was sung in Italian which, as with the semi-staging of *Acis and Galatea*, seems yet another indication that the rationale of oratorio, clear as it may seem in retrospect, was far from obvious at the time. But it is also the case that there was no time for

Henry Carey. Mezzotint after Worsdale. Librettist of the immensely popular *The Dragon of Wantley* and other light-hearted skits on Italian opera.

even Samuel Humphreys to run up a singing translation, and the English word-book that did appear shows clear signs of being produced in haste. Since Handel was again to revive *Il Trionfo del Tempo* in 1757, this time in English, and with additional though not original music, he must have thought highly of it, but it is hard to see why. In editing his 1707 score Handel cut some of the more mannered chromaticisms, presumably in the interests of blandness: that chromaticism could still play an essential part in his musical vocabulary, however, is made abundantly clear in *Saul*.

The nuns of Aix, we are told by Handel's first biographer, on hearing Handel play the organ only a few hours after having subjected himself to a spell in the vapour baths almost three times longer than was normal, considered his recovery from partial paralysis miraculous. It is tempting to extend their diagnosis to a full-scale conversion to oratorio, but nothing quite so neat occurred. The winter of 1737 saw the opening of *The Dragon of Wantley*, a gloriously anarchic burlesque which contrives to send up even its own form since it is not merely a ballad opera but an opera based on a ballad; it was printed with the libretto *Cum Notiis variorum*. The author, Henry Carey, himself an able musician, continued the joke by dedicating the result to the composer John-Frederick Lampe, who had first suggested the squib, recalling the 'joyous Hours' they had spent endeavouring 'to display in *English* the Beauty of Nonsense, so prevailing in the *Italian Operas*' and congratulating himself on the complaint of 'the Morose, the Supercilious, and Asinine' part of mankind that it was 'low, very low' since 'Lowness (figuratively speaking) is the Sublimity of Burlesque: If so, *this Opera* is, consequently, the tip-top Sublime of its Kind'. It repeatedly reflects on Handel; the Dragon itself parodies the sea-monster in *Giustino*, the opera which Handel had brought out in February, and the part was taken by Henry Reinhold, who had sung for Handel in opera, and would do so again in oratorio. But there were equally pointed jibes at the expense of the nobility, and though the production was full of topical touches the satire was general, the more intelligent opera lovers were greatly amused, and Handel, with good reason, thought well of Lampe's music. What he might understandably have resented was the clear directive contained in the conclusion of the opera. The Hero, Moore of Moor Hall, has killed the Dragon 'by a kick on the back-side', in recognition of which feat Gaffer Gubbins permits him to wed his daughter:

Most mighty *Moore*, what wonders hast thou done?
Destroyed the Dragon, and my Marg'ry won.
The Loves of this brave Knight, and my fair Daughter,
In *Roratorios* shall be sung hereafter.

The final chorus begins the process:

Sing, sing, and roario
An *Oratorio*
To gallant *Morio* . . .

But Handel was to stage four new operas – *Faramondo* (1738), *Serse* and *Giove in Argo* (1739), and *Deidamia* (1741) – before he accepted Carey's helpful indication as to where the future lay. In March 1738, severely pressed to pay his singers for the season that had just ended, he was persuaded by friends to test the gratitude of his public with a benefit concert, calling the hotch-potch of favourite arias, a drastically pruned *Deborah* and *Zadok the Priest*, an 'Oratorio'. This it certainly was not, although it was attended by well over a thousand people, was much appreciated, and made Handel a satisfactory and much-needed sum of money.

The title of oratorio could not, however, be denied the work upon which he embarked on 23 July 1738 – the setting of *Saul*, which is presumably the libretto sent him by Jennens in 1735. Here for the first time Handel had a thoughtful and well-written text constructed with real dramatic flair. The process of composition was far from straight-forward and at least twice he was misled into attempting musical solutions to his problems which did not take account of the dramatic situation, saw the error of his ways (in one instance they were pointed out by Jennens, who visited him while the work was still in progress) and had to start the relevant sections again from scratch. That his mind had most seriously turned to oratorio is also confirmed by evidence of a quite different kind. Jennens, reporting on his visit to Lord Guernsey, a cousin, told him that Handel had ordered from Jonathan Morse of Barnet an organ 'so constructed that as he sits at it he has a better command of his performers than he used to have, and he is highly delighted to think with what exactness his Oratorio will be performed by the help of this organ; so that for the future instead of beating time at his oratorios, he is to sit at the organ all the time with his back to the Audience'. Jennens made a joke of this prodigal expenditure when Handel was financially beleaguered – very inappropriately, because the fact the composer was taking oratorio so seriously would have, in due course, significant and gratifying consequences for Jennens. Not the least part of Handel's eventual success with oratorio was the way in which he established a ritual for his performances, the running-in of the pit to the boxes, the disposition of the stage, his own entry preceded by a valet with candles for the music-desk at the organ. Nor did the fact that Handel's back was to the audience preclude him from communicating his emotion to them; for those who knew how to read the signs, his satisfaction or otherwise could be deduced from whether there was, or was not, a just perceptible tremor to his wig.

Saul opened on 16 January 1739 at the Haymarket and received five more performances that season. The *London Daily Post* maintained that it was 'met with general Applause by a numerous and splendid Audience', and there is no reason to doubt this, though another revival of *Alexander's Feast* was as widely noticed, both in the press and in private correspondence. On 20 March Handel gave it (very appropriately) as a benefit for the newly founded Fund for the Support of Decay'd Musicians and their Families. Performing music for a charitable object was not new; the annual meeting of the Sons of the Clergy had had grand church music as its main attraction for many years, but a secular concert for an institution rather than an individual was a novelty. It became an annual event.

Saul is a tragedy full of incident and violence, which offers points of comparison with *King Lear* and *Macbeth*; *Lear* for Saul's madness, *Macbeth* for Saul's commission of a series of crimes that leads him to lucidity, desperation and an ignominious death. It begins with a song of triumph and ends with an elegy. The only elements that have significance for the Christian revelation are the truth of prophecy exemplified in Samuel, and the hope of Jewish survival expressed in the conclusion, and embodied in David. Both Samuel, called back to earth by the Witch of Endor, and David, who orders the execution of the Amalekite who brings him the news of Saul's bungled suicide, are devoid of mercy. Any pity that we might feel for Saul is neutralised by his ferocious vindictiveness until the last act. No one could pretend that it is in any way an edifying story. The action, of which there is a great deal, is improbable when transferred to a stage. Saul, who is the point of the whole oratorio, emerges almost entirely through recitative; indeed, the proportion of recitative to arias (just three) in his part would have been quite unacceptable in opera. And if Saul is the hero of the oratorio, he is so in the same way that Satan is the hero of

Paradise Lost. The turmoil evident in the manuscripts, the discarded sections, the scorings-out, the rewritings which have scratched their way through the paper, is famous. What holds all this emotional incoherence together is the presence of the chorus and of the leading tonalities with which it is associated. The chorus is, as Winton Dean says, a character as important in the oratorio as the King himself, immediately involved with the action at every point, and actually, through its glorification of David after he kills Goliath, thereby inciting Saul to envy, precipitating it. It is only if we empathise with the Israelite's fortunes that we can see, by the end of the oratorio, the significance of the story: it is about a hope for Israel. The scoring of *Saul* is elaborate and unusual throughout; and the carillon which illustrates not Saul's madness, as Jennens had thought, but Israelite jubilation, proved a great popular success.

The second new oratorio brought out by Handel early in 1739, *Israel in Egypt*, was only successful in arousing controversy. It is a choral work with just four arias. The librettist is unknown; it might have been Jennens (though contemporary hearsay pointed to Handel himself), but if so, he chose not to paraphrase and expand the biblical story in blank verse as he had, to notable effect, in *Saul*, but took his words from scripture verbatim. This invited trouble. Church music itself had been under continuous if ineffectual attack since the reinstitution of the cathedral choirs at the Restoration; at the various Cecilian celebrations there were usually sermons in defence of the art. A particular object of the campaign against indecency on the stage, which had crystallised at the turn of the century and never let up since, had been 'blasphemy', which included both the citation of the scriptures in plays, and the satirical representation of the clergy. There were many churchgoers whose principles or whose pastors forbade them from attending the playhouse. The Licencer of Plays was as sensitive to religious as to political transgressions, and the day after the first performance of *Israel in Egypt* on 4 April the *London Evening Post* congratulated the 'Patrons and Lovers of Musick' on the 'Miracle' that Handel had worked in obtaining a permit for the performance. When the oratorio was next given, a week later, it was for artistic reasons 'shortened' and for opportunistic ones 'intermix'd with songs'. In a letter to the *Evening Post* an anonymous writer who was present deplored the smallness of the audience, but praised the sublimity of the words. An additional and more successful performance followed on 17 April, which elicited another much longer letter by a further correspondent, again praising the words, but urging the audience to 'have a Truce with Dissipation, and noisy Discourse, and to forbear that silly Affectation of beating Time aloud on such an Occasion', particularly in view of the sanctity of the words. The writer also alludes to the 'stupid, senseless *Exceptions* that have been taken to so truly Religious Representations, as *this*, in particular, and the other *Oratorios* are, from the *Place* they are *exhibited* in'. It is the longest piece of writing to have been provoked by any of Handel's works up to this point in his career and it was thought important enough to be reprinted in advance of the revival of *Israel in Egypt* the following year; yet it is essentially a defence of the propriety of what Handel was doing, and an indication of the strength of the opposition. What it recommends so far as the deportment of the audience is concerned is mostly good manners, but modern commentators have been irked by its defence of the seriousness of Handel's intentions.

The winter season of 1739–40 opened on 22 November with a new ode for St Cecilia, whose day it was, a setting of Dryden's poem originally written for 1687. A shortened version of *Alexander's Feast* preceded it and two Concerti Grossi, together with an organ concerto, were also given. It thus neatly symbolised the contribution of the English Cecilian odes to the more extensive and varied forms that, in part, grew out of them. It was a winter of bitter weather and the management had to take special precautions to keep the auditorium heated but not fuggy, and to prevent the poor and homeless from coming into the passages of the theatre to stay warm. Handel's one work 'Never perform'd before' was *L'Allegro, il Penseroso ed il Moderato*. In order to make a synthesis out of John Milton's original thesis and antithesis of exuberance and melancholy, Handel requested Jennens to write these 'two independent poems in one Moral Design'. Jennens set to and did a very adequate job, at least as adequate as that by the Reverend Mr Dalton when he converted *Comus* into a workable stage masque for Arne. Both men have attracted the inevitable modern criticisms, and as Jennens himself reported to his friend Edward Holdsworth, his effort fell foul of the sharp-tongued at the time: 'I overheard one in the Theatre saying it was Moderato indeed, & the Wits at Tom's Coffee House honour'd it with the Name of Moderatissimo . . .'. It is significant that Handel suggested the plan; perhaps the ideal of moderation to the instincts caused him to value *Il Trionfo del Tempo*, and here he found an adequate musical equivalent for them. It is a long way from the vortex of *Saul*, and as far again from the solemnities of *Israel in Egypt*; it was also instantly popular, and Handel needed success. He had been wise in not venturing an opera; Burney, describing his rivals' efforts, paints their difficulties vividly:

> The opera, a tawdry, expensive and imperious lady, who had been accustomed to high keeping, was now reduced to a very humble state, and unable to support her former extravagance. Instead of the sumptuous palace which she used to inhabit, she was driven to a *small house* [The New Theatre in the Haymarket], in the neighbourhood of her former splendid mansion, where her establishment was not only diminished, but her servants reduced to half-pay.

These economies only made the lady even less attractive, and two of the three works given were pasticcios.

Something potentially more interesting was happening at Hickford's Rooms, a concert hall in Brewer Street, for which J. C. Smith, a pupil of Handel's and the son of his amanuensis and aide, had composed an English opera, *Rosalinda*. This did not amount to much, being less than full-length and minimally staged, but it did achieve several performances (the music is lost). The libretto was by John Lockman, the 'poet of the gardens' who supplied innumerable Vauxhall lyrics, combining this with the Secretaryship of the British Herring Fishery and miscellaneous writing. He had written an oratorio, *David's Lamentation over Saul and Jonathan*, which was set by both William Boyce and J. C. Smith, and also an exceedingly ambitious Cecilian ode, set by Boyce. To *Rosalinda* he prefixed an essay on *The Rise and Progress of Operas and Oratorios*, and another on the effects of *Operas, Lyric Poetry, Music, &c*. Neither essay is profound, but they are lively and an involuntary testimony to oratorio as a major aspect of musical life, even though Lockman sees the fact that oratorios are performed in the theatre as setting a limit to their 'solemnity' and – a word that will come to have a particular significance for *Messiah* – 'sublimity'. The composer's own revivals of *Saul*, *Esther* and *Israel in Egypt* kept oratorio in the public eye; the Academy of Ancient Music under Dr Pepusch, at the Crown and Anchor Tavern, also performed *Saul*. But that autumn Handel once more turned to the composition of opera, completing *Imeneo*, which he had begun two years earlier and laid aside, on 10 October, and *Deidamia*, to a text by Rolli, on the 27th; they are both studiously lightweight works, *Imeneo* not claiming to be more than an 'operetta' or, when Handel revived it without action in Dublin, a 'serenata'.

Paolo Rolli. Mezzotint by Vandergucht. Rolli was the librettist of several of Handel's operas, including his last, *Deidamia*. His letters are full of malicious gossip about the 'Saxon bear'.

Deidamia was remarkable for the amount of chorus work involved, which is why, in 1955, it became the first Handel opera to be revived on the London stage, having been the last to appear on it under the composer's direction (the last in any form was a mutilated *Giulio Cesare*, staged at George III's request in 1787). *Imeneo* ran for two nights. *Deidamia* went one better, closing on 10 February 1741, and was not published until after it had closed – John Walsh failed to raise a subscribers' list, despite publishing the first act as a specimen.

Handel's operatic days were over. Baron von Bielfeld, a Prussian diplomat, who did not write letters without a thought for their future publication, summed up the matter to a Berlin friend:

> During my first voyage to London, in the year 1736, I found two Italian opera companies. . . . The eminent skill of the composers, the extraordinary quality of the voices, the rivalry in performances – all this made London then the centre of the musical world. But today [7 February 1741] it seems that Europe has abandoned the shores of Albion and we have nothing left but the *Oratorio*, that is, a kind of sacred concert, which Mr. Hendel occasionally puts on.

A more confessional note was struck by 'J. B.' in the *London Daily Post* of 4 April, urging attendance at Handel's last oratorio concert of the season, advertised for 6 April:

> He has charmed me from my Childhood to this Day, and as I have been so long his Debtor for one of the greatest Joys our Nature is capable of, I thought it a Duty incumbent upon me at this Time, when it is become a Fashion to neglect him . . . to recommend him to the public Love and Gratitude of this great City, who have, with me, so long enjoyed the Harmony of his Composition. *Cotsoni* [Cuzzoni], *Faustina*, *Cenosini* and *Farinelli*, have charmed our Ears: We ran mad after them, and entered into Parties for the one or the other with as much vehemence as if the State had been at Stake. Their Voice indeed was grateful to the Ear; but it was *Handel* gave the persuasion. . . . His influence prevail'd, tho' his Power was invisible; and the Singer had the Praise and the Profit, whilst the Merit, unobserved, and almost unrewarded, was the poor, but the proud Lot of the forgotten Master.

It was not an analysis which would have displeased Handel, even if it is only a part of the story.

Some time late in 1741 Alexander Pope began entirely to overhaul his poem *The Dunciad*, first published in 1728. He began by writing a completely new conclusion, Book IV, which has been admired ever since, even by those who have found the three preceding books excessively topical. It tells how the Empress Dullness, aided by all the enemies of art, comes to reign omnipotent over England. Pope had no love for music, and never owned to any involvement in either *Acis and Galatea* or *Esther*. Here he took Handel to illustrate his case. In doing so he had to treat the composer's lifelong commitment to opera as an aberration, since for Pope Italian opera was the means by which Dullness lulled the intellect to sleep, but oratorio was another matter; so, too, were large orchestral forces:

> But soon, ah soon Rebellion will commence.
> If Music meanly borrows aid from Sense:
> Strong in new Arms, lo! Great Handel stands,
> Like bold Briareus, with a hundred hands . . .

Nevertheless, even this would not avail, and Pope clinched his case by reporting the latest news of the composer's activities:

> Arrest him, Empress; or you sleep no more –
> She heard, and drove him to th' Hibernian shore.

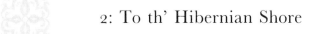

2: To th' Hibernian Shore

WHAT WAS IT THAT WAS SO IRONIC ABOUT 'TH' HIBERNIAN shore'? If Handel had retreated to one of the German states Pope could have represented the Empress Dullness as driving him 'to the Gothick shore', which would have been one up against the Hanoverians, whom Pope detested, but would have been defused by the fact that Handel was German anyway. Ireland was another matter. The *Dunciad* had as its model John Dryden's *Mac Flecknoe*, which personified Dryden's bitter enemy, the playwright Shadwell, as Dullness, and in so doing triumphantly substantiated the claim by representing him as an Irishman. When Shadwell protested that he had no connection with that island it merely added to the jest. The melancholy fact is that for most eighteenth-century Englishmen Ireland was the apotheosis of dullness. Alexander Pope, although he numbered the Irishmen Congreve and Swift amongst his closest friends, shared this opinion. Ireland was a by-word, a joke; indeed, it had come to define a kind of joke, called 'the Irish bull': a contradiction in terms never seen as such by the Irishman who perpetrated it. Ireland, to put it as a bull, was the barren mother. It was to that ultimate desolation, that rain-swept bog, that sound, sense and Handel had been driven. It was in Ireland, though Pope was never to know how time would improve his rough-and-ready irony, that Handel's greatest work was first performed, first acclaimed, and first made part of a standard repertoire – in itself a novel concept. These are sufficient reasons to excite our curiosity about the city and country in which it saw the light of day.

The question nevertheless remains as to whether *Messiah* was actually intended for Dublin. There is no doubt as to when and where it was written: London, August to September 1741. There is equally no doubt as to when and where it was first performed: Dublin, 13 April 1742. What is lacking in the documentary record is any precise demonstration of the connection between these two events. It is clear that the Duke of Devonshire, the Lord Lieutenant of Ireland, gave his support to Handel's visit. The Duke's motive can reasonably be inferred. It leaves us with another bull, of a kind: the Prince of Peace was enlisted in the cause of war. The Lord Lieutenant's problem, in 1741–2, was to guarantee the continuing support of the Irish parlia-

ment for the war with Spain; anything that he could do to improve
the Dublin winter season would both help to ensure the attendance of
members and encourage them to vote with the Government. A further
irony was that the War of Jenkins' Ear was unwillingly entered into
by, and eventually brought about the downfall of, Walpole's essentially
pacific ministry. As it was, Dublin welcomed *Messiah* with an open-
heartedness that London, a year later, failed to evince. That Handel
himself accorded to *Messiah* a particular significance amongst his works
(something that is disputed by those, who for one reason or another,
resent its pre-eminence) is attested by the grand likeness of Handel
painted by Thomas Hudson in 1747 (and reproduced as the frontispiece here) where the manuscript under his left hand is, prominently,
that work. Since, by then, *Messiah* had been performed in London only
five times, it is an assertive statement. It is also significant that the
first engraving of this portrait was by Andrew Miller of Dublin; the
fashionable John Faber of London did not follow suit until the following year.

But Pope was not the only poet to whom the Hibernian shore offered
a bleak prospect:

> From the last Isle, along whose shore extends
> The waste Atlantick, and where Europe ends,
> On whose wild plains, to ancient fame unknown,
> Nor Roman Arms, nor Grecian Science shone . . .

At this point Thomas Tickell, Pope's rival as a translator of Homer,
abandoned his effort, perhaps because he was overcome by the desolation he set out to describe, perhaps because he knew it to be untrue.
It was his habit to scribble on official paper in Dublin Castle, where
from 1724 he held the important post of Secretary to the Lords Justices,
who acted for the Governor of Ireland, the Lord Lieutenant, in his
absence. Tickell had previously been an Under-Secretary of State in
London, and was lucky to retain office and receive promotion when
his patron, Lord Carteret, was offered the Lieutenancy. As it happened, his father had been at Trinity College, Dublin, and within two
years of landing Tickell made an advantageous marriage into the
Eustace family, which had been in Ireland for five hundred years; by
this he became a considerable landowner in Co. Kildare. He died the
year before Handel made his visit to Dublin, but he tells us a great
deal about the country that Handel went to, though he does so by
accident rather than design.

Dublin from the spire of St George's, Hardwicke Place, by James Mahoney.

One would not guess, from the tone of his lines, that by 1750 Dublin would be, with a population of 125,000, the eleventh largest city of Europe. It lagged way behind London with its 676,000 and Paris with its 560,000, but it was bigger than Madrid, Milan, Berlin or Hamburg, none of them thought of as remotely provincial. Its expansion had been rapid (a careful account put the number of its inhabitants at 40,508 in 1695) but it had, by and large, been well handled by a government concerned to impress, and a commercially ambitious municipality. St Stephen's Green was a piece of town planning the equal of anything in contemporary London. The native Irish had not been a city-dwelling people, but the rigour of the Penal Laws, enforced after William III's victories in 1690 and 1691, drove the Catholic upper classes into exile and many of the lesser landowners and their tenants off their properties. The constant upheavals of the seventeenth century had vastly increased the urban population, and Dublin, as both administrative centre and principal port of entry, grew accordingly. The Protestant aristocracy maintained town houses in Dublin or added to the constellation of mansions that clustered around the city. They were soon joined by speculators of all kinds who profited by the fluidity of Irish affairs and could easily assimilate themselves in a society where even three generations of residence in Ireland seemed historical. Residence is of course a relative term: Swift, in the seventh

Drapier Letter, estimated that one-third of Irish rents were spent in England, while Prior's *List of Absentees* for 1729, a publication which appeared both in Dublin and London, as factually detailed as it was practically ineffectual, calculated that £621,499 was spent abroad. Both these complaints testify to a movement for reform, as does Samuel Madden's *Reflections and Resolutions proper for the Gentlemen of Ireland, as to their Conduct for the Service of their Country* (1738). (In his efforts for agriculture 'Premium' Madden was, indirectly, the founder of the Dublin Horse Show.)

The poverty defied description; George Berkeley, Bishop of Cloyne, asks in *The Querist* (1735), 'whether there be on earth any Christian or civilised people so beggarly, wretched, and destitute as the Common Irish?' Yet the edification of Dublin, in stone and brick, went on apace, until by 1783 there were only ten wooden houses left in the entire city. Edward Pearce's Parliament House, now the Bank of Ireland, was begun in 1729; grander and more practical than its English counterpart, it was also, in principle, more democratic, since the gallery of the Commons had room for seven hundred strangers. Pearce died before it was completed, but not without having amused Mrs Pendarves's musical friend, Mrs Donellan, by his evident tiredness at a ball. Churches were built or rebuilt: St Michan's in 1686; St Mary's, Mary Street, still wonderfully intact (as of 1991: any statement of this kind which has to do with Dublin must be carefully dated), in 1697; St Nicholas Within, a ruin of a ruin, in 1707; St Werburgh in 1715, but rebuilt later in the eighteenth century, and originally boasting a wonderfully inept hexagonal dome and drum; St Ann's, Dawson Street, fine behind its stunted nineteenth-century façade, in 1720; St Mark's, Pease Street, a mysteriously glum affair, in 1729. They were Protestant churches; the Mass chapels were sequestered, but marginally tolerated. In a city where half the population – but the lower half – was Catholic, this was probably a necessity. Within a couple of years of each other Lord Middleton was proposing that, by Act of Parliament, all Catholic priests should be castrated, and Lord Molesworth was arguing that they should be maintained by the state. Trinity College assumed a considerable architectural presence; the Laboratory and Anatomical Theatre were completed in 1711, Thomas Burgh's great library in 1732 and Richard Castle's Printing House in 1734, a year in which some undergraduates murdered the Dean, although it must be said in mitigation that he had had a shot at them first. In that year also troops had to be called out against the weavers, who were mostly Protestant and many of them comparatively recent immigrants. It is perhaps excessive to allege, as Sir Edmund Sullivan did of the country later in the century, that 'The character of Ireland was then an anomaly in the moral world', but Dr Maurice Craig's judgement that Dublin in this period offered 'an extreme example of tendencies generally diffused' invites assent.

The conundrum is most evident in the case of Swift, who was Dublin-born and educated at Kilkenny Grammar School and Trinity College. He then spent a decade in England before returning in 1699 to Ireland, where he had already been inducted to a prebend which could be enjoyed *in absentia*; he now acquired the living of Laracor and a better prebend at St Patrick's Cathedral, of which, after several years spent largely in England engaged in political writing, he became, through Tory interest, Dean in 1713, continuing in the post until his death, writing the tracts and satires and practising the personal charity that made him a hero to the Dublin poor; 'an absolute monarch in the *Liberties*, and King of the Mob'. No one, it might be thought, could have had their heart more in Ireland. Yet he often cursed the country, and often expressed the wish to be out of it, although he realised, as he wrote to Tickell in 1725, that he was 'tyed to this Kingdom'. Bishop Berkeley, after Swift Ireland's greatest writer of the age, and as great a patriot, retired to Oxford.

What is evident here is not a lack of conviction, but an oscillation. When Boswell asked Johnson, one of Ireland's steadiest friends amongst the Englishmen of his time, 'Should you not like to see Dublin, Sir?' the Doctor replied, 'No, Sir. Dublin is only a worse capital.' His opinion was second-hand, but it reflected the views of some who had been there, and of some who lived there.

Those who lived there did not, however, repine; when they could, they set out to do things on a scale that would redress the balance; besides Pearce's Parliament House we have such substantial buildings as the Royal Hospital, Kilmainham, The Royal Barracks (now the Collins Barracks) and, though it has been refaced, The Mansion House. There were great town houses, too, on a London scale, Pearce's imitations of Kent in Henrietta Street, at Iveagh House, and at 85 St Stephen's Green. That they often stood solitary, waiting on flankers who were slow to join them if they were ever joined at all, is an aspect of the devil-may-care attitude that gives them a distinctive *élan*, even though they may not be great architecture. In the matter of their entertainments Dubliners were less reckless, but equally

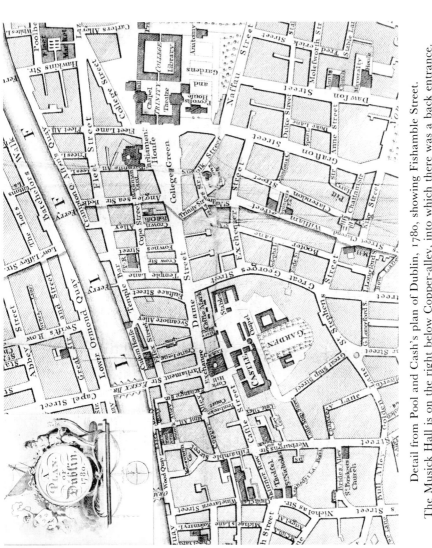

Detail from Pool and Cash's plan of Dublin, 1780, showing Fishamble Street.
The Musick Hall is on the right below Copper-alley, into which there was a back entrance.

determined to emulate and even exceed what could be achieved in London.

The first Dublin theatre had been established shortly before the Civil Wars and lasted just four years. The patentee, John Ogilby, recommenced with a new Theatre in Smock-Alley in 1662; nine years later the building fell down, with some loss of life, during a performance of Jonson's *Bartholomew Fair*. It was rebuilt, and functioned (with brief periods of closure for political reasons) until it again collapsed, with heavier loss of life, during a performance of Shadwell's *The Libertine* in 1701. Despite puritanical admonitions it was gamely reconstructed in 1705 and stayed in business, to be joined by a second theatre which was built in Aungier Street in 1733. Both theatres were well if rowdily patronised, they were interested in attracting talent from the London stage, while actors who learned their craft in Dublin might, as in the case of the tragedian Charles Macklin or the comedienne Peg Woffington, triumph in London.

Dublin was well provided with newspapers which, by and large, give a better coverage of events in the early eighteenth century than their London equivalents. At the time of Handel's visit there were three principal papers, all well established, *Pue's Occurrences*, the *Dublin Gazette* and Faulkner's *Dublin Journal*; they contained regular announcements of forthcoming performances and kept their readers informed of theatrical affairs. They also carried announcements of music although, as in London, the public concert had still not fully developed, and the principal venues were the rooms which the larger taverns kept for public meetings and dances. But it is unlikely to have been by chance that Handel's visit coincided with the opening of two halls purposely built for music. As in London, the main musical institutions were the cathedrals and the Court, but in Dublin the Court was that of the Lord Lieutenant, and its band was known as The State Music. The cathedrals, of which Christ Church is the older but St Patrick's the grander, both had permanent choirs in theory, but the majority of the vicars choral served both establishments.

We learn something about the larger choir, St Patrick's, from Swift's correspondence. He was no more musical than Pope, and regarded music in the cathedral as, at worst, a necessary evil and at best a joke – 'I have the honour to be Captain of a band of nineteen musicians (including boys) which are I hear about five less than my friend the D. of Chandos' – but many of the circle of friends upon whom he so much depended for amusement, and – when he could bear it –

Pool et Cash. del.

Ifaac Taylor fculp.

The PARLIAMENT HOUSE.

Publish'd according to Act of Parliament January 1 1780.

The Parliament House, Dublin. Engraving by Pool and Cash. Sir Edward Lovett Pearce's masterpiece; the foundation stone was laid in 1729. Now the Bank of Ireland.

company, were enthusiasts. Patrick Delany, the Chancellor of the Cathedral, who in 1743 was to marry Handel's friend Mrs Pendarves, loved a ballad as well as he did an opera song; Prebendary Edward Synge, consecrated Bishop of Clonfert in 1730 and of Elphin in 1740, was an attentive listener and involved in the St Cecilia's Day celebrations; when Swift's poetical protégé Matthew Pilkington, a penniless curate, took his wife by storm, she found him installed in her parents' home 'his harpsichord placed in the parlour, which, with a cat and an owl, were all his worldly goods'. Delany and Synge pressed Swift to fill vacancies in the choir, neglected by his predecessors, because of its importance in the city's musical life; he turned to them for informed opinions on the individual merits of members of a body which he thought slovenly and unreliable, noting in 1734 of Mr Fox, whom he believed not untypical, 'Daily losing his voice by intemperance. Neglect in his attendance. Scandalous in conversation and behaviour'. But two years later Synge was able to report favourably on Mr Hughes ('adequate voice, but desirous to improve himself') and the choirs were capable of creating a good impression when they combined for special occasions.

Since 1728 the State Music had been in the hands of Matthew Dubourg. His predecessor, Johann Sigismund Cousser, was a Bohemian, born at Bratislava; he had worked at Versailles, in Hamburg, Stuttgart and London. He was a competent and prolific composer who maintained his connections with the Continent and had an extensive music library. He composed an annual Serenata to mark the royal birthday, and those for 1712 and 1727 appear to have been staged – probably the nearest that Dublin came to music theatre until *The Beggar's Opera* was given, very shortly after its London opening, in March 1728. Dubourg, by contrast, was only an occasional composer, but was a virtuoso violinist who had begun his career in London as a child prodigy, playing Corelli standing on a high stool; he first visited Dublin in 1724. The exact size of his official orchestra is unknown, but, by calling on the services of other musicians as well, he could muster a band of eighteen, besides the kettle-drummers and trumpeters who officiated on ceremonial occasions. Dubourg had been taught by Francesco Geminiani, the composer and celebrated performer born at Lucca who had been resident in London since 1714. In 1728 Geminiani was offered the Dublin post but felt, although he was an ardent Freemason, unable to renounce the faith into which he was born. However, Dubourg invited him to Dublin on several occasions and it was there that, at a great age, he was eventually to die. During his two visits in the 1730s the venue he used in Spring Gardens became known as 'Geminiani's Great Room'. He was not the only internationally celebrated musician to perform in Dublin; the castrato Nicolini had given concerts in 1711, and one of the foreigners who made a living by teaching and playing in Dublin was Francesco Scarlatti, brother to the then famous Alessandro, and uncle to the now famous Domenico. Italy was as much a *summum bonum* for musical Dubliners as it was for those rich enough to build. Indeed, they were often the same people: Patrick Delany and Edward Synge had put up the money to erect the tower and dome of St Werburgh's. In 1709 the Dean and Chapter of St Patrick's and the music lovers of the city had subscribed to send Thomas Roseingrave, the son of their organist, to study in Italy, where he had met Domenico Scarlatti. As with so many initiatives of this kind, the project benefited the world but not Dublin; Roseingrave went from Italy to England where he became organist of Handel's church, St George's, Hanover Square, returning to his birthplace only after he had been incapacitated by recurrent insanity.

There was, therefore, a keen awareness in Dublin of what Europe at large had to offer musically. That there was a corresponding unawareness of Ireland's own musical resources should come as no surprise; as in England and Scotland, art music and popular music were distinct, although there were always points at which the borders might be crossed: Dubourg, a notorious wag, disguised himself as a fiddler, the better to see Duboyne fair, and tried to play in character but failed; he was nevertheless successful in introducing variations on 'Ellen Aroon' into the concert room. Within a year or so of arriving in Ireland Thomas Tickell had written a ballad beginning 'Of *Leinster*, fam'd for Maidens fair' to an 'Irish' tune; in England such tunes, of a more convincing kind, had been used by Byrd, imitated by Purcell, and appropriated by Gay for *The Beggar's Opera*. But Dublin's need to import music was as urgent as London's, even though Italian opera had never been attempted there, and it had become the more so during the 1730s when the city's concert life had rapidly developed along new lines: although these same tendencies were apparent in London, they were never anything like as significant, and to a certain extent imitated the course of events across St George's Channel. The essential element was the appropriation of music to a charitable purpose.

Catholics required objects of charity to achieve salvation through works; *refrigexiet caritas multorum*, 'the charity of many shall wax cold'

(Matthew 24:12) was cited without reference to its context as an encouragement to immediate and personal acts of generosity. The Authorized Version defused Christ's saying by translating *caritas* as 'love'; Protestants sought institutional solutions to the problems, so subversive to any ordered state, of poverty, vagrancy and disease. So too did some Catholics; particularly rulers who resented the clerical line that only the Church could act as intercessor in these matters. Between 1716 and 1717, as part of his campaign to reduce ecclesiastical interference in his dominions, the cunning and determined Victor Amadeus of Savoy banned begging in Turin, reorganised the finances of the Ospizio di Carità, clad all identifiable paupers in uniform, brought them to Mass in the cathedral followed by a public dinner at which they were served by the nobility, and marched them off to segregation, forced labour and compulsory prayer. British protestants might have secretly applauded this solution, but it could not be re-enacted in a constitutional monarchy where principles of *laissez-faire* (if not precisely freedom) were as jealously proclaimed as they were little understood. More subtle, though no less practical, approaches were explored and given ironic expression by the Dutch-born doctor, Deist and versifier, Bernard de Mandeville, in his *The Fable of the Bees, or Private Vices, Public Benefits* (1714), a work which attracted a good deal of attention in Dublin, but little understanding. Viscount Molesworth and Bishop Berkeley both seem to have missed the complexities of its irony; Swift, to whom this would have been child's play, would have strongly disapproved of Mandeville on religious grounds, and did not comment. Yet nowhere can we see Mandeville's principle that supposed luxuries actually help support the needy more immediately translated into action; the poor of Dublin, severed from their land, disenfranchised by their faith (though we should not forget the progeny of Cromwell's settlers, often as violently displaced and disowned), had much to gain from the conspicuous expenditure of the rich on building, entertainment and other luxuries. Amongst these we can include a sense of guilt, which in effect put the seal on Mandeville's argument.

The Dublin poor did not allow themselves to be ignored, and were less reticent – perhaps because they had less reason to be – than their English counterparts. Beggars abounded; Swift, who hated for the sake of love, inveighed against them: 'they have in this Town been frequently seen to pour out of their Pitcher good broth that hath been given them into the kennel; neither do they much regard Cloaths, unless to sell them; for their Rags are part of their Tools with which

The Front of St Warburghs Church.

St Werburgh's Church. From Brooking's Map of Dublin, 1728. The bottom part of the façade, by Alessandro Galilei, is all that remains. The tower and dome were paid for by Dr Patrick Delany and Dr Edward Synge.

they work'. They wanted money for drink; they were 'Thieves, Drunkards, Heathens and Whore Mongers'. The gaols were vile, and in 1729 a Committee of the Irish House of Commons investigated matters at least as thoroughly as a Committee set up at the same time in the English House. They found one room in the Sheriff's Marshalsea in Newhall Market (it was known as 'The Nunnery' because street-walkers were confined in this chamber when picked up by the watch) so noxious that they were only able to stay there for as long as it took them to measure it. Moreover, poverty was a respecter of neither confession nor nationality; debtors were as likely, in that fast-gambling city, to be members of prominent ascendancy families as to be the tradesmen who, attempting to cope with such customers, had failed to balance their accounts.

During Handel's stay in Ireland two cases involving peers were simmering; both were brought to trial before the Irish House of Lords. Neither of them can be regarded as typical, but both demonstrate extreme examples of tendencies perhaps mercifully diffused. In the Annesley peerage case (1743) Lord Altham had long concealed the fact that he had a son, in order to raise money from his expectations of his great-uncle's estate. On Altham's death his brother took advantage of this concealment to usurp the title; he subsequently kidnapped the son (who had been fostered by a butcher) and sold him into slavery in America. After thirteen years the son escaped and in 1743 established his claim to the title and estates; he died in 1760, having failed to dislodge his uncle from either. In 1744 Viscount Netterville was finally brought before the House charged with murder; the excitement was such that it necessitated the postponement of the first revival of *Messiah*. The Viscount was acquitted, the two principal witnesses for the prosecution having died before the trial was convened.

Ireland of the 1740s was by no means a land without law, but it was often, and conspicuously, a land without justice. It was also a land where the charity sermon, and the establishment of charitable foundations, had a strong emotional appeal. In Dublin a public surgery had been opened in 1718; Dr Richard Steevens' hospital, the building of which was seen through after his death by his sister Grizell, was completed in 1733. To a handsome if old-fashioned design by Thomas Burgh, it stands around a quadrangle, and brother and sister are prominently commemorated over the gateway. Several of the beds were endowed by subscriptions from the gentry. Mercer's Hospital was founded in 1734, and other institutions planned though not built in 1742 included a hospital for incurables and a lying-in hospital, while Dean Swift had signified his intention to endow a hospital for the insane.

Musical life in Dublin, occasions of Church and State aside, was a matter of benefits for professional musicians and 'music meetings' made up either entirely of amateurs or of professionals leading amateurs, along the lines of the London societies such as that which met at the Apollo's Head Tavern, where *Esther* had first been revived. They met regularly in convenient 'great rooms', and by 1732 the Philharmonic Society (formerly the Musical Academy) seems to have acquired the exclusive use of such a room in Crow Street, which was known as 'The Musick Hall', but was primarily suited for instrumental music. Such societies naturally desired, on occasion, to perform to a larger audience than their own members and their immediate friends; it was appropriate to charge a fee to restrict entrance and to pay the professionals, but inappropriate for gentlemen amateurs to pocket the surplus. A charitable purpose provided both solution and absolution: the solution to the question of the surplus, and absolution from the charge of playing merely to show off (even though it probably ensured larger audiences). It was also beautifully calculated to quiet any residual pangs of conscience amongst ladies in the audience who might otherwise have feared they were merely indulging themselves. For more ambitious concerts, involving predominantly professional performers, the rationale was slightly different but the charitable element was equally important. The only places large enough, and equipped with organs, were churches; the music had to be sacred. The precedent was that of the annual London service in St Paul's for the Society of the Sons of the Clergy. What was probably the first performance of any of Handel's sacred works in Ireland took place at what was also the first benefit for Mercer's Hospital, on 8 April 1736 in St Andrew's Church. There were over seventy musicians, 'among whom', *Pue's Occurrences* reports, 'were several noblemen and gentlemen of distinction, besides the best publick Hands in the kingdom'; the leader was Dubourg, and the principal singers, John Church, William Lambe, James Baileys and John Mason, would all in due course take part in the first performance of *Messiah*. They gave, before a large audience which included the then Lord Lieutenant, the Duke of Dorset, and his Duchess, the Utrecht *Te Deum* and *Jubilate* and one of the coronation anthems; it is natural to assume that this was *Zadok the Priest*, requiring oboes, bassoons and three trumpets, but it is unlikely that at that time it could be managed with Dublin resources.

The occasion appears to have been a great success, but preparations for it had not run at all smoothly. It was originally announced for 31 March, but had to be postponed; postponement of musical performances in Dublin was so frequent as to be almost the norm, but this time a change of place was required. What seems to have happened is that it was originally arranged with St Michan's Church, which had a good recent organ by Jean-Baptiste Cuville, a pupil of Renatus Harris. However, a rumour got around, and possibly a press advertisement was placed (though this does not survive) to the effect that what was to be given was an oratorio. This so alarmed the parochial officers of St Michan's that they refused permission for the concert even though the rumour was unfounded; it had therefore to be re-advertised for St Andrew's. Obviously, though no such thing as an oratorio had yet reached Ireland, the threat was an occasion for alarm.

The reasons are clear from the controversy caused by St Cecilia's Day celebrations in St Patrick's Cathedral in 1731. A year or so before, Swift, in a poem 'To Himself on Saint Cecilia's Day' had wryly predicted that by permitting this celebration he was inviting trouble:

> Grave Dean of St Patrick's, how comes it to pass,
> That you, who know music no more than an ass,
> That you, who so lately were writing of Drapiers,
> Should lend your Cathedral to players and scrapers?
> To act such an opera once in a year,
> So offensive to ev'ry true Protestant ear,
> With trumpets, and fiddles, and organs, and singing,
> Will sure the Pretender and Popery bring in.

In 1731 the preacher was Thomas Sheridan, a divine, schoolmaster, amateur musician and close friend of Swift's with a genius for getting into hot water; newly presented to a living at Rincurran, Co. Cork, he was asked to preach in Cork on Sunday, 1 August 1725. He obliged with a sermon on Matthew 6:34: 'Sufficient unto the day is the evil thereof'. He had forgotten, but his congregation had not, that it was the anniversary of the accession of George I. A sermon in St Patrick's on St Cecilia's Day 1730 had also given offence, which is why he decided to publish the one he delivered in 1731, to show how innocent the proceedings were. He once again exercised his inimitable gift; presumably acting on the principle that attack is the best method of

Jonathan Swift, by R. Barker. Dean of St Patrick's from 1713 until his death in 1745. He viewed his friends' enthusiasm for music satirically but tolerantly.

defence, he punctuated his judicious and moderate observations on
the proper role of music in churches with withering and not strictly
necessary jibes at dissenters, concluding, for instance, a warning
against improvised voluntaries ('what the organist pleases to run off
his fingers without any regard whether melody or harmony be in it')
by going for the throat with 'It is too like extempore prayer, and that
is saying enough'. Not surprisingly, this provoked a reply which set
out to demonstrate that both instrumental music in church and the
celebration of saints' days were Popish abominations. Undeterred, the
Musical Society marked 22 November in the following year by asking
Sheridan to preach again and by holding an even more elaborate
service, which, quite unprecedentedly, included a concerto by Corelli
– something which had never been ventured in England and neatly
demonstrates the Dublin propensity to carry things a little further.

Several months after the first Mercer's Hospital Benefit the bugbear
of oratorio once more alarmed Dublin. On 22 November 1736 the
Dublin Daily Advertiser published a 'Prologue', by 'The Ingenious
Mr. Thomas Griffith, comedian', which he had written to be spoken
by himself before an oratorio. This was allegedly to have been given
by Italian performers, so it seems possible that something had been
projected by the cellist Pasqualino, who (together with the soprano
Anna Strada del Pò) had played in the first performance of *Alexander's
Feast* at Covent Garden on 19 February, had presumably also done so
in the subsequent revival of *Esther*, and who was in Dublin by 8 April
to lead the cellos in the Mercer's concert. Whatever was in the wind,
however, failed to materialise, and the *Daily Advertiser*, which liked its
little joke, prefaced Griffith's poem by professing relief that the Italians
had not 'honour'd our Isle with their Appearance, and condescended
to pick our Pockets of more Money than we could spare; but we are
happy enough not to be worth their notice'. The importance of the
substance of the prologue is the part it attributes to the Lord Lieutenant in what might have happened:

> Yet while a Dorset lives to cross the Maine,
> The Muses still will follow in his train:
> Where Sackville is, the syrens will be found,
> And raise new Musick on Parnassian Ground.

Lionel Sackville, Duke of Dorset, lived long – long enough to serve a
second tenure of the Lord Lieutenantship fifteen years later. When he
finally left in 1754, his going was greeted with jubilant bell-ringing:

> He played Cat-in Pan,
> Says the bell of St. Ann . . .
> You're a very bad parcel,
> Says the bell of the Castle.

But when he left office for the first time in 1737 he was still popular, mainly because he did very little during his lieutenancy. His successor, William Cavendish, 3rd Duke of Devonshire, took the point and did even less. He was 'plain in his manners, negligent in his dress'. His wife was still plainer; Horace Walpole reported that 'The Duchess of Devonshire was more delightfully vulgar than you can imagine: complained of the wet night and how the men would dirty the room with their shoes, called out at supper to the Duke, "Good God, my Lord, dont cut the ham – nobody will eat any!" ' The Duke appears to have taken no offence when Swift, at least half insane, encountered him at dinner at the Lord Mayor's and, seeing his Garter ribbon, addressed him as 'You fellow, with the blue string'. Thomas Tickell found Cavendish a most agreeable master, and amenable to a joke. He wrote to him in the character of a local poetaster, John (or James) Ward, petitioning for a post:

> Some pretty neat portion in th'Army or State,
> For Life not too small, nor for Virtue too great.

This was apposite because the new Lord Lieutenant, though he had little taste for political activity, was, if circumstances demanded, an energetic patron of the arts. When his London house burned down he asked William Kent to rebuild it. When he saw that Dublin had an appetite for music that local practitioners could not assuage, he invited Handel to Ireland. For those of us who owe so much to his initiative it is frustrating that this modest man seems to have left so few traces behind him. In politics he was a loyal though not subservient adherent of Walpole and Newcastle. His reports on matters of state are shrewd and pragmatic; he knew that it was foolish to attempt to exert influence beyond a certain point, and declined to do so. He was a patron of music and theatre, a friend of Handel and of the actor James Quin, though just what this patronage amounted to, beyond taking his large family to the shows the season offered, is unclear. Yet his personal involvement in Handel's visit is testified to by all the advertisements for and reports of Handel's Dublin concerts and, in a letter to Charles Jennens, by Handel himself.

*

1741 was a year of much musical excitement and anticipation in Dublin. The Musical Academy of Crow Street announced that having 'brought Instrumental Musick to so great Perfection, and as there is such great deficiency in Vocal Musick, they are determined to send to Italy for those of that kind that shall excell, in hopes of bringing the one on a Par with the other . . .'. Their scheme, although much advertised, did not succeed; if by 'those of that kind that shall excell' castrati were intended, they had chosen a bad year; the War of Jenkins' Ear was under way, and Farinelli's ascendancy at the Spanish Court a matter of common ridicule and contempt. After this failure the Musical Academy appear to have transformed themselves into the Philharmonick Society and to have set their sights on new premises; they were established in a large room opposite St John's Church in Fishamble Street by the autumn of 1742. Presumably they were prompted to do this by a desire to emulate the Charitable Musical Society, whose more ambitious plans must have been formulated at least by Christmas 1740, since they involved the construction of a purpose-built Musick Room, to be 'finished in an elegant manner, under the direction of Capt. Castle'. Richard Castle was of German origin, had settled in Ireland and married a Huguenot girl in the 1720s, and was a prolific architect capable of excellent work: Russborough, Co. Wicklow, with a 700-foot façade in a magnificent setting, was going up at the same time as the Musical Society's modest exploitation of a difficult site at an awkward corner of the ancient street that descends the hill from just beyond the eastern end of Christ Church to Wood and Essex Quays. Of this, in 1991, the walls improbably survive – improbably because neither they nor the structure of which they once formed a part can ever have been substantial, despite the fact that, at a pinch, the hall could seat seven hundred together with an orchestra and choir. The internal construction must been wholly of timber and large galleries would have been necessary to accommodate so large an audience. If we can form no very clear picture of its appearance today, a contemporary poet found it no easier:

> Adorn'd with all that workmanship can do
> By ornaments and architecture too.
> The oblong area runs from east to west,
> Fair to behold, but hard to be exprest . . .

Russborough shows what Castle could do in the way of decoration, and it was no doubt on this that the subscribers and their treasurer,

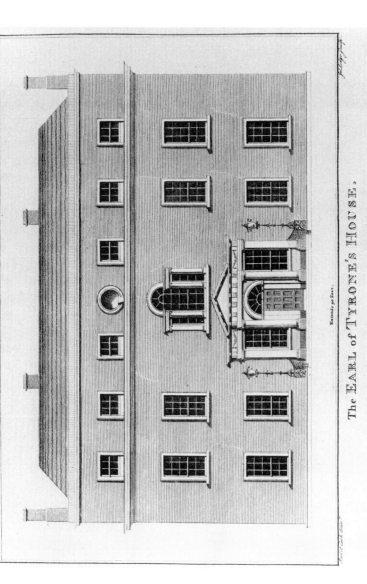

The EARL of TYRONE's HOUSE.

Published according to Act of Parliament, March 1. 1770.

Tyrone House, Dublin. Engraving by Pool and Cash. Built for Sir Marcus Beresford by Captain Richard Castle in 1740, this characteristic, although grand, town house of the *Messiah* period still stands in Marlborough Street.

William Neale, laid out their money to most effect. Neale had a music
shop in Christ Church Yard, published music in partnership with
William Manwaring who also had a shop, Corelli's Head, on College
Green, and advanced money to make building the Hall possible; it
was a shrewd move, because the 1740s were to see an extraordinary
growth of public music-making in Dublin, for which the opening of
the Fishamble Street hall, which eventually took place on Friday,
2 October 1741, was a precondition. It must also have been a precondition for Handel's visit. It offered what London lacked – a substantial
auditorium for oratorio which was, nevertheless, not a theatre. At the
same time it was part and parcel of the interaction between music and
the charitable societies, which by 1741 had become interdependent.
The governors of Mercer's Hospital spelled things out in a com-
mendably direct advertisement for their musical service of 14 February
in St Andrew's Church: 'N.B. The Benefit arising hereby is the main
support of the Hospital for the Expense this last year, ending the
1st November 1740, amounted to £548 10s. 4d. where the annual Subscriptions thereto are but £201 11s. 9d. 1179 Persons were under the
Care of the Hospital in the said Year.' It is hard to imagine where,
apart from Dublin, deficit budgeting on so bold a scale would have
paid off. The remarkable thing is not only that it did pay off, but that
there proved to be slack in the system which remained to be taken up.
But it is easy to see now, and it must have been more urgently apparent
then, that this could not be accomplished without a major injection of
imported talent. One of the few things that we know for certain about
Devonshire (his reports to Newcastle show it again and again) was
that he was a good listener. The charitable music lovers had offered
hostages to fortune. They urgently needed a return on their money.
There had never been such a thing as Italian opera in Dublin, though
the travesties of it had flourished, and it was not to arrive until 1753.
If Devonshire, who liked relaxed cheerfulness, listened as sensitively
to social gossip as he did to political – all the indications are that he
did, and the one in any case served the other – then no enormous effort
of diplomacy was necessary, with Handel disaffected and restive in
London, to match need for need.

It has been questioned whether Handel specifically intended *Messiah*
for Dublin. The short answer to this is that Faulkner's *Dublin Journal*
reporting the first rehearsal on the day after, refers to 'this Noble and
Grand Charity for which this oratorio was composed'. The obvious
response is 'Blarney', the injustice of which is implicit in the fact

that for ten years nobody bothers either to repeat or to challenge the assertion. The evidence against is that Handel did not communicate his intention to go to Dublin to Charles Jennens, who had evidently hoped that he would set *Messiah* for use in London during Passion Week, and that having completed *Messiah* Handel went on almost immediately to write *Samson*, which, as first envisaged, called for orchestral forces unavailable in Dublin. The considerations that must modify this evidence are that Handel was notably uncommunicative in his dealings with Jennens (not answering Jennens's letters was a way of maintaining his independence; all the signs are that he found letter-writing uncongenial, and Jennens was in any case the kind of correspondent who should not be encouraged), and that Handel's bursts of creative energy often carried him on from an immediate aim to a hypothetical one. Thus in the summer and late autumn of 1738 he had drafted *Saul* and *Imeneo*, subsequently overhauling *Saul* for performance in the New Year, but leaving *Imeneo* in the rough, finally finishing it in September 1740. Among the many things to distinguish *Messiah* from all Handel's other oratorios is the factor that has caused so much subsequent debate: that it was devised in a simple, transportable form, requiring, if necessary, no more than four solo voices and no orchestral forces beyond strings, continuo, a pair of trumpets and drums (although there are oboe parts in the autograph score, they are for the choral version of 'Their sound is gone out into all lands', which was inserted at the very end after Handel had composed it for the London performance of 1749).

In this simple form we might regard *Messiah* as a 'portmanteau' oratorio; not in Lewis Carroll's sense of something that collects everything together, but in the sense that it could be produced from a portmanteau and adapted to suit whatever the composer found at his journey's end. It is hard to imagine that Handel could have had any other destination than Dublin in mind. Dubourg had played a 'new Concerto' by him (which does not seem to survive) as early as 1719; James Baileys, a vicar-choral of the two Dublin cathedrals, had been in London in 1737 and sang the tenor part of the funeral anthem for Queen Caroline; Pasqualino's connection we have already observed. He could not have set out without reasonable assurances, above all that the Fishamble Street Music Hall had been completed (it had taken longer than was anticipated), but also that the co-operation of the Cathedral choirs was likely and that he had adequate lodgings for the season. Such arrangements could not have been made haphazardly. And even if we cannot be absolutely certain about this, there can be no doubt that Dublin received *Messiah* with rapture and within two years began the custom of annual performance, whilst its introduction to London was by no means an unqualified success, and it was a decade before performances became annual.

Mainwaring, Handel's first biographer, started a historical hare when he mistakenly supposed that *Messiah* was first performed in England, but he was right in assuming that Dublin, 'famous for the gaiety and splendour of its court, the opulence and spirit of its principal inhabitants, the valour of its military, and the genius of its learned men', was particularly congenial to Handel, and right also in his comment that 'The reception that he met with, at the same time that it shewed the strong sense which the Irish had of his extraordinary merit, conveyed a kind of tacit reproach on all those on the other side of the water, who had enlisted in the opposition against him.' It is time to investigate the contents of his portmanteau.

3: 'Begin the Song':
Jennens's Libretto

WE DO NOT KNOW EXACTLY FOR HOW LONG HANDEL HAD HAD in front of him, or in a drawer, the word-book for *Messiah*, when he began the business of setting it on 22 August 1741. Some six weeks is a reasonable guess, since on 10 July Charles Jennens had written to his friend Edward Holdsworth, reporting that:

> Handel says he will do nothing next Winter, but I hope I shall perswade him to set another Scripture Collection I have made for him, & perform it for his own Benefit in Passion Week. I hope he will lay out his whole genius & Skill upon it, that the Composition may excell all his former Compositions, as the Subject excells every other Subject. The Subject is Messiah.

Some of Jennens's earlier dealings with Handel have already been touched upon. He was the heir of Gopsal, a large estate in Leicestershire. He had been at Balliol College, Oxford, but had not taken a degree because, on grounds of conscience, he refused to swear fidelity to George I, regarding him as a usurper. Jennens was, in fact, a non-juror, an Anglican faithful to the dwindling body of clergy who had been forced out of their livings (or been ordained by bishops who had been forced out of their sees) after the Glorious Revolution because they would not abjure their oaths to James II. So, too, was Holdsworth, who until his death in 1746 was Jennens's closest friend, passionately interested, as was Jennens, in literature, music, painting and architecture, and, of the two, the finer intellect. Holdsworth's devotion was Virgil, and his particular study the geographical and archaeological setting of Virgil's poems. Denied by his political and religious convictions what promised to be a brilliant career as a classical tutor at Magdalen College, Oxford, he had the compensation of being able to explore Italy as thoroughly as he could wish – one reason why his correspondence with Jennens was so extensive. In 1746 he died as a result of a recurrent rheumatic fever contracted a few years earlier in an exploration of a drain dug by the Emperor Claudius for emptying a lake. Jennens, who survived, unmarried, until 1773,

mourned him for the rest of his life and in him lost a friend whose
shrewd views of men and affairs had acted as a check on his extra-
vagances. Indeed, most of the stories which abound of Jennens as
'Solyman the Magnificent', overbearing and ostentatious, date from
the years after Holdsworth's death and after Jennens's succession to
Gopsal in 1747.

As early as 1731 their correspondence had assumed the supremacy
in music, of Handel. Jennens had been a subscriber to all his works
since the publication of *Rodelinda* in 1725. Handel's letter of 28 July
1735 (which we have seen) presumes a prior acquaintance, and by
that time Jennens is being furnished with manuscript copies of the
composer's latest works. *Saul*, which was probably the work referred
to in the letter, demonstrates the most surprising thing about Jennens:
that despite his notorious arrogance, combativeness and love of opulence, in matters concerning the scriptures he was a master of economy
and tact. (There was also another side to his personal character: his
unostentatious charity to fellow non-jurors, which only emerged after
his death.)

When he compiled 'another Scripture Collection' (whether what
had preceded it was never set and is now lost, or whether it was *Israel
in Egypt*, remains uncertain), he had no guarantee that Handel would
compose music for it, and no possible expectation of financial reward
or, save in a minute circle of friends who already knew his talents, of
personal celebrity. When he wrote that 'the Subject excells every other
Subject', he knew perfectly well that the dangers inherent in tackling
it were commensurately heightened. The subject had attracted great
poets, including the man who was, to Jennens and Holdsworth, the
greatest of them all – Virgil. He had treated it in his *Pollio*, the fourth
eclogue, which Jennens, fond of and careful of mottoes, quoted on the
title-page of the word-book, 'MAJORA CANAMUS'. This was
from the poem's first line, 'Sicelides Musae, paulo majora canamus'
('Muses of Sicily, we sing a grander strain'), or, in the words of Pope's
imitation:

> Ye Nymphs of *Solyma*! begin the Song:
> To heav'nly Themes sublimer Strains belong.

The fourth eclogue was not merely one of Virgil's most intricately
wrought imaginings; for Jennens and his contemporaries it was a pic-
torial restatement of a Sybilline prophecy announcing the birth of
Christ:

Jam redit et Virgo, redeunt Saturnia regna,
Jam nova progenies caelo demittitur alto –

literally, 'Now [the cycle of all ages and] the Virgin returns, returns
the age of Saturn; now from heaven on high a new generation is sent
down', or, in Pope's fusion of Virgil and Isaiah (since he 'could not
but observe a remarkable parity between many of the thoughts' – a
jejune comment; the similarities had been exploited for 1500 years):

Rapt into future Times, the Bard begun,
A *Virgin* shall conceive, a *Virgin* bear a Son!
From *Jesse*'s Root behold a Branch arise,
Whose sacred Flow'r with Fragrance fills the Skies.

The greatness of Jennens's text was to know all this, and other
treatments besides, such as Vida's *Christiad* (an early sixteenth-century
recasting of the life of Christ in the form of a neo-Latin heroic poem,
intended to stem the tide of scholarly Renaissance paganism) and to
reject their basic premise, that the scriptural story was best served by
amplification and ornamentation. Dr Johnson, who at Oxford had
achieved fame through his translation of Pope's *Messiah* into Latin as
a Christmas exercise, and who shared with Steele the astounding
opinion that Pope's imitation excelled the *Pollio*, nevertheless qualified
his encomium by observing that this was 'no great praise, if it be
considered from what original the improvements are derived', the
'original' being Isaiah. Earlier Abraham Cowley, on whom Jennens
had drawn for the word-book of *Saul*, had used his innovative and
extravagant English recreation of the form of the Greek Pindaric ode
in an attempt to evoke the intensity of feeling aroused by the contem-
plation of *Christ's Passion, The Resurrection* and *The 24th Chapter of Isaiah*.
Jennens took the whole business a stage further, or perhaps backwards.
Seeing how his precursors had tried but never wholly succeeded, he
simply constructed a cento, a patchwork of direct quotation from the
Bible which made up a new and constant whole.

But 'simply' is misleading. Constructing coherent and appropriate
texts for music from scriptural fragments was a common seventeenth-
and early eighteenth-century task, and the Anglican sub-deans, pre-
centors and other clergymen who undertook it in the course of their
duties were simply continuing in the vernacular a practice familiar to
the compilers of the Roman Breviary. Purcell's *My Heart is Inditing*, for
the coronation of James II, is a familiar example, though it does not

Charles Jennens by Mason Chamberlin the elder. Besides *Messiah*, he
provided the words for *Il Moderato*, *Saul* and *Belshazzar*.

involve more than a drastic editing of Psalm 45 and the addition of a verse from Isaiah. The words of Handel's *Funeral Anthem* for Queen Caroline in 1737 were assembled from Psalms 16 and 51 by Edward Willis, the Sub-Dean of Westminster Abbey; an anecdote which dates from the time of the coronation service ten years earlier reports that then, when there was some difficulty over texts, Handel had claimed that he knew his Bible at least as well as any bishop, and was perfectly able to contrive his own selections. But no one had ever attempted anything on the scale, or of the nature, of *Messiah*. *Israel in Egypt* may have been the other 'scripture-collection' referred to by Jennens in his letter to Holdsworth of 10 July (and it is suggestive that Cowley had written yet another Pindaric on *The Plagues of Egypt*), yet, compared with *Messiah*, it is a work of dismaying literal-mindedness. It attempts to make an epic out of a charade, and emerges as something episodic, and nowhere deeper than the Red Sea.

Messiah disdains narrative and from its first words commands attention because of what it does not explain. It uses, with very slight editorial modifications of phrasal detail, the language of the Authorised Version of the Bible or, in the case of 'Psalms', the Book of Common Prayer. Those modifications must have their origins more in Jennens's sense of euphony than in his sense of what might be fit for music, since they occur even in the quotation from the First Epistle to Timothy (3:16) which, on the title-page, follows the motto from the *Pollio*:

And without controversy, great is the Mystery of Godliness: God was manifest*ed* in the Flesh, justify'd by the Spirit, seen of Angels, preached among the Gentiles, believed on in the World, received up in[to] glory.

Here, as well as the expansion and contraction noted, capitalisation and the spelling of 'controversie' and 'justified' are Jennens's. But at points he goes further.

O Zion, that bringest good tidings, get thee up into the high Mountain; O Jerusalem, that bringest good tidings, lift up thy voice with strength; lift it up, be not afraid; say unto the cities of Judah, Behold your God!

by adopting the Vulgate sense, given as a marginal alternative in the Authorised Version, emerges as the far more incisive and rhythmic:

O thou that tellest good Tidings to *Zion*, get thee up into the high

Mountain: O thou that tellest good Tidings to *Jerusalem*, lift up thy
Voice with Strength . . .

Here, however, Jennens has had to choose an alternative, rather than
actively to alter. But in 'He was despised and rejected of Man, a Man
of Sorrows, and acquainted with Grief', 'He was despised' has been
moved from the present to the past tense; the past is in fact implicit
in the continuation of the verse from Isaiah 53:3, and Jennens's regu-
larisation brings it into line with 50:6: 'He gave his back to the Smiters,
and his cheeks to them that plucked off the hair; he hid not his face
from Shame and Spitting', though here Jennens has had to achieve a
further conformity by changing I ('I gave my back to the Smiters') to
'He' throughout, thus preserving the impersonality of the narration
and avoiding the disruption that would be caused if the Man of Sorrows should directly address his listeners. The process reaches its
climax in 'Behold, and see, if there be any Sorrow like unto his Sorrow',
where, in the twentieth century, reputable singers have been known
to achieve disreputable effect by reverting to the original form in
Lamentations: 'Behold, and see, if there be any sorrow like unto my
sorrow'.

We presumably owe to Handel the greatest departure from the
Authorised Version, the duet and chorus version of 'How beautiful are
the feet', with a text derived from Isaiah 52:7–9 rather than the
development of the same passage in Romans, since it was used to
replace the Romans passage when Handel modified his score to suit the
practicalities of performance in Dublin. The evidence of subsequent
contention about the passage suggests that here Handel provided his
own text, although it was eventually to be grudgingly incorporated by
Jennens. That Jennens should emerge as so consistently faithful in his
adherence to the word of scripture should not surprise us; late in life
he became involved in editing Shakespeare, and consequently the
object of bitter sarcasm by a rival in that contentious field, George
Steevens. Yet Jennens's object, though not immediately apparent
today, was to present the text warts and all, so that a reader could
make his own decisions. The words of *Saul*, where the biblical story
was too tangled to allow of direct quotation, are remarkably free of
conscious literary artifice. *Messiah* achieves the ideal, a minimum of
tampering with the actual words of scripture and a maximum of effective collocation, of revealing their full significance through a sequence
of new conjunctions.

Gopsal Hall, Leicestershire. Engraving by J. Throsby, 1789. Jennens did not inherit and commence enlarging Gopsal until 1747, but his improvements show the scale on which this bachelor squire lived. Demolished in 1951.

These might have surprised both the uninformed and the knowledgeable. While the former were still wondering who it was that was prophesying to comfort his people, and why, the latter would have been grappling with the realisation that when Isaiah (and the exceptionally informed would have been asking the question 'Which Isaiah') uttered these words it was in conjunction with a prophecy of the Babylonian captivity, and if the message was ultimately one of hope it carried with it a measure of imminent deprivation and misery. The words were as challenging to the initiate as to the neophyte.

Messiah is, for all its lack of stated plot, a drama, though one in which the momentum is primarily internal and intellectual rather than external. It is notably daring (and indeed modernistic) in that the listener's knowledge of, or capacity to deduce, the historical narrative is assumed, so that it becomes a commentary on the Nativity, Passion, Resurrection and Ascension, framed by, at the beginning, the promises of God uttered by the prophets and, at the end, the ultimate fulfilment of these in redemption. There is a constant exemplification of this in the interplay of Old and New Testament material, revealing the relation of the two covenants. All of this was central to the Anglican theological tradition, and Jennens regarded himself, despite and because of his position as a non-juror, as a guardian and interpreter of that tradition. But it had been explored even more fully by Lutherans, and must immediately have recalled to Handel the teachings of his youth. What Jennens created was above all an *affective* poem, a believer's meditation on the supreme goodness of God in offering to the world his only Son; on the sufferings of this sacrificial victim; and on the hope of salvation for mankind now that the risen Christ stands at the right hand of God. Christ's Incarnation and Passion were conventional subjects of Continental oratorio, but *Messiah*, although the title is accurate, is entirely original in making them episodes subsidiary to the benevolence of God the Father. This emphasis has the inevitable consequence of making the treatment to an extent abstract; it certainly achieves an enormous simplification, and in human terms a reduction, of the dramatic element. Yet drama is not necessarily human.

Here Jennens had a purpose which we might find unexpected in an oratorio, not usually thought of as a medium for theological instruction. To him, as to many educated and devout Anglicans of his time, conformists or non-jurors, though particularly to the latter since they compensated for their internal exile by regarding themselves as the bastion of true orthodoxy, the greatest contemporary threat to their faith was from 'natural religion' or 'Deism'. Deists believed in a Supreme Being, but only in the sense of the original creating force from which material life derived; they denied revelation, the super-natural divine intervention in human affairs. They found much susten-ance in the writings of John Locke, though he would not admit himself to be a Deist, and were severely assailed by two Anglican bishops, George Berkeley (who for four years employed the cellist Pasqualino to teach the children music in the episcopal palace at Cloyne) and Joseph Butler; from different angles of attack they sought to demon-strate that the self-evident truths with which the Deists supported their case were by no means self-evident at all, and that their faith in human reason generally, and in their own reasoning in particular, was misplaced. It is quite wrong to imagine, despite the laxities of the Church, the universities and of society, that the Deists were in the ascendant. *Messiah*, with its insistence on God's free ('gratuitous' in the true sense of the word) gift of his Son, on the historical fact of the Incarnation and the supernatural fact of Redemption, was an assertion of everything that the Deists sought to deny, and if the listener, con-fronted by Jennens's selection from scripture, had to infer much of this, then the act of comprehension, the movement towards a recognition of the greater narrative from the fragmentary presentation, was analo-gous to the supercession of glimmering reason by faith which Dryden had described in one of the first and greatest assaults on Deism, *Religio Laici*. The light of the moon and stars is only borrowed:

> And as those nightly Tapers disappear
> When Day's bright Lord amends one Hemisphere;
> So pale grows *Reason* at *Religion*'s sight;
> So *dyes*, and so dissolves in *Supernatural Light*.

The text of *Messiah* is profoundly religious. (Whether the same can be said of what Handel made of it is another matter.) It will command the assent of many (but not all) Christians; it requires the suspension of disbelief in non-Christians. It is open to criticism on two grounds, theological (which will primarily concern Christians, but coherence of thought is a legitimate cause for concern among non-Christians) and aesthetic. The chief theological objection to the words is that, by wrenching them from their context, Jennens implied applications that were not justified. It was the case when he wrote (and remains so today) that there was considerable doubt as to whether the prophecies of Isaiah, chapter 40 onwards, which appear not to have been made by the prophet of the earlier part of the book, actually concerned the Messiah. This calls into question much of Part I, from the very first words, and important interjections thereafter. For different reasons the opening of Part III raises problems of which biblical critics, in Jennens's day and, increasingly, later on, were well aware. Despite its similar place in the Burial Service, 'I know that my redeemer liveth' in the Authorised translation is a highly conjectural reconstruction of perhaps the most obscure piece of Hebrew in the whole of the Old Testament, the translators themselves telling us in their marginal gloss that 'yet in my Flesh shall I see God' might read 'out of' or 'without' my Flesh, while, though this was not glossed, 'Redeemer' in Job's language meant, under the Mosaic law, 'blood avenger'. The centrality of this contentious text to *Messiah* is merely one of the ways in which it owes as much to the decisions of the makers of the *Book of Common Prayer* as to the scripture more universally interpreted.

The aesthetic problems, only marginally easier, are at least more open to discussion; it is a measure of Jennens's success that his solution has remained largely unquestioned. The Dublin word-book was printed well away from his editorial hand; it records what Handel set before his Irish audience, with the adaptations that he made to accommodate local circumstances. The 1743 Covent Garden word-book shows Jennens firmly in control and divides up each Part as though it were an act in an opera, that is, into numbered verses (in opera, these did not indicate set changes, but the introduction of new material or a new situation through the entry or exit of a character). Accordingly we have:

    I (i) The prophecy of Salvation; (ii) the prophecy of the coming of Messiah and the question, despite (i), of what this may portend for the World; (iii) the prophecy of the Virgin Birth; (iv) the appearance of the Angels to the Shepherds; (v) Christ's redemptive miracles on earth.

    II (i) The redemptive sacrifice, the scourging and the agony on the cross; (ii) His sacrificial death, His passage through Hell and Resurrection; (iii) His Ascension; (iv) God discloses his identity in Heaven; (v) Whitsun, the gift of tongues, the beginning of evangelism; (vi) the world and its rulers reject the Gospel; (vii) God's triumph.

    III (i) The promise of bodily resurrection and redemption from Adam's fall; (ii) the Day of Judgment and general Resurrection;

MESSIAH.

AN

ORATORIO.

As it is Perform'd at the

THEATRE-ROYAL

IN

COVENT-GARDEN.

Set to Mufick by Mr. HANDEL.

MAJORA CANAMUS.

And without Controverfy, great is the Myftery of Godlinefs: God was manifefted in the Flefh, juftified by the Spirit, feen of Angels, preached among the Gentiles, believed on in the World, received up into Glory. In whom are hid all the Treafures of Wifdom and Knowledge.

LONDON:

Printed by and for J. WATTS; and Sold by him at the Printing-Office in *Wild-Court* near *Lincoln's-Inn-Fields:*

And by B. DOD at the *Bible* and *Key* in *Ave-Mary-Lane* near *Stationers-Hall.*

[Price One Shilling.]

Messiah, word-book, 1752. A London printing, hence the spacious quarto format.

(iii) the victory over death and sin; (iv) the glorification of the Messianic victim.

The word-books of oratorios seem to have been at least as necessary to the audience as were the libretti of operas; since there was no need to print a translation they came in a larger format (quarto rather than octavo in London, though provincial printers were to prefer octavo). Early word-books of *Messiah* are today extremely rare; issued roughly stitched in sugar-paper wrappers, they were both fragile and, evidently, intently read: this despite the fact that, amongst all Handel's large-scale works, *Messiah* is outstanding for the way in which Handel consistently ensures that the vocal line is audible (partly a consequence of the modest orchestral forces). The words were seriously pondered by *Messiah*'s early audiences at least, a fact voluminously attested to by the Reverend John Newton who, in 1784 and 1785, preached no fewer than fifty 'Expository Discourses on the Series of Scriptural Passages, which form the subject of the Celebrated Oratorio of Handel', his purpose being to redeem them from the frivolity of the recent Commemoration of the composer in Westminster Abbey. He nevertheless assumed from the start that 'The arrangement or series of these passages, is so particularly disposed, so well connected, and so fully comprehends all the principal truths of the Gospel, that I should not attempt either to alter, or to enlarge it.' It is a great tribute to Jennens from a critic whose theological standards were severe, and whose fundamental absurdity is to fail to see that others, who did not share his aversion to the embodiment of sacred truths in what he regarded as secular music, did not grasp at least a part of what he so copiously expounded.

But Jennens's arrangement of his materials is not unassailable, though it might seem to be if we paid attention to a characteristically bland half-truth of Goethe's, who, when confronted by his old friend Carl Friedrich Zelter's opinion that *Messiah* (which both men particularly admired) had not been planned as a whole, but was an anthology of religious settings by Handel, observed that the notion was plausible 'since fundamentally it does not matter in the least whether the unity is formed at the beginning or the end; it is always the spirit that produces it in either case and here the unity was implicit in the Christian purpose of the work from the very outset'.

In so far as the whole significance, to a Christian, of biblical prophecy is its fulfilment, this is a truism, and one of the fundamental devices of the *Messiah* word-book, typology – the fulfilment of Old Testament prophecies in the New – stems directly from it; indeed, the theological criticism of the text, that the two Isaiahs are not prophesying the same thing, arises from an over-exact application of typology. The aesthetic problem is most apparent in II (i), where the chorus changes role in a way that both confuses and contradicts the logical development of the theme. At the end of Part I it has pronounced what we might well (with two more parts to come) suspect to be an untested truth, 'His Yoke is easy, his Burden is light', though this has the authority of the Gospel. At the beginning of Part II the chorus assumes an almost priestly function with the announcement: 'Behold the Lamb of God, that taketh away the sin of the world'. After the alto solo 'He was despised' it moves through sympathy ('surely He hath borne our Griefs'; 'And with his stripes we are healed') to penitence ('All we, like sheep, have gone astray'). It then becomes, quite abruptly, and with no more of a cue than the accompanied recitative 'All they that see him laugh him to scorn', the voice of the crowd mocking Christ on the cross, if we follow the gospels of Mark and Matthew; the voice of the malefactors, if we follow Luke; or the voice of the crowd replying to Pilate, if we follow John (though this is implicit in the other Gospel narratives).

There is nothing inappropriate about such a choric function. It is an essential part of the German Passion, and Handel, when he set it, responded to it accordingly. It is reasonable to suppose that the crowd that hailed Christ's entry into Jerusalem on Palm Sunday was not so different from that which vilified him in his hour of despair. What is inconsistent about Jennens's treatment is that the account of the incarnation in Part I (iv) has led us to expect narrative where the gospel story is used. In Part II (i) this pattern is not followed. From 'Surely he hath borne our grief' to 'the Lord hath laid on Him the iniquity of us all' the chorus appears to have learned a lesson of which it has lost all idea in 'He trusted in God, that he would deliver him'. H. R. Haweis, in a devout, highly subjective account of *Messiah*, accommodated this abrupt severance by supporting first of all an interior vision 'as of some beloved disciple who stands aside comprehending in part the nature of the tragic spectacle before him, and a prey to all its desolating influences', and secondly:

the outside world laughing Him to scorn . . . till at last the disciple who stands by can bear the sight no longer, and, as he hears the

Saviour cry out, 'Eloi, Eloi, lama sabachthani!' he himself turns away, overcome with remorse, exclaiming 'Thy rebuke hath broken his heart.'

It is a good example of the kind of exposure which Jennens's text can both demand and command. It remains the case, however, that this may be the one point at which the technique of implicit reference and connection is pushed too far. Another, not readily answerable explanation of it, would be the assertion that the Passion masks the dislocation of all ordinary references of time and place. The problem is that words and music have to continue in time and place.

If this criticism has any substance, its force is simply to indicate the magnitude of Jennens's achievement. For all kinds of reasons Jennens made enemies easily. He is often represented as over-bearing, when in fact he seems, rather, to have been unduly fussy, a stickler for details, who in pursuit of them lost all sense of proportion. The wholly unfounded nineteenth-century assertion that *Messiah* was in fact the work of a Reverend Mr Pooley, Jennens's chaplain, presumably stems from somebody's jocular observation that *Messiah* was the kind of thing one could get one's chaplain to put together for one. Quite the opposite is the case. It is the justification of Jennens's perfectionism. It achieves its highly ambitious end with the absolute minimum of elaboration or alteration. There is not a redundant phrase or word in it. To cut it is not only to modify its balance but to distort its meaning. Handel was quite capable of standing up to Jennens; he had no obligation to set the texts he was offered, and though he did ultimately place the Hallelujah in *Saul* at the end of Part I, which was where Jennens intended it to be, it was only after determined efforts to put it at the end; there, as Jennens pointed out to Holdsworth, 'Grand as it is, [it] comes in very nonsensically, having no manner of relation to what goes before.' But Handel's one alteration to Jennens's text in Dublin, where he was quite free of any possible interference, was the replacement of the sequence from Romans:

How beautiful are the Feet of them that preach the Gospel of Peace, and bring glad Tidings of good Things. Their Sound is gone out into all Lands, and their Words unto the Ends of the World.

This, which he had set as a da capo aria, with 'How beautiful are the Feet . . .' as the repeated A section, became a setting for duet and chorus of the verses in Isaiah to which St Paul was alluding:

P A R T III.

S O N G.

Know that my Redeemer liveth, and that he shall stand at the latter Day upon the Earth: and though Worms destroy this Body, yet in my Flesh shall I see God. For now is Christ risen from the Dead, the first Fruits of them that sleep.

CHORUS.

Since by Man came Death,
By Man came also the Resurrection of the Dead;
For as in Adam all die,
Even so in Christ shall all be made alive.

RECI-

RECITATIVE, *accompany'd.*

Behold I tell you a Mystery: We shall not all sleep, but we shall be all changed in a Moment, in the twinkling of an Eye, at the last Trumpet.

S O N G.

The Trumpet shall sound, and the Dead shall be raised incorruptible, and we shall be changed. For this Corruption must put on Incorruption, and this Mortal must put on Immortality.
[Da Capo.

RECITATIVE.

Then shall be brought to pass the Saying that is written, Death is swallowed up in Victory.

D U E T.

O Death, where is thy Sting?
O Grave, where is thy Victory?
{*The Sting of Death is Sin,*
And the Strength of Sin is the Law,

CHO-

> How beautiful are the feet of them that bringeth glad Tidings,
> Tidings of Salvation; that saith unto Sion, thy God reigneth,
> Break into Joy, glad tidings, thy God reigneth.

When *Messiah* was first given in London the next year, and Jennens
had had a chance to scrutinise it, he allowed Handel's Isaiah text
stand, though apparently insisting on the scriptural 'feet of him
(rather than Handel's back-formation from St Paul, 'feet of them
but he persuaded Handel to reinstate 'Their Sound is gone out in
all the Lands', and these words (though the 1743 solution of an ar
setting was abandoned in 1745 when they became a chorus) stood
the text thereafter, providing the motivation for 'Why do the Natio
so furiously rage together', which must, in Dublin, have constituted
transition too obscure even in terms of the logic of prophesy on whic
Messiah depends.

In 1763 Dr John Brown, a Newcastle clergyman with a reputation
an educationalist and most of the consequent professional deformiti
(grotesque certainty in his own judgement, prodigious powers
inexact generalisation; he eventually killed himself) published a *Disse
tation on the Rise, Union and Power, the Progressions, Separations, and Corru
tions, of Poetry and Music*. The essence of his argument is in his title; t
book is a plea for the recovery of that chimerical union. The discussio
of English oratorios is necessarily a discussion of Handel's, 'who
exalted Genius [the Writer] reveres'. It comprehensively finds fau
on the grounds of the 'Weight of Dulness' that he had to set, thoug
Brown's attempt to identify a cause will not do. Because Handel intro
duced oratorio into England, he argued:

> it became a Matter of Necessity, that he should *employ* some Write
> in his Service. Now this being a Degradation, to which Men o
> Genius would not easily submit, he was forced to apply to *Versifiers*
> instead of *Poets*. Thus the Poem was the *Effect* either of Hire or
> Favour, when it ought to have been the voluntary *Emanation* o
> *Genius*.

If Jennens ever read this, he would have had reason to howl with rag
Brown amplified his point; in oratorio Handel 'was in the situation
a great Painter, who should be destined to give Life by Colours, to
dead and unmeaning Design'. Having said this, honesty constraine
him to add a footnote: 'The *Messiah* is an Exception to this gener
Remark.' This admission, however, proved too much for pedagog
amour propre:

> Though that grand Musical Entertainment is called an *Oratorio*, yet it is not *dramatic*; but properly a Collection of *Hymns* or *Anthems* drawn from the Sacred Scriptures: In strict Propriety, therefore, it falls under another Class of Composition . . .

Messiah, according to Brown, succeeded because it was not an oratorio; it was a 'Scripture Collection' (which was, after all, Jennens's own description of it). The question of classification is not of any significance; it is a distinction without a difference, and *Israel in Egypt* is not made more cohesive by being a scripture collection which incorporates real anthem material. The tribute to *Messiah* shines all the more brightly by reason of Brown's wrongheadedness. Though his reasons are a welter of prejudices and arbitrary formulations, he cannot deny the exceptional quality of *Messiah*. To turn his castigation of all Handel's other oratorios into praise for this exception: it is not a composition which anyone could accuse of being 'unconnected, weak, and unaffecting'; we do find an actual 'Succession of pathetic Songs and Choirs' which 'heighten each other by a combined Progression'; there is, throughout the work, an 'Accumulation of Passion'. Totally against the drift of his argument Brown offers an encomium for *Messiah*, and for Jennens, which is uncannily like the praise given it by its first identifiable critic, Edward Synge, Bishop of Elphin.

4: 'The Ravished Ear':
The Music of *Messiah*

THE MANUSCRIPT OF *MESSIAH* IS REMARKABLE FOR CLARITY achieved in evident haste. We do not need Handel's careful record – Part I begun on Saturday (the days are distinguished by their astrological signs) 22 August 1741 and finished on Friday 28 August; Part II finished on Sunday 6 September; Part III on Saturday 12 September; and the whole work *ausgefüllt*, 'filled up', on 14 September – to see how rapidly it was written. There are blots, smudges, passages abruptly scored out, show-throughs from an over-inked quill, and traces of what looks like an upset ink bottle. There are occasional tailless notes (most are deliberate abbreviations); there is the odd excess crotchet, an unfilled bar in the viola part, and there are a few places where a principal part has been revised and part of the accompaniment has not been adjusted to conform to it. In 259 pages such slips of the pen are extraordinarily rare, and almost as many (sometimes more) occur in subsequent transcriptions by professional copyists. The hand is bold and vigorous throughout, written with a generous expressiveness. At the end Handel has inscribed SDG, *Solo Deo Gloria*, 'To God alone the glory'; it is not evidence that when he wrote (as the ineradicable story implausibly has it) he felt that he 'saw all heaven before him', but a customary, if by then rather old-fashioned, acknowledgement of the gift of craftsmanship. (The youthful Henry Purcell charmingly concluded the manuscript of a collection of his anthems: 'God bless Mr. Henry Purcell'). The autograph is an oblong folio in a binding put on after Handel's death. It was bequeathed by Handel to J. C. Smith the elder, from whom it was inherited by his son, who presented it to George III; from 1911 it was on loan to the British Museum, to which, with the rest of the Royal Music Library, it was given by the Queen in 1957. Two leaves containing the last sixty-one bars of the overture and the opening of 'Comfort ye') were missing from an early date. There is an appendix of six leaves which relate to the London performances of 1743 and 1749.

But *Messiah* was not written straight down, with a few minor mistakes and revisions, as a letter might be. In the Fitzwilliam music collection there are sketches for parts of the 'Amen' chorus, for 'He was despised' and for what, rather unnervingly, Handel variously thought of as 'Let all the Angels of the Lord' (i.e. 'God' in the finished version), or 'Let us break their bonds asunder'. The 'Amen' sketch is the most developed and comes amongst other partly worked fugal fragments. Each is in the nature of an outline but germinative subject, a phrase of music, emerging from words, tested back against those words. From such sketches, we know, Handel could begin to compose at length, writing the music in outline first, then adding the words, and completing the infilling last of all. How many more such fragmentary formulations as these were necessary we cannot now begin to tell; they were the kind of jottings which might also include, as these do, the address of a banker, or a tune (interestingly by *Der arme Irische Junge*, the poor Irish boy) heard in the street.

Before looking at the contents of the three parts, which are distinct though related entities, and (because of the way the future and past of a text based on prophecy interreact) short-circuit conventional narrative development, making it possible for the work to be convincingly performed, as at Oxford in the 1750s, over two days – it is important to ask to what extent the work is governed by any general principle of musical unity. Attempts have been made to reconstruct a tonal scheme but these are essentially banal. The 'Hallelujah' chorus and 'Worthy is the Lamb that was slain' end Parts II and III in D major because this was the obvious and, if the players were unknown, the safest key for trumpets. The A minor trumpet obbligato, 'With honour the desert be crown'd', in *Judas Maccabeus*, is a deliberate and extreme abnormality. D major is naturally enough the key of 'Glory to God in the highest' in Part I – the only extraordinary thing would be the treatment by Handel of these choruses in any other way, although the omission of the conventional drums in 'Glory to God' can be read as a deliberate withholding of effect, leaving something in reserve for Parts II and III. But that is a matter of orchestration. This is not to say that keys and key relationships are anything other than considered and subtle in *Messiah* – in its context 'He was despised' extracts as much from this element of design as any constituent part could – but *Messiah* is not an *oratorio a chiave*, sustained by particular significances for given keys: it is constructed in blocks of keys, which establish their local centres, and work through these, rather than according to any overriding rules of reference. In Part I the blocks fall neatly into a recitative, chorus and aria pattern; thereafter they are more complicated.

Another possible way of unifying an oratorio would be by motif rather than key, something that Rudolf Steglich believed Handel achieved in *Messiah* through what he called the 'fourth of certitude', decisively asserted in the ascending fourth on '*I Know* that my Redeemer liveth', and '*and that He* shall stand at the latter day'. Again we find this in '*He was* despised' and emerging, emphasised by the re-entry of the basso continuo, out of the opening phrases of 'Comfort ye' with '*Speak, ye com*fortably to Jerusalem'. The frequent recurrence of the interval is undeniable; that Handel intended this melodic commonplace to have a specific significance is implausible, although the phrase 'fourth of certitude' is beguiling.

A third unifying element has been identified, in an unassuming way, by Arnold Schering in his study of Handel and the protestant chorale. That Handel had chorale melodies, known to him from his earliest years, in his mind when he considered his texts, which frequently drew on the same sources, can hardly be doubted. That these were particularly insistent when he came to compose the choruses, seems very probable and is substantiated by, say, the use in the fugue theme of 'Let all the Angels of God worship Him' of the last line (modified) of *Wachet auf*; this occurs again in the 'And He shall reign for ever and ever' of the Hallelujah chorus. The presence of the influence is undeniable; it is why Handel's choruses seldom sound anything like Purcell's. But it is not, in the end, more than a factor contributing to stylistic unity, interesting in that it is there, but not particularly informative beyond the fact that it tells us that Handel, for all his eclecticism, was sustained by his roots. If its presence is stressed too much (and it is revealing that it has primarily been noted by North European protestant critics, who have been exposed to the sources as no one from an English-speaking tradition has), it becomes part of that 'divide and school' tendency that would teach us that Handel oratorios are compounded of Italian da capo arias, the English anthem tradition, the German chorale tradition, etc., and have us hear in a fragmented way what in fact has been formed into a natural whole. Indeed *Messiah*, where Handel first transmuted the A-B-A da capo aria into the form A-B-Chorus, as in 'Why do the nations – The kings of the earth rise up – Let us break their bonds asunder', is the work which, more than any others, makes nonsense of this. The unity of *Messiah* is a consequence of nothing more arcane than the quality of Handel's attention to his text, and the consistency of his musical imagination.

PART I

The overture (originally 'Sinfony') has generally been thought an admirable introduction to what follows; the one exception is Jennens, who had apparently advised Handel to excise it, but, as he told Holdsworth, 'He retain'd his Overture obstinately, in which there are some passages far unworthy of Handel, but more unworthy of the Messiah'. In the nineteenth century Horatio Townsend objected to this with an unabashedly subjective reading of the *Grave*, 'with its grand succession of chords that come rolling in, one after the other, like great billows of the ocean'. But he hesitated to concur with those who discerned in the fugue 'the development of a great theme or design', and we might well prefer to admire the abstract quality of the whole, noting the absence of modulation (which we half anticipate) into the major in the allegro, and the further, most unusual, absence of a minuet. As Dr Burney put it, 'How exquisitely are judicious ears disappointed' when they mistake the prelude to 'Comfort ye my people' for a preparation for the dance movement they expect. Though the judicious ears and the anticipation have long since gone, the transformation from the E minor of the overture to the E major recitative can still create an effect of pleasurable surprise, and the new key is to be recalled when the believer expresses the redemption of the promise that the words contain in 'I know that my Redeemer liveth'. The change from accompanied recitative to simple chordal punctuation in bar 30 adds to the effect of the ritornello of the air that follows.

In the autograph and the copies nearest to it 'crieth' ('The voice of him that *crieth* in the wilderness') is, as Burney points out, a monosyllable; so too, though not always, is 'Glory' in the first chorus; so too is 'cometh' in 'Rejoice greatly', and instances of the tendency can be multiplied, as can also instances of monosyllables set as disyllables, notably 'were' in 'There *were* shepherds abiding'. The process of 'correcting' these began with John Walsh's publication, *The Songs in Messiah*, which, though not issued until after Handel's death, was probably engraved c. 1750. It has continued in modern editions, yet in fact the autograph settings can be negotiated by confident singers and even a slight awkwardness is preferable to the losses that are caused by tampering.

The tenor continues with 'Every valley': this falls musically into two complementary halves in which the same text is differently treated, though the technique of restrained illustration through word-painting ('Ev'ry valley shall be *exalted*', 'the *crooked* straight and the rough places *plain*') remains the same. The section concludes with the A major chorus 'And the glory of the Lord', where the jubilance of the first phrase, rising eventually to a top a″ on 'Lord', is answered but also checked by the descending figure on 'shall be revealed', a figure that is continued in an altered form and kept going by alternate pairs of voices while the other intones 'for the mouth of the Lord hath spoken it'.

The next group was written to the same pattern, but originally (there were to be many changes in performance) with a bass singing the recitative and aria. Its sombre theme, the Judgment that will attend the coming of the Saviour, is appropriately matched by the sequence D minor–G minor. The accompanied recitative establishes the urgency of the Lord's message with a simple dotted rhythm and rudimentary ascending motif, subsequently modified into semi-quavers in imitation of the soloist's onomatopoeic treatment of 'shake'. 'Desire' in 'and the desire of all nations shall come' is also handled in this way; but here the device conveys not movement but urgency. The accompaniment is again radically simplified at the end, so as to obtain the maximum effect from the entry of the ritornello to 'But who may abide the day of His coming', set in what Burney called 'a Sicilian pastoral style', and once more binary in form. The voice that Handel first had in mind must have been what we would describe as baritone, since in the elaborate treatment of 'when He *appeareth*' (simplified in the alto version) it is required to leap to a top f′, which, contrasted with the interrogatory fifths and octaves that close each question ('But who may abide the day of His *coming*?'), sets, against this unimaginable event, the all too apparent frailty of man. Whether the alto version, which simplifies the first part of the aria in order to offset the elabor-ation, now emphasised by a change of tempo to prestissimo, of 'For He is like a refiner's fire' is preferable, as Handel apparently thought, will always be debatable; it makes the chorus 'And He shall purify the sons of Levi' a meditation on the aria rather than a continuation of and climax to it. It throws all the force of the music into the simile – just that aspect of Italian opera that Gay so deftly satirised. Contrary to what is usually said, the bass version is at least as difficult techni-cally, though less obviously virtuosic.

To call a busy allegro chorus a 'meditation' may seem perverse, but

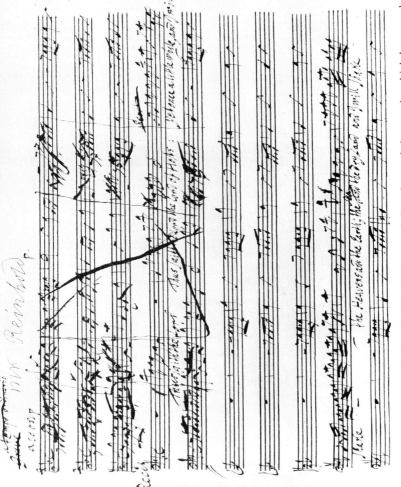

'Thus saith the Lord', showing Handel's second thoughts and the way in which he turned what he had originally intended as an arioso which was to be either *a tempo ordinario* or *grave* into a (recitativo) *accompagnato*.

the long passages for single parts, only coming together when, at 'that they may offer unto the Lord an offering in righteousness', they join homophonically, have that effect. This is one of the five self-borrowings in *Messiah*, from the last movement of the Italian chamber duet *Quel fior che all'alba ride*, written as recently as the beginning of July 1741. Some of these borrowings, all from the Italian cantatas, were known to Burney, and also to George III, which is hardly surprising since several of the duets were written for, and more were performed by, the monarch's sisters. After 1784 they could have been identified by any enquiring Handelian. Here the effective part of the chorus is the inter-polation, the homophonic passage, which, raised a fifth and with changed harmonies, brings it to its conclusion.

The third section of Part I concerns the prophecy of the birth at Bethlehem. It is longer than the preceding sections and the solo parts are taken by two voices; the alto commences with the *secco* (accom-panied by the continuo only) recitative, 'Behold a Virgin shall con-ceive', a marvel of simplicity, all within the compass of a seventh, and continues with the air, 'O thou that tellest good tidings to Zion', which leads into the chorus to the same words and using the same thematic material, with the strings playing a vigorous counter-melody developed from the two-bar motto of the opening phrase, the demi-semiquavers of which enliven the whole number. 'For behold, darkness shall cover the earth, and gross darkness the people' is the recitative which brings in the bass; the dissonant sevenths in the accompaniment are insistent, and the harmony only clarifies when, with 'but the Lord shall arise upon thee', the voice is liberated from its syllabic bonds and climbs to a D. The air, 'The people that walked in darkness' is what might be rather cumbrously described as a 'double binary aria'; that is, it is in two distinct halves, each of which also contains two halves. The overall structure is determined by the essential parallelism of Hebrew rhetoric:

> The People that walked in Darkness have seen a great Light;
> And they that dwell in the Land of the Shadow of Death,
>   upon them hath the Light shined . . .

where the repetition of the idea of light clinches the two halves of the prophet's utterance (in the Psalms such parallelisms are the equivalent of, in English verse, rhyme); this is the basis of Handel's musical disposition. The air carries forward one of the features of the recitative since, in Charles Burney's words, 'the chromatic and indeterminate

modulation seems to delineate the uncertain footsteps of persons
exploring their way in obscurity'. The chorus 'For unto us a Child is
born', is again derived from an Italian chamber duet, *No', di voi non vo
fidarmi*, another product of July 1741. It also depends for its effect
on homophonic statements which finally take over from the tripping
movement of the duet material, and are reached by means of the new
theme announced in the tenor, 'and the government shall be upon His
shoulder', which leads to the culminating 'Wonderful, counsellor, the
mighty God, the everlasting Father, The Prince of Peace'. Burney,
again in his account of the great Commemoration of Handel in May
1784, reports that 'During the performance of [*Messiah*], I made three
several pencil marks, expressive of the degrees of comparative good
with which my ears were affected, by particular movements', and he
'found the sign of superlative excellence stamped on [this] chorus'. He
praised in particular the fugal subjects and the violin accompaniments,
but above all the 'clearness and facility which reign through the whole'.

The Incarnation is the subject of the fourth section, which possesses
a radiance of feeling all its own. It introduces the soprano soloist,
whose voice is the more effective for having been hitherto withheld. It
begins with an unashamedly naturalistic device, the *pifa*, an imitation
of the tunes played by shepherds from the Abruzzi who came with
their bagpipes into the streets of Rome during the Christmas season.
But Handel did not expect his listeners to know that at first hand; the
similarity to the last movement of Corelli's Concerto Grosso opus VI
no. 8, 'fatto per la Notte di Natale', would have been sufficient to
convey the point. The recitative to which it acts as a prelude is in four
sections, alternately *secco* and orchestrally accompanied, the accompanied sections evoking, with their running chordal figures, first the
arrival of the angel of the Lord, and then the appearance of the angel
host. Burney noted, although in 1784 he attributed this in part to the
powers of Madame Mara, 'an effect far beyond what might be effected
from such few and simple notes, without air or measure: they were
literally made "*melting sounds*" to every hearer of sensibility present'.
The last recitative, 'And suddenly', leads directly into 'Glory to God
in the highest', unprepared for by any orchestral prelude and bringing
in – an effect to which Handel gave particular consideration – the
trumpets *da lontano e un poco piano*, 'from far off and rather soft'. They
were originally to have been *in disparte*, 'from elsewhere', or 'hidden',
effective if it could have been managed, but not really practical. The
tessitura of all the parts is kept high, except for the basses, held back

until their dramatic entry with a simple falling octave on 'And peace on earth'. Burney had to resort to French to express his delight and admiration: 'There is more *claire obscure* in this short Chorus than perhaps had ever been attempted at the time it was composed'. He meant disguised learning, particularly in the fugal imitations of 'goodwill towards men', that need not be at all apprehended for the piece to have its full effect; but the particular aptness of the phrase is that it also conveys that sense of the luminous ('myriads of flame-like faces, sublime and tender . . . the air vibrates with the pulsation of their innumerable wings', wrote H. R. Haweis, a century later) which the chorus seems invariably to suggest.

The final section concerns the ministry of Christ on earth, which foreshadows what he will achieve for man in Heaven. It has a historical point of reference in Palm Sunday, but does not attempt to re-create it dramatically as the appearance of the angels to the shepherds had been in the last episode. It begins not with a recitative but an aria, in B flat, 'Rejoice greatly, O daughter of Zion', and there is no change of voice; the soprano sings this as she does the subsequent recitative and aria. In the autograph it is an operatically grand da capo aria with a binary A section and in 12/8 time. Handel very soon shortened it (probably for Dublin), and subsequently rewrote the shortened version in common time, thus differentiating it rhythmically from the next aria, 'He shall feed his flock', and reducing the very considerable burden of solo work that falls on the soprano in the last two sections of this part. 'A brilliant and difficult air', says Burney of the final version; not so brilliant, but difficult (though for different reasons), we might say of the first. There has been critical unease with this section, charitably expressed by Haweis: 'The great artist knows when the eye requires rest, and lays on his middle tints, until our emotion has been subdued . . .' Handel's revisions certainly attempted to wind it up to a higher level of musical interest. But it restores the human dimension as it relaxes the tension. The recitative, with its brief narrative of Christ's ministry of healing, 'Then shall the eyes of the blind be open'd', concentrates this element, and the *siciliano*, 'He shall feed His flock', with its reminiscences of secular pastoral, continues it; it has always been popular and is as unaffectedly simple, and perfectly judged, as the *pifa*. Handel's final version, with the first half sung in F major by an alto, the second in B♭ major by a soprano, effectively breaks the long run of B♭ major and of a single voice. The text of the chorus carries forward the passage of St Matthew with which the aria concludes. Once more the setting derives from the chamber duet *Quel fior che all'alba ride*, this time from the first section, so that 'The flower which laughs at *dawn*' becomes 'His yoke is *easy*', the substitution explaining what Sedley Taylor, in his pioneer study of Handel's borrowings, called 'a piece of word-painting, quite appropriate in its original position, but grievously out of place where it now stands'. But Sedley Taylor also tells us to look for the stroke of genius which comes in the added four-part conclusion, in which he sees a mingling of 'beauty and dignity'. 'Elegance' might be a more appropriate word; it brings Part I neatly to an end without prejudicing the range of emotions to be explored in what is to come.

PART II

Part II begins with the Eucharistic invitation, 'Behold the Lamb of God, that taketh away the Sin of the World', and the first section is concerned with Christ's Passion. Burney gave the chorus one good mark, for solemnity, but the dotted rhythm makes for a dramatic declamatory opening, and the idea of a fugued beginning, even though it is more apparent than real, is also unexpected and arresting. Jens Peter Larsen points to the resemblance of the initial motif to that of 'He shall feed His flock', and though the atmosphere is so different, the connection seems inescapable: innocence is now precipitated into an alien and uncomprehending world. 'He was despised' is, somewhat unexpectedly in E♭ major, a full da capo aria for alto, linked back to the G minor of 'Behold the Lamb of God' by the use of that key in the conclusion of the B section. It is not a display piece, but calls, with its fragmented vocal line constantly semi-echoed instrumentally, for the utmost in controlled expression. In the B section the unrelenting dotted rhythm of the strings' accompaniment and snatched phrases of the vocal line suggest accompanied recitative; the return to the A section relaxes the tension. Burney said the air 'has impressed me with the highest idea of excellence in pathetic expression, of any English song with which I am acquainted'.

It is followed by a sequence of three choruses, the first two in F minor, the third moving from F major to conclude in F minor. 'Surely, He hath borne our griefs' is as unexpected as the opening chorus. The introduction, which continues the dotted figure used to depict scourging in the B section of the air, leads us to anticipate an accompanied recitative, which essentially it is, but the recitation is by a homophonic chorus, and the effect to make the 'our' of 'our griefs', 'our sorrows', 'our iniquities', a statement of collective identity and responsibility. If there is an incipient emotionalism in this it is expunged by the austerity of 'And with His stripes we are healed', a (for Handel) severe fugue on a theme which had been used by earlier composers and would be used by later, where the instruments have no other function than to double the vocal parts. If there is any symbolism to be observed in the piece it is simply in the fact that the exchange of parts between the voices in the fugue mirrors the process that the seven-word text describes. 'All we like sheep' again has its origin in the chamber duet *No, di voi non vo fidarmi*, but this time is taken from the last part, and with an altered opening. As Sedley Taylor points out, the consequence of applying music originally written as a denunciation of the tyranny of 'blind love and cruel beauty' to this new text is that it breathes 'a certain heaven-defying recklessness which a less dramatically minded composer than Handel would hardly have read into the English words'. Nor is the determined straying of short duration. It is when the words 'and the Lord hath laid on Him the iniquity of us all' are introduced by the cessation of the insistent running bass, the change of tempo to adagio, and the return to the minor key which governs the group of choruses, that the theme of repentance is re-established.

The accompanied recitative 'All they that see Him' reiterates the scourging motif and prepares the way for the scorn and mockery of 'He trusted in God that He would deliver Him', where the assertive contemptuousness of the chorus is achieved largely through the driving note (syncopated) on 'He' (as it refers to God): 'He trusted in God that *He* would deliver Him'. The effect of the fugal structure here is, as with 'And with His stripes', to generalise the sentiment, but in this case it does not in any way depersonalise or abstract it; we encounter a characterised but unanimous crowd, and this is the moment when *Messiah* comes closest to a German passion. The tenor* then again takes up the thread, in a sequence in which a slow accompanied recitative, *arioso* and accompanied recitative culminate in the andante air 'But Thou didst not leave His soul in hell', having carried us through a series of sharp keys into A major. What is, for Handel, an emphatic use of modulation and of unexpected progressions characterises the recitatives, particularly 'Thy rebuke hath broken His heart',

---

* Those early scores which carry authority suggest that Handel 'did not count on a performance in which all five numbers were sung by the same singer' (Larsen). But the contrary is hard to show, and this is not so long as the preceding soprano sequence.

which concludes with the rigidly unexpressive 'to comfort Him'. 'Behold and see' uses a similar device, the opening-up of the invocatory 'Behold', first perfect fifth, then an augmented sixth, but concludes with the deadened descending third and monotone, varied only by a mordant, on 'like unto His sorrow'. 'He was cut off out of the land of the living' moves us, in opposition to the sense of the text in detail ('for the transgressions of Thy people was He stricken') from B minor to A major, the key of 'But Thou didst not leave His soul in hell', short, free-flowing, liberating, and causing Larsen, a comparatively severe critic, to continue, unwittingly, Haweis's metaphor from the end of Part I: 'Once again we seem to see the clear blue colours of old Italian Masters of painting, their purity enhanced by contrasting greyness.'

The chorus 'Lift up your heads' in Jennens's division of the word-book constitutes a section in itself. It is exceptional, in that he makes a brief but effective use of a double chorus, achieved in no more complicated a way than by making the altos work overtime, now a bass to the divided sopranos, now a treble to the tenors and basses. Economy of means, as is the case throughout *Messiah*, proves extraordinarily effective. Here the parallelism of *Psalms*, in its straight question-and-answer form, determines the musical structure, and the final response to the insistent question 'Who is this King of Glory?', 'The Lord of Hosts', unites the chorus in four parts and generates some jubilant writing as the strings unashamedly cross parts and, in the case of the first violins in bar 51, soar to heights they may not have thought themselves equipped to scale.

The fourth section describes, as briefly, Christ's reception into Heaven. The tenor recitative effects a necessary transition of key to another chorus, but also does what by now we have recognised as customary in the oratorio: it puts the divine words into the simplest possible musical dress: 'Unto which of the angels said He at any time, Thou art My Son, this day have I begotten Thee?' The chorus 'Let all the angels of God worship Him' induced a state of near ecstasy in Burney:

This spirited fugue, seemingly on two subjects, is, perhaps, the most artificial that has been composed in modern times. Handel, in order to exercise his abilities in every species of difficulty which the most learned and elaborate Canonists and Fughists of the fifteenth and sixteenth centuries were ambitious of vanquishing, has composed

Larghetto
How beautiful are the feet of them that
preach the gospel of peace
them that preach the gospel, how beautiful are the feet
of them that preach
how
and bring glad ti-dings
glad tidings of good things, and

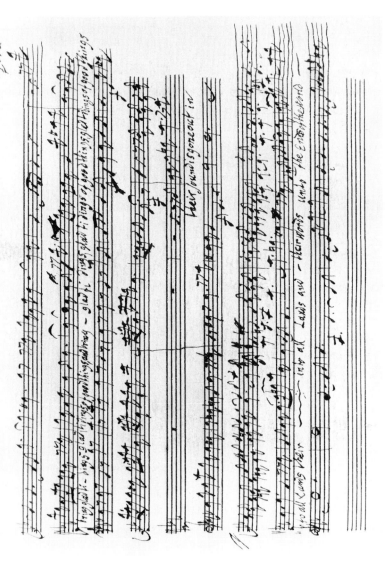

Messiah, the autograph. The opening of 'How beautiful are the feet' as a dal segno aria including the section 'Their sound is gone out'. For Dublin Handel replaced these words from Romans 10 with words from Isaiah 52 arranged as a duet and chorus.

this movement in what ancient theorists call *minor Prolation*; in which the reply to a subject given, though in similar intervals, is made in notes of different value: as when the theme is led off in semibreves and answered in minims, or the contrary.

This is a very fair explanation, but it is only in a footnote, recommending the study of the piece to 'Professors', that he really finds his words for what is achieved: 'an exercise for ingenuity often practised about two hundred years ago, on a few slow notes . . . but never before, I believe, in so many parts, with such perfect airy freedom, or little appearance of restraint and difficulty'.

Perhaps one can go further than Burney here, by attempting to identify the factor which required him to make two attempts at trying to explain the profound feelings that 'Let all the angels of God' evoked in him. Church music of the Renaissance had inherited much from the middle ages that was largely forgotten by the eighteenth century – above all an underlying concern with the mystery of number and proportion. By drawing on this composers attempted to make statements that were primarily symbolic rather than emotional. Their splendour and strangeness was dependent on the listener's sense of their abstract content; and it is that aesthetic that Handel recalls to make manifest the idea of the angelic choir.

The next section of this longest part of *Messiah* treats of Whitsun and, after the gift of tongues, the preaching of the Gospel. It is the point in the oratorio at which alternative versions make matters particularly complicated. But the autograph remains the most reliable guide. Whitsun itself is described in 'Thou art gone up on high', originally for bass, organised in the subdivided variant of binary form which Handel so frequently employs. In the original version it is dominated by a ritornello which frequently appears to be telling us something that the words are not; Handel subsequently endeavoured to prune this. That Christ should disappear from the world in order for God to dwell in it is a misreading of the text, but the one that is liable to occur at first hearing, and it is not easily annihilated. But, in each of its three variants (revised for alto, revised for soprano, and simply transposed from the original version for soprano), the idea of a triumphant ascension is clearly conveyed. The chorus that follows opens with the tenors and basses singing, unaccompanied and in unison, 'The Lord gave the Word'; it then rockets off like an Italian toccata, one of the infrequent but notable moments when Handel is reminiscent of Monteverdi.

'How beautiful are the feet' was originally a da capo aria for soprano, which was replaced by the alto duet and chorus to the Romans text (see page 74) at the first performances of *Messiah* in Dublin and London, but itself subsequently replaced in a shortened version of the original, which also exists transposed for alto. When the original aria was cut, its B section, 'Their sound is gone out into all Lands, and their words unto the Ends of the World', became first an *arioso*, then an independent chorus. Handel, therefore, probably never performed what he originally wrote. The history of the evolution of *Messiah* is also that of the gradual elimination of the da capo element, and here the closed nature of the form militated against the direction of the words; the return of the *siciliano*, after an expansive treatment of 'Their sound is gone out' in the B sections, is only logical from a musical point of view. Paradoxically, in the duet version the problem is primarily with the inserted text, 'Break forth into joy, thy God reigneth', which even in terms of the subliminal motivations of *Messiah* does not explain why, at this, the nations should rage together. The provision of a further setting of 'Their sound is gone out' restores the sense, but Handel was evidently dissatisfied with the scale of his first solution, the tenor *arioso*, though it is an effective piece of writing, making an unshowy but dramatic use of the high register. The choral version economically re-uses the same material, but is constructed on a bass which twice soars and descends with a spaciousness more common in sixteenth-century a cappella writing than in the works of Handel's contemporaries.

The next aria and chorus, 'Why do the Nations so furiously rage together?' and 'Let us break their bonds asunder', form the penultimate section of this part, and describe the persecutions which greeted the spread of the Gospel. Both the first part of the aria and the chorus are in C major, making possible the fusion of the two already mentioned. The aria is of a stock operatic type, illustrating a worldly response to actions divinely inspired. It could easily have been mere bluster, but it is sufficiently focused to convey the anger of institutions whose whole justification is called into question. For Dublin it was shortened, and it is once more reasonable to assume that, as with 'How beautiful are the feet', it was never performed in its original version. The ferocity of 'Let us break their bonds asunder' is apparent from its abrupt opening, and from the closeness of the entries, which come falling over one another and create a concentrated release of splenetic energy.

The final section, in a recitative, air and chorus, depicts God's victory. The recitative and air are for tenor, the recitative, 'He that dwelleth in Heaven shall laugh them to scorn', being only three bars long, and the more effective for its brevity. The air, 'Thou shalt break them with a rod of iron', is marked by powerful ritornelli, not directly related to the vocal line, which reiterate the flagellation figure and dominate the piece. It is sufficiently taxing for Handel to have replaced it with a recitative at the Dublin performance, but he subsequently reinstated the air. If it is slight compared with what is to come, then perhaps this is because God's power exercised on earth is seen as but a trivial aspect of his omnipotence, now to be attested in the 'Hallelujah' chorus. 'It is not easy to speak of it', says Haweis; 'I hasten to speak of it', says Burney. The anonymous author of *An Examination of the Oratorios which have been performed this season* (1763), a work which followed immediately in the wake of Dr John Brown's discourse, and which resolutely refused to admit that any number was beyond criticism, was nevertheless forced to concede it 'truly striking and sublime, by the most perfect conduct it rises by degrees to the utmost pitch of sublimity and pathos, till music exhausts her utmost powers in the noble expression of *King of Kings, and Lord of Lords*'. Burney is more use and keeps his *o altitudino* – a comparison with Dante's *Paradiso* improved with a touch of Milton – for a separate paragraph:

> The opening is clear, cheerful and bold. And the words 'For the Lord God omnipotent reigneth', set to a fragment of canto fermo, which all the parts sing, as such, in unison and octaves, has an effect truly ecclesiastical. It is afterwards made the subject of fugue and ground-work for the Allelujah. Then as a short episode in plain counterpoint, we have '*The Kingdom of this world*'. . . . But the last and principal subject proposed, and led off by the bass – '*And He shall reign for ever and ever*', is the most pleasing and fertile that has ever been invented since the art of fugue was first cultivated. It is marked, and constantly to be distinguished throughout all the parts, accompaniments, counter-subjects and contrivances, with which it is charged. And, finally, the words – '*King of Kings, and Lord of Lords*', always set to a single sound, which seems to stand at bay, while the other parts attack it in every possible manner, in '*Allelujahs – for ever and ever*', is a most happy and marvellous concatenation of harmony, melody, and great effects.

The end of the Hallelujah chorus, with Handel's note that he completed Part II on Sunday (indicated by the astrological sign) 6 September, 1741.

To this several things could be objected; that the fugal element is often more impressionistic than actual, that the 'most pleasing and fertile' subject is in fact the last line, a little altered, of *Wachet auf*, that the real artifice comes in the rhythmic pacing of the piece as a whole, the alternation and eventual simultaneous presentation of a simple melody of a *cantus firmus* type and strongly marked chordal motifs. A context is established in which every detail works to its maximum advantage: 'The Kingdom of this world' is perhaps the supreme example. There are two moments in *Messiah* which I find have an effect out of all proportion to their length or to anything that there is to say about them. This is one; the other is the first appearance of the phrase 'He is the righteous Saviour' in 'Rejoice greatly'. In both the strings simply double the vocal parts; both are figures based on a descending fifth; both create an illusory sensation of ritardando; both suggest reflection amongst jubilation and are of exceptional poignancy.

PART III

'The third part of the *Messiah* is purely theological,' says the Reverend Mr Haweis, a little dauntingly, 'yet the interest does not flag.' It can hardly do so. The unfinished business after the Hallelujah chorus is the point of what has gone before. Listening to Madame Mara singing 'I know that my Redeemer liveth' with which it opens and which, with the chorus 'Since by Man came Death', makes up the first episode, Burney, 'though long hackneyed in music', could not forbear to shed a tear. He made another less personal comment. Mara's 'power over the sensibility of the audience seemed equal to that of Mrs Siddons' – the greatest tragic actress of the century. The strength of the aria is in its effective simplicity. The violins accompany the voice in unison. The aria is in three parts: 'I know that my Redeemer liveth'; 'And tho' worms destroy this body'; 'For now Christ is Risen'. In the last Christ is named for the first time in *Messiah*, and finally recognised as 'the anointed one' of prophecy. The vocal line maintains a gentle tension between consolation – the lulling rhythms suggesting rest, and exaltation – the leap of an augmented sixth on 'My Redeemer', the long ascending octave scale on the final 'For now Christ is Risen'. The word setting has often been criticised, and caused acute dissatisfaction to Jennens, who spent a long time trying to improve it. His efforts are wholly destructive of the musical line. Handel intended what he wrote and attempts to regularise it eradicate those shifts of emphasis which force even an unresponsive singer to adapt to the declamatory accents of the speaking voice. The unaccompanied *grave* opening of the following chorus, 'Since by Man came Death', leads into the allegro 'by man came also the resurrection of the dead', an effect that is mirrored in the second half.

The second section also consists of two numbers, the brief accompanied recitative, 'Behold, I tell you a Mystery' and 'The trumpet shall sound', both for bass, and describing the general Resurrection on the Day of Judgment. The instrumental figures at the end of the recitative presage the strange motif of the aria itself, which is intensified by the initial opposition and subsequent imitation of trumpet and bass. Here, the victory won, the da capo form makes perfect sense, and although Handel subsequently shortened the aria, he preserved its shape. The B section, 'For this corruptible must put on incorruption', is accompanied only by the continuo, making this long and (I maintain) essentially meditative aria decidedly conservative in form. The held high notes and descending scale of a seventh at '*on* incorruption' are odd on paper, natural in practice, a temporal gesture towards eternity.

The penultimate section of the oratorio foretells what cannot humanly be told, the victory over death and sin. The alto recitative, 'Then shall be brought to pass', commands attention (as do all the recitatives) by its undemonstrative succinctness; the duet for alto and tenor which it introduces has no orchestral accompaniment, and the abstraction of the treatment ('O death, where is thy sting?' is only formally a question) and clarity of exposition are implicit in the first bar, where the 'walking bass' immediately proclaims the affirmative character of the movement. The source is again an Italian duet, this time an early, not a recent composition. It is a self-borrowing of genius, to my mind the most completely successful of such borrowings in the work; what was originally an injunction to forgo the transitory pleasures of love seems even more appropriate in its new context. It runs directly into the chorus 'But thanks be to God', which foreshortens motifs from the duet and is built as an extension of the same bars. The final aria, 'If God be for us', for soprano, continues the mood of 'O death, where is thy sting?'; it is reflective rather than triumphalist, something conveyed by its assured movement over a bass that moves almost entirely in crotchets, and by the exchanges between the voice and the unison violins that depend on long rests in which one part listens to what the other has to say. It is perhaps the only piece in *Messiah* that might have been (rather than could have been) written by Bach.

The three concluding choruses, thought John Mainwaring, reveal Handel 'rising still higher' than he did in that 'vast effort of genius, the Hallelujah chorus'. The eighteenth century seems to have been less troubled by the doubt that beset the nineteenth, as to whether the end of Part II was not the true climax (indeed the proper conclusion) of *Messiah*. George III, annotating Mainwaring, was determined to put the Hallelujah in its place, preferring the Dettingen *Te Deum*. He even ventures that the *Te Deum* might be finer than 'Worthy is the Lamb' and 'the unexpected Amen at the close', but he certainly makes clear that 'Worthy is the Lamb' was usually regarded as the apogee of Handel's choral writing. Burney, of course, would not have agreed, but his admiration is expressed in terms comparable to those that he applies to the Hallelujah, though here he stops short of metaphor, noticing particularly the different characters of the three: 'Worthy is the Lamb', 'in solemn, simple counterpoint, and modulation, is slow; with alternate strains of an accelerated movement, to which there is a very ingenious and pleasing accompaniment for the violins, totally different from the voice-parts'; 'Blessing and honour, glory and power', remarkable for its long subject, judicious emphasis and the way in which 'with a fire, spirit, and resources peculiar to Handel, this admirable Chorus is wound up with reiterations of the words "*for ever and ever*" '; the 'Amen', where, 'unembarrassed by words' he 'gave a loose to genius, liberated from all restraints but those of his own art'.

'Worthy is the Lamb' is in two complementary sections, largo–andante, largo–andante, the largos largely homophonic, the andantes contrasting descending semiquavers in the strings with ascending quavers in the vocal parts. 'Blessing and honour' is a splendid exercise in free fugato, a use of the elements of fugue with reinforced entries and stretti, leading to an apparently premature conclusion on the dominant, A, rather than the anticipated D. But this ushers in an 'Amen' which satisfies every kind of contrapuntal curiosity with a dazzling display of learning and inventiveness, yet is nevertheless not, as a whole, strictly constructed; it is, in fact, a written-out example of the kind of inspired improvisation which made Handel's fame as an organist, here transferred to another medium and made permanent.

5: 'That Generous and Polite Nation': The Dublin Performance

HANDEL ARRIVED IN DUBLIN ON WEDNESDAY 18TH NOVEMBER 1741. He had sailed from Parkgate rather than Holyhead, a sea journey of double the length, but saving the 60 miles of bad Welsh roads which faced the traveller from London after Whitchurch. Parkgate, a village on the banks of the Dee from which, weather permitting, packets sailed to Ireland four times a week, is 12 miles from Chester, where he was watched 'narrowly' by a fifteen-year-old schoolboy who was 'extremely curious to see so extraordinary a man'. The youth was Charles Burney, the future historian of music, not long since introduced to the art by Edmund Baker, the organist of Chester Cathedral, 'who being distressed for an assistant during a fit of the Gout, taught [him] to play a Chant on the Organ before he knew his Gammut or the names of the keys'. By now music-mad, Burney watched the great composer 'smoke a pipe, over a dish of coffee, at the Exchange Coffee-house'. Handel was forced by prevailing westerly winds to remain at the Golden Falcon inn for several days, and asked Baker 'whether there were any choirmen in the cathedral who could sing *at sight*; as he wished to prove some books that had been hastily transcribed, by trying the choruses which he intended to perform in Ireland'. Baker obliged and a time was fixed for a private rehearsal at the Golden Falcon, the bass being a local printer called Janson or Jeynson. There, according to Burney (who told the story often but did not claim to have been present), 'alas! on trial of the chorus in the *Messiah*, "*And with his stripes we are healed*", – Poor Janson, after repeated attempts, failed so egregiously, that Handel let loose his great bear upon him; and after swearing in four or five languages, cried out in broken English: "You schcauntrel! tit not you dell me dat you could sing at soite?" – "Yes, sir", says the printer, "and so I can; but not at *first sight*" '.

We do not know who, besides his servant, accompanied Handel, but it is possible that John Christopher Smith travelled with him.*

* If Smith went with Handel to Dublin, as Jennens apparently thought, this might explain why the fair transcript of Handel's autograph, the 'conducting' or 'Tenbury' score, is on a cheap unwatermarked paper, unlike any other used by Smith. The Chester anecdote,

Smith, born Schmidt, was from Anspach and had been a fellow-student of Handel's at the University of Halle; he had come to England in 1716 to act as his treasurer as well as his amanuensis; as Handel's fame grew and demand for more complete copies of his music than were available in print grew with it, Smith became, in effect, the head of an informal scriptorium, sub-contracting a good deal of this work. The same issue of Faulkner's *Dublin Journal* that welcomed 'the celebrated Dr Handell, a Gentleman universally known by his excellent Compositions in all Kinds of Musick, and particularly for his *Te Deum, Jubilate, Anthems*, and other Compositions in Church Musick, (of which for some Years past have principally consisted the Entertainments in the Round Church, which have so greatly contributed to support the Charity of Mercer's Hospital) to perform his Oratorios' also carried a report from Chester, dated 5 November, of the visit of a Mr Maclaine, en route for Dublin, who had been invited to play on the cathedral organ and had 'performed so well . . . that some of the best Judges in Musick said, They never heard that Organ truly played on before; and his Performance was allowed to be very masterly, and in the finest Taste'.† The *Dublin Journal* went on to connect the two musicians; in order to present his oratorios Handel had engaged 'Mr Maclaine, his Wife, and several others of the best Performers in the Musical Way'. Mr Maclaine and his wife are shadowy figures, but since Mrs Maclaine did indeed sing in *Messiah* it must be assumed that the Dublin journalist, even though he had been over-enthusiastic in awarding Handel a doctorate and wrongly presumed him to have sailed from Holyhead, had otherwise got his facts right. The next issue reported the arrival 'in the Yacht from Parkgate, Signiora Avolio, an excellent Singer, who is come to this Kingdom, to perform in Mr Handel's Musical Entertainments'. (The 'Yacht' was the rather superior packet that

---

however, implies that, since parts were available, the fair copy had already been made, though they could have been made directly from the autograph. It is not possible to show from the conducting score itself whether Smith was in Dublin or not.

† The identity of MacLean may not be impenetrable. English professional organists are better documented than most musicians, and there is no candidate. But the Scottish violinist and composer Charles McLean not only taught the spinet and harpsichord at the Aberdeen music school; St Paul's Chapel in that city had what was thought, in 1726, to be the only organ in a public church in Scotland. In 1738, having held his Aberdeen appointment for little more than a year McLean took off for Edinburgh and became a violinist employed by the Edinburgh Musical Society. In 1740 he disappears from the Edinburgh record, but there are indications that he was still active musically in the 1760s. He was just the kind of itinerant professional who might have tried his luck in Dublin.

ferried the Lord Lieutenant and was reputedly safer than the ordinary traders.) The rival *Pue's Occurrences* simply plagiarised the *Dublin Journal*, as it often did, and reported the coming of Handel, who was 'to perform here this Winter, and has brought over several of the best performers in the Musical Way'. But they evidently journeyed separately, and whether there were others besides the mysterious Macleans and Christina Maria Avoglio, of whom this is the earliest record apart from a possible appearance as Cleopatra in Handel's *Giulio Cesare* at Hamburg in 1729, is not known. What is perfectly evident is that Handel felt no need to arrive in Dublin with a galaxy of celebrated performers. As we have seen, he knew musicians there already: Dubourg, Pasqualino, James Baileys, and even, should he need him, a French horn player named Winch who, a month earlier, had played a concerto between the acts at the Smock Alley Theatre, billed as having 'perform'd several years in Mr Handel's Operas and Oratorios'. Moreover, Handel waited for over a month before giving his first concert, on Wednesday 23 December.

During that month he had to establish himself in his house in 'Abbey Street, near Lyffey Street', and to find his way around Dublin, geographically and musically. He seems to have done so cautiously (which accords with the way he ran his opera and oratorio seasons in London). He was at once approached to play the organ at the Mercer's Hospital Benefit on 10 December, when his *Te Deum, Jubilate* and two anthems new to Dublin were performed, along with an anthem, 'Blessed is he who considereth the sick', specially commissioned from William Boyce. Handel must have played some part, since two days after the performance, the governors of the Hospital ordered John Wynne, the precentor of St Patrick's, to thank him 'for his attendance', but it is curious that there is no notice of it in the journals.

Meanwhile, on 3 December, there had been another arrival from England, that was to prove, fortuitously, of great importance to Handel. This was the actress Susannah Cibber: whilst Handel came to Dublin in the full confidence of his great reputation, it seems likely that Mrs Cibber ventured on to the Dublin stage partly in the hope that here her past would be unknown. She was twenty-seven, a younger sister of the composer Thomas Augustine Arne. In 1734 she had married Theophilus Cibber, son of the Poet Laureate and former actor-manager Colley Cibber, who was now an actor-manager in his own right. She made her début as a singer in J. F. Lampe's English opera *Amelia*; this was followed by the pirate performance of *Acis and*

Galatea referred to in Chapter 1, in which she played Galatea. The following year her brother acquired full control (hitherto shared with his father, Lampe and Henry Carey) of the English Opera and produced his own first stage-work, a setting of Joseph Addison's *Rosamond*, which proved a great success, with 'Was ever Nymph like Rosamond', sung by Susannah Arne, its most popular air.

Theophilus Cibber had many of his famous father's less amiable characteristics but none of his genius. As a manager he was unable to control his company; as an actor he played to the least reputable part of the gallery; personally he was recklessly extravagant, drank to excess and frequented prostitutes. He shortly gave his wife two children, who both died soon after birth, and venereal disease. He married her largely for her box-office potential, but he lacked appropriate vehicles to display her talents as a singer at Drury Lane. It was his father, Colley, now free of financial involvement in the theatre but still keenly interested in its affairs, who thought little of Susannah's ability as a singer ('not the best, and if not best, 'tis nothing') but felt there might be merit in her speaking voice. Trial proved that there was; Colley Cibber was an excellent coach, and she turned out to be the ablest pupil he had had in forty years' experience of the stage.

In 1736 Susannah came out in the title role of Aaron Hill's translation of Voltaire's *Zara* and played this notable pathetic part with enormous effect. Later that year Theophilus cast her as Polly in the *Beggar's Opera*, a part that in the past had belonged to her rival in the company, Kitty Clive; the result was violent public partisanship, fuelled by Theophilus, who resented his wife's refusal to enter into the spirit of this deliberate bid for publicity, and begrudged in particular the loss of the anticipated revenue. Early in 1737 he broke into her dressing-room, removed her jewels and costumes, and sold them. One of his major creditors was a young country gentleman, William Sloper, of West Woodhay, Berkshire. To alleviate the situation Cibber demanded that Susannah receive Sloper socially, and when, in the course of time, acquaintance ripened into a love affair, he was complaisance personified. But when his presence, despite the amenities of inter-connecting bedrooms (so that Mrs Cibber could undress in her husband's room, and then go next door until she and Sloper were awakened by Cibber's morning knock), became irksome, and she and Sloper eloped, thus cutting off his source of financial relief, Cibber's temper changed. He had already taken the precaution of acquiring a dossier of part of their relationship, compiled in meticulous, indeed clinical detail by a Mr Hayes, the husband of the landlady from whom Susannah's former maid had rented rooms, ostensibly to return to her old trade of mantua-making, actually to provide a place of assignation for Mrs Cibber and Mr Sloper. They did not know that Mr Hayes had bored two holes through the wainscot from a closet, and that from there he could watch and record every move they made. In the autumn of 1738 Cibber abducted and imprisoned his wife, who was rapidly rescued by her brothers Thomas and Henry, at the head of a large body of men. Mrs Cibber then swore peace against her husband, and he sued Sloper for 'assaulting, ravishing, and carnally knowing her'.

The trial delighted London and made the reputation of the junior defending counsel, the future Lord Mansfield, who persuaded the jury to award Cibber, not the £5000 he asked, but £10. Mr Hayes's evidence, despite reporting restrictions, and despite the fact that he was cut off in full flow* by the Lord Chief Justice, Sir William Lee, became a minor classic of voyeurism. Susannah Cibber and William Sloper retreated into the country for three years, where she bore him a daughter. In 1741, though her relationship with Sloper continued (their last child, a son, Charles, was born a decade later), she took the remarkable decision to return to the stage. She seems to have done so at the instance of James Quin, the leading London tragedian, who in June had gone to give a season in Dublin at Aungier Street with Kitty Clive, in part for the ironical reason that they had been supplanted in the favours of their London audience by Charles Macklin and Peg Woffington, both of them Irish. Quin had acted with Mrs Cibber at Drury Lane, and the initiative is almost certain to have been his, since the managers of Aungier Street would not have known how to contact her in her seclusion. The Arne family were certainly in Quin's mind; after playing Falstaff and Henry VIII he gave the first Dublin performance of Arne's *Comus*, with Mrs Clive as Euphrosyne. It was a great success and showed what could be done in Dublin:

> the Orchestra was enlarged, several eminent Hands being added to the Band, for the Occasion, particularly Signor Pasqualino: the Musick was finely performed, having – as we hear – been a long time in Practice under the Inspection of Mr Dubourg: and the whole

---

* 'Between five and six in the evening he let down the turn up bed softly, she laid herself upon it, upon her back, and pulled up her clothes. Her body was bare. He unbuttoned his clothes, hung up his bag wig upon a sconce, let down his breeches, took his privy member in his hand, and lay down upon her.' Here Sir William Lee intervened: it was the third such incident described.

Entertainment that Night was executed with a Decorum and Taste so elegant, as has never been attempted in this Kingdom. The sublimity of the great Milton, the Eloquence of Mr Quin, and the Harmony of Mrs Clive, delighted and charmed everyone.

But late in August Mrs Clive had her benefit performance in Fielding's *The Miser*, sang the 'celebrated song call'd Ellen a Roon' and returned to London. Mrs Cibber was her belated replacement, and during her stay was required to work very hard indeed, repeating a number of Mrs Clive's parts and many more besides. Her first appearance was in Steele's *The Conscious Lovers*, playing Indiana, the heroine, who, beautiful and defenceless, trusts in the sincerity of the man who loves her, even when he is forced into an apparently duplicitous course of conduct. Steele intended his play to be 'consonant to the Rules of Religion and Virtue', and by commencing her return to the stage with it, Mrs Cibber pointed up her challenge to Dublin society. On the first night it seemed as though she had lost – the house was worth a mere £10. But just under a week later, a performance of Otway's *Venice Preserved* was given 'by their Graces special Command', the presence of the Duke and Duchess of Devonshire was the necessary sanction for the house to be filled, and Susannah Cibber was consistently successful thereafter. Bellamira, in Otway's play, is another trusting, innocent woman, but there is no happy ending; only madness and death can release her from the nightmare of conspiracy and sexual corruption that invades her waking world. Readers of *The Tryal of a Cause for Criminal Conversation, between Theophilus Cibber, Gent., Plaintiff, and William Sloper, Esq, Defendant* would not have been disappointed.

From Monday 14 December the *Dublin Journal* announced: 'Attendance will be given at Mr Handel's house in Abby Street, near Lyffey Street, from 9 o'clock in the Morning till 2 in the Afternoon, in order to receive the Subscription Money for his six Musical Entertainments in the New Musick-Hall in Fishamble Street, at which Time each subscriber will have a Ticket delivered to him, which entitles him to these Tickets each Night'. A few days later the programme was announced for the first of these, on 23 December: *L'Allegro, il Penseroso ed il Moderato*, with two concertos 'for several instruments' and an organ concerto. Of the performance we know no details, beyond that the *Dublin Journal* thought that the audience at Mr Handel's 'first Oratorio' was 'more numerous and polite . . . than ever was seen upon the like Occasion' and that 'the Performance was superior to any

The Musick Hall, Fishamble Street. Wood-block after a watercolour by
E. Fairholt. This is the state of the entrance c. 1800.

Thing of the Kind in this Kingdom before'. Handel recorded his c
reactions in one of his rare letters, which glows with satisfaction.
addressed it to Jennens:

Dublin Decem^{br}. 29 17

Sr

        it was with the greatest Pleasure I saw the Continuation
Your Kindness by the Lines You was pleased to send me, in Ord
to be prefix'd to Your Oratorio Messiah, which I set to Musi
before I left England. I am enboldned, Sir, by the generous Conce
You please to take in relation to my affairs, to give You an Accou
of the Success I have met there. The Nobility did me the Hono
to make amongst themselves a Subscription for 6 Nights, which d
fill a Room of 600 Persons, so that I needed not sell one single Tich
at the Door. and without Vanity the Performance was received wi
a general Approbation. Sig^{ra} Avolio, which I brought with me fro
London pleases extraordinary, I have form'd an other Tenor Vo
which gives great Satisfaction, the Basses and Counter Tenors i
very good, and the rest of the Chorus Singers (by my Direction)
exceeding well, as for the Instruments they are really excelle
Mr Dubough being at the Head of them, and the Musick sour
delightfully in this charming Room, which puts me in such Spi
(and my Health being so good) that I exert my self on my Org
with more than usual Success. I opened with the Allegro, Pensero
& Moderato and I assure you that the Words of the Moderato i
vastly admired. The Audience being composed (besides the Flow
of Ladyes of Distinction and other People of the greatest Quality)
so many Bishops, Deans, Heads of the Colledge, the most emine
People in the Law as the Chancellor, Auditor General, &tc.
which are very much taken with the Poetry. So that I am desi
to perform it again the next time. I cannot sufficiently express
kind treatment I receive here, but the Politeness of this gener
Nation cannot be unknown to You, so I let You judge of the satisf
tion I enjoy, passing my time with Honnour, profit, and pleasu
They propose already to have some more Performances, when
6 Nights of the Subscription are over, and My Lord Duc the L
Lieutenant (who is allways present with all His Family on th
Nights) will easily obtain a longer Permission for me by His M
esty, so that I shall bee obliged to make my stay here longer th
I thought. . . . I expect with Impatience the Favour of Your Ne

concerning Your Health and wellfare, of which I take a real share, as for the News of Your Opera's, I need not trouble you for all this Town is full of their ill success, by a number of Letters from Your quarters to the People of Quality here, and I can't help saying that it furnishes great Diversion and laughter. The first Opera I heard my self before I left London, and it made me very merry all along my journey . . .

Informative as it is about Handel's reactions, the letter adds little to the notices which appeared in the journals, though it is useful confirmation that the writers were not exaggerating the attendance and that Handel thought as well of the musical standards, as did the audience. That Avoglio is the only singer mentioned by name suggests that Susannah Cibber's presence in Dublin was not prearranged by Handel, and indeed there is no reason to suppose that she was yet singing for him; we have no references to her other than as an actress until March. The tenor 'form'd' by Handel was probably John Church, since in James Baileys he already had a tenor who had sung under his direction, and it was Church and Baileys whom he was to choose as soloists in *Messiah*. 'My organ' tells us what we might otherwise have deduced from the fact that the Fishamble Street Musick Hall did not have an instrument of its own until the next autumn. Handel must therefore have brought his own, and this suggests a bureau organ, such as was built in large numbers by Johann Snetzler, though his instruments post-date Handel's Dublin visit. The model followed by Snetzler and others was made to resemble the piece of furniture that gives it its name, equipped with carrying handles; it had a keyboard which folded out, a stopped diapason, a 4-foot flute, a fifteenth and a mixture. The best surviving examples display surprisingly mellow diapasons and flutes, all of wood, and bright and forward fifteenths (2-foot ranks) and mixtures. Accurately voiced and tuned, so modest an instrument could perfectly well display not just 'a fine and delicate touch, a volant finger, and a ready delivery of passages the most difficult', which the music historian Sir John Hawkins considered to be 'the praise of inferior artists', but also the superior excellencies of Handel, 'his amazing command of the instrument, the fullness of his harmony, the grandeur of his style, the copiousness of his imagination, and the fertility of his invention'. Organ concertos were a feature of all Handel's Dublin concerts, including *Messiah*, and that they were so successful is a reminder that neither great volume

Dr Charles Cobbe, Dean of Christ Church, subsequently Archbishop of Dublin, who gave the permission necessary to ensure the participation of the cathedral choirs in *Messiah*.

nor great technical elaboration is essential to musical effect. It is illuminating that Handel should have taken his obligations to the King seriously, and substantiates the importance that, Sir John Hawkins reported, his pensions assumed for him at times when his other finances were precarious. He also casts a glance over his shoulder to his London base when he mocks the pasticcio *Alessandro in Persia*; he had left a stricken field to triumph elsewhere. Seen from beyond the fray, the lesson that hitherto he had been so reluctant to learn was obvious. The immediate prospect consisted of five fully subscribed concerts, to be held weekly on Wednesdays from 13 January 1742 onwards, and a call for more when the series was completed.

Although there were difficulties, they do not seem to have impinged on Handel directly. The problem was one of conflicting interests in an area where empiricism and opportunism coalesced: the mutually dependent spheres of charitable enterprise and marketable musical accomplishment. Mercer's Hospital had profited by the activities of the Philharmonick Society in the past and hoped to do so in the future; the Philharmonick Society was now established in Fishamble Street, in a potentially uneasy proximity to the Charitable Musical Society and its New Musick Hall. The limited supply of experienced singers meant that to mount a choral work the cooperation of the Cathedral choirs was necessary, and this was complicated by the fact that the majority of the vicars-choral were on the establishments of both cathedrals and thus served two deans and chapters. The Dean of Christ Church was Dr Charles Cobbe, whose official residence was in Fishamble Street and who was himself a Trustee of Mercer's Hospital. The Dean of St Patrick's was, of course, Jonathan Swift, who was frankly unmusical and had now, as his friend Laetitia Pilkington put it, fallen into a 'deep melancholy', having taken a 'wrong turn in his brain', or, as he himself graphically said, pointing to an expiring specimen, had become a tree 'dying at the top'. The Sub-Dean, Dr John Wynne, who dealt with musical matters, was also involved with Mercer's Hospital, as a governor, and was a member of the Charitable Musical Society. When the Board of Mercer's Hospital met on 4 January they resolved to ask the Dean and Chapter of St Patrick's to allow such of their choir as were willing to take part in the Philharmonick Society's concerts for the Hospital's benefit, adding that the Dean and Chapter of Christ Church had already granted their permission. The reply that they received was conditional: St Patrick's would cooperate provided that Christ Church would extend their permission not just for the Philharmonick Society's benefit for the Hospital, but also for Handel's concerts, since he had also promised a benefit, and this would raise a considerable sum without detracting from the Philharmonick Society's contribution. But St Patrick's was also concerned that this would create a precedent, and took the opportunity to pass on a message to Christ Church: some 'proper rule' had to be devised to prevent members of either choir 'performing in any publick Musical Performance excepting in Churches without the joint permission of both Deans and Chapters first had & obtained'.

   This was a sensible if belated response to the fact that Dublin now had as active a concert life as any city in Europe, if anything strengthened by its lack of that contentious and expensive symbol, an Italian opera house. The Deans and Chapters attempted to confront a situation which their opposite numbers at Westminster and St Paul's had largely evaded, partly because a further extension of musical pluralism joint tenure of Court and cathedral appointments, made the London situation impossibly complex. As it happened, the Dublin chapters were to prove virtually powerless, and internal squabbles in the choirs posed a greater impediment to concert activity than decanal rulings. But the immediate threat came from Swift, who having apparently granted permission for six of his choir to play in the benefit, decided he had done no such thing, and in a draft letter to the Sub-Dean and Chapter stated that:

> whereas it hath been reported that I gave a license to certain vicars to assist at a club of fiddlers in Fishamble Street, I do hereby declare that I remember no such license to have been ever signed or sealed by me; and that if ever such pretended license should be produced, I do hereby annul and vacate the said license; intreating my said Sub-Dean and Chapter to punish such vicars as shall ever appear there, as songsters, fiddlers, pipers, trumpeters, drummers, drum-majors, or in any sonal quality, according to the flagitious aggravations of their respective disobedience, rebellion, perfidy and ingratitude.

Whether or not this splendid tirade, which might have come from a character in a play by Ben Jonson, had any effect we do not know within a few weeks Swift's insanity was obvious and his duties were taken out of his hands. But when, in March, the performance of *Messiah* was mooted, the Committee appointed for the three charities which Handel designated as beneficiaries – Mercer's Hospital, the Charitable

Infirmary and the Charitable Musical Society – were careful to make approaches to the Deans and Chapters of both cathedrals. The popularity of the subscription concerts put a severe strain on the amenities of Fishamble Street, and the organisers attempted to direct the circulation of coaches (down rather than up this difficult declivity), to make the passage of sedan chairs easier, and to provide better waiting-rooms for the footmen. These arrangements obviously proved satisfactory as the one-way system was taken over for the popular Saturday assemblies, also held at the New Musick Hall, and when a second subscription series was announced early in February the only chairs allowed to stand at the new exits into Copper Alley were 'hazard Chairs' – chairs plying for hire which would take the first comer rather than private chairs which would hold up the 'emptying of the House' while they waited for their owners to emerge.

The success of the concerts does not, however, seem to have affected theatre attendance, and an important event in January was Susannah Cibber's first appearance as a singing actress. Her brother's *Comus* had reached Dublin the previous year; she herself had played the Lady at its original Drury Lane opening in 1738. In Dublin she took the part of the nymph Euphrosyne, representing mirth. As casting this was far less appropriate than the solemn and assailed Lady, but at Drury Lane the Lady had not sung at all, and 'Sweet Echo, sweetest nymph', which belongs to her part, was performed off-stage by Susannah's sister-in-law, while she mimed the action. Euphrosyne, of marginal dramatic importance, had by contrast three songs and a recitative, and the largo in her last song, 'Ye Fauns and ye Dryads', contains some of the most expressive music in the entire masque. The recitative, 'Love, the greatest bliss below', though short, also contains dramatic possibilities. Handel knew *Comus* and it had influenced his melodic style as well as his choice of text in *L'Allegro, il Penseroso ed il Moderato*; indeed, the character of Euphrosyne in Arne's *Comus* had been imported from Milton's original poem *L'Allegro*, by the adaptor John Dalton, to expand the seventeenth-century masque into a piece of operatic length. As we know from other testimony besides his own account to Jennens of his visit to *Alessandro in Persia*, Handel took an active interest in the doings of the opposition. In the circumstances of Dublin the Aungier Street Theatre did not even rate as that, and it seems far more probable that a sympathetic visit to Aungier Street, rather than any prearrangement, led to his discovery, in Mrs Cibber, of the second soprano soloist whom he needed for *Messiah*. That he had to transpose and partially revise those numbers which she sang seems to clinch the matter. *Comus*, a perfectly judged stage-piece in Dalton's version (this is not to denigrate Milton, to whom it owes everything, but a seventeenth-century household masque and an eighteenth-century theatre masque were quite different things), seems to have held Dublin as captivated as, on stage, was the Lady in her enchanted chair.

On 1 February Handel played the organ at evensong at St Patrick's and a large congregation gathered to hear him 'show the best abilities of the best Organist in Europe, upon the fine Organ belonging to that Cathedral'. They might have disagreed in Leipzig, but the *Dublin News-Letter*'s opinion would have passed almost anywhere else. Two days later Handel gave Dublin its first true oratorio, *Esther*, 'with additions'; as Winton Dean has remarked, ' "additions" meant subtractions'. The two anthems were cut, as also were many of the recitatives; several of the airs were redistributed amongst the characters. The cast is not known. A repeat closed the first subscription series, but the new series could be subscribed for and tickets collected from the Music Hall, or at Handel's home in Abbey Street. One hundred and fifty subscriptions only were offered, which meant, if they were all taken up, a theoretical capacity audience of four hundred and fifty (each subscriber was entitled to three tickets for every performance; these had to be claimed on the day before, or on the day of, the concert). *Pue's Occurrences* announced as in the press 'A Poem by Laurence Whyte on the General Effect and Excellency of Musick, particularly, on the famous Mr Handel's performance, who had been lately invited into this Kingdom, by his Grace the Duke of Devonshire . . . for the Entertainment of the Nobility and Gentry'. The Duke and his family left for London on the 16th, but the Lords Justices gave support by proxy and in March the Charitable Society on College Green put off their regular concert so that it should not conflict with Handel's, whilst a foreign gentleman, a Mr de Rheiner, was forced to delay his benefit 'on account of all the best Musick being engaged to Mr Handel's concert' (he believed his 'unhappy situation' was 'pretty well known to the Publick', and though he had never appeared on a stage before, hoped to entertain them with singing, and by playing Sir Harry Wildair in Farquhar's *The Constant Couple*).

On 6 March we have our first evidence of Handel's use of Mrs Cibber as a singer, through the postponement, on a regular subscription evening, of 'the new Serenata called Hymen' on account of her 'sudden illness'. *L'Allegro, il Penseroso ed il Moderato* was given instead – yet another indication that Handel had not used her in the latter work. *Hymen* finally opened on 24 March and was advertised as 'long delayed'; it was in fact an adaptation of Handel's opera *Imeneo* and its repetition a week later was his last performance of one of his own operas – but as an oratorio. During that week the *Dublin Journal* had carried an announcement:

> For Relief of the Prisoners in the several Gaols, and for the Support of Mercer's Hospital in Stephen's Street, and of the Charitable Infirmary on the Inns Quay, on Monday 12th April, will be performed at the Musick Hall in Fishamble Street, Mr *Handel's new Grand Oratorio, call'd the* MESSIAH, in which the Gentlemen of the Choirs of both Cathedrals will assist, with some Concertoes on the Organ, by Mr Handell. Tickets to be had at the Musick Hall, and at Mr Neal's in Christ-Church-Yard, at half a Guinea each. N.B. No Person will be admitted to the Rehearsal without a Rehearsal Ticket, which will be given gratis with the Ticket for the Performance when pay'd for.

This was repeated in the *Dublin News-Letter* which, however, called *Messiah* a 'New Grand Sacred Oratorio' and added that 'Books are also to be had at a British Sixpence each'.

The requisite permissions from the Deans and Chapters had been obtained without difficulty, but the dates of both rehearsal (not announced until 3 April, when it was set for 8 April) and the performance itself had to be postponed, the rehearsal because it clashed with a stage performance by Mrs Cibber at Aungier Street, where she was in arrears to the management because of illness in March, the performance 'At the Desire of several Persons of Distinction'. In the absence of the Lord Lieutenant these might well have been the Lords Justices, but throughout his career Handel was always quick to identify those who were attentive to his music and was, in his turn, attentive, though certainly never obsequious, towards them. What friends he made in Ireland we cannot tell, partly through the destruction of records in the Troubles (though this tends to be exaggerated); partly because of the wonderful whimsicality of nineteenth-century Irish historians, who were so often poets and novelists *manqué*; partly because Handel himself did not readily put pen to paper – his letter to Jennens of 29 December must have exhausted his epistolary powers for months. It is difficult to believe that he ever had a chance to make that dash to Cork which Martha Wilmot supposed when she wrote about Lota in 1856; he very probably did visit Clontarf Castle, where his German friend Dorothy Vernon (*née* Grahn) lived, but it is as well to remember that Clontarf Castle is in Co. Dublin and not, as some authorities suppose, in Cork. As for the numerous chamber organs on which Handel's fingers allegedly rested or, rather, tirelessly refused to rest, they are a product of that enthusiasm for the instrument which his playing evoked. At Newhall, Co. Clare, Charles McDonnell even contrived to mock the vogue by having his hall cupboard constructed in the shape of one – an airy nothing.

The rehearsal eventually took place on the morning of Friday 9 April, the doors opening at 11 a.m. Although subscribers got in free, others had to pay, and the advertisements are clear in calling it 'public'; Handel played organ concertos which would have involved extemporisation and were therefore in the nature of a performance; Mrs Cibber notoriously required prolonged coaching, which Handel undertook because, as Burney put it, her 'voice and manners had softened his severity for her want of musical knowledge', and this had certainly been completed long before she appeared in a new part. For her he had significantly modified the disposition of the oratorio.

To take Handel's alterations to the portmanteau manuscript in order, assigning the reasons when they are apparent:

(1) He cast the opening of 'Thus saith the Lord, the Lord of Hosts', which was originally an *arioso a tempo ordinario* with three bars of instrumental introduction, as an accompanied recitative with just a single bar of introduction, which is much more dramatically effective.

(2) He rewrote the original setting of 'But who may abide the day of His coming', a bass air in D minor, as a bass recitative. The authenticity of this revision has been doubted, but the Dublin word-book prints it as a recitative and the John Matthews copy of the score, now in Archbishop Marsh's Library, Dublin, says firmly: 'If the foregoing song is to be left out as it was in the performance in Dublin, sing this recitative upon the very same words.' The recitative, if the singer has the nerve to take it slowly enough and the audience can forget Handel's subsequent development of the original bass air into the bravura alto piece (albeit often sung by a bass) that he composed for Guadagni, moves us quite naturally to 'And He shall purify'.

(3) He altered and shortened 'Rejoice greatly, O daughter of Zion'. It was originally a da capo aria (ABA) with a very long A section which lacked coherence in its last half; this he cancelled, expunging

Susannah Cibber. Mezzotint by J. Faber after Thomas Hudson.

the da capo instruction, and used the cancelled material, rewritten, as a concluding section. Both versions were in 12/8 time. The version in 4/4 is a further modification, made after Dublin.

(4) He transposed the recitative 'Then shall the eyes of the blind be open'd' and its air 'He shall feed His flock like a shepherd' from the soprano to the alto voice, so that the air is in F major rather than B♭ major; the duet version for soprano and alto is later. This was for Mrs Cibber and is an evident improvement on the original run of soprano arias from 'There were shepherds abiding in the field' to the end of Part I.

(5) As we have seen in Chapter 3, he provided a new text, from Isaiah, for the original da capo soprano air on 'How beautiful are the feet' as the words appear in Romans: it is for two male altos and chorus.

(6) He revised the conclusion of 'Why do the nations', shortening the original in the interest of cohesion and drama (as in 'Rejoice greatly', though the air was not da capo but, having proceeded as though it was about to be, ran into 'Let us break their bonds asunder' where the repeat of the A section might have been anticipated). The new ending, as a recitative, has been called, by John Tobin, a 'truncated, misshapen alternative', but in fact it does the same job in a different way.

(7) He altered 'The trumpet shall sound' from its original da capo form to a dal sequo without the repeat of the opening ritornello; this is in line with the general reduction of da capos from the work as originally composed.

(8) He almost halved the length of the alto/tenor 'O death, where is thy sting'.

(9) He transposed 'If God be for us' from G minor into C minor, so that it could be sung by Mrs Cibber.

For our knowledge of this we are dependent on Handel's autograph, on J. C. Smith's fair copy, which was what Handel used to conduct from in Dublin, and on an annotated copy of the word-book, in which the anonymous purchaser endeavoured to write the names of the singers against some of the items. Whether these referred to the first or second performance is unknown, and sometimes the names have been wrongly aligned: Mrs Cibber manifestly did not sing the chorus 'Behold the Lamb of God' at the beginning of Part II. If all of the combined choirs took part there were sixteen men, Messrs Baileys, Carter, Church, Colgan, Hall, Hill, Jones, Lambe, Mason, Phipps,

Smith, Tavenor, Taylor, Ward, Woffington and Worrall; there were also sixteen boy choristers. The soloists were James Baileys (tenor); John Mason and John Hill (basses; Hill sang only one number, 'Why do the nations so furiously rage together?'); Joseph Ward (alto; he sang 'Then shall be brought to pass' and the alto part in 'O death, where is thy sting'); and William Lambe (also an alto; he sang 'Behold a virgin shall conceive' and presumably also 'O thou that tellest good tidings to Sion' as well, apparently, as 'He that dwelleth in Heaven' and 'Thou shalt break them', though these are normally taken by a tenor). The names of 'Baley', 'Hill', 'Ward' and 'Masson' are still indistinctly visible on the much-used conducting score. There are references to Mrs Maclaine but none to Signora Avoglio. Her part in the first *Messiah* was reported in the press; it has been surmised that the word-book annotator may have been at the second performance, but Signora Avoglio was still in Dublin when that took place, and it seems most improbable that Handel dropped her since she sang in the first London *Messiah* the following year, and also in *Saul*, and in *Samson* and *Semele* the year after. She may of course have been ill for the second performance; there was a serious flu epidemic in Dublin which had possibly caused Mrs Cibber's indisposition earlier, but the question remains puzzling. It is also conceivable that the annotations refer to the rehearsal.

The accounts of the rehearsal in the *Dublin Journal* and *Dublin News-Letter* left the authors with few superlatives in hand for the description of the performance itself. The *Journal* reported that:

> Yesterday Mr Handell's new Grand Sacred Oratorio, called, The MESSIAH, was rehearsed . . . to a most Grand, Polite and crouded Audience; and was performed so well, that it gave universal Satisfaction to all present; and was allowed by the greatest Judges to be the finest Composition of Musick that ever was heard, and the sacred words as properly adapted for the Occasion.

It went on to announce the revised time for the actual performance (noon on 'Tuesday next', the 13th) and to add that:

> Many Ladies and Gentlemen who are well-wishers to this Noble and Grand Charity for which this Oratorio was composed, request it as a Favour, that the Ladies who honour this Performance with their Presence would be pleased to come without Hoops, as it will greatly encrease the Charity, by making Room for more company.

The *Dublin News-Letter* contrived different phrases for the same sentiments:

> Yesterday Morning . . . there was a public Rehearsal of the Messiah, Mr Handel's new sacred Oratorio, which in the opinion of the best Judges, far surpasses anything of that Nature, which has been performed in this or any other Kingdom. The elegant Entertainment was conducted in the most regular Manner, and to the entire satisfaction of the most crowded and polite Assembly.

It scored in point of accuracy by explaining that the 'grand performance' was to be for 'the benefit of three very important public Charities', rather than, as the *Dublin Journal* implied, one only.

A notice on the 13th – though the papers would have been off the press the night before – reinforces the sartorial injunction and more directly indicates its source. It is not a nebulous group of ladies and gentlemen, but 'The Stewards of the Charitable Musical Society', who 'request the Favour of the Ladies not to come with Hoops this Day to the Musick-Hall in Fishamble Street: The Gentlemen are desired to come without their Swords'. Both were a sacrifice.* A few seasons earlier Mrs Pendarves had reported: 'The fashionable hoops are made of the richest damask, trimmed with gold and silver, fourteen guineas a hoop.' But she had no business to exclaim; her own minute and fascinated accounts of fabrics ('The Duchess of Queensbury's clothes pleased me best; they were white satin embroidered, the bottom of the petticoat *brown hills* covered with all sorts of weeds, and *every breadth* had an *old stump of a tree* that run up almost to the top of the petticoat, broken and ragged and worked with brown chenille, round which twined nastersians, ivy, honeysuckles, periwinkles, convolvuluses and all sorts of twining flowers which spread and covered the petticoat'; this is just the first half of what she noted) could never have been penned had not the petticoats themselves been spread, which was the function of the hoop. Its management was a matter of deportment; those to whom it did not come readily might have been happy to swap the opportunity for display for the comparative simplicity of entering a sedan chair without one. Swords were worn longer in

---

* So far as I am aware no student of semiotics has pointed out the significance of this initiative. At Handel's behest, the audience was compulsorily unsexed, involuntarily precipitated into the loose-gowned, swordless future when sentiment was to collapse into romanticism. Was this physical manipulation of the audience perhaps the chief reason for *Messiah*'s peculiar success?

Dublin than in London, although it is unclear whether this was because of the readiness of the gentry to call each other out, or because Dublin lagged behind in matters of fashion. But 40-inch Spanish blades were not uncommon, and as demanding to manage as a hoop.

The Stewards managed to override not only fashion, but also faction. Jennens had hoped that Handel might perform *Messiah* 'for his own Benefit in Passion Week'. Handel, to Jennens's chagrin, had decamped to Dublin. He nevertheless did perform *Messiah* in Passion Week (Easter Sunday fell on 18 April), although not for his own benefit. There was, as Thomas Sheridan's experience eleven years earlier indicated, at least a fair chance of sectarian objection. When, the following year, *Messiah* was first performed in London, prejudice was just as marked. But there is no evidence that it existed in Dublin, though the fact that it was Passion Week might have helped persuade the audience to put off their finery. There seems to have been nothing to cloy the delight, extending (if the report which appeared in almost identical form in the *Dublin Journal*, the *Dublin News-Letter* and the *Dublin Gazette* is to be taken at its face value) even to self-congratulation, experienced by those who first heard the finished and rehearsed thing:

On Tuesday last [the 13th] Mr Handel's Sacred Grand Oratorio, the MESSIAH, was performed at the New Musick-Hall in Fishamble-street; the best Judges allowed it to be the most finished piece of Musick. Words are wanting to express the exquisite Delight it afforded to the admiring crouded Audience. The Sublime, the Grand, and the Tender, adapted to the most elevated, majestick and moving Words, conspired to transport and charm the ravished Heart and Ear. It is but Justice to Mr Handel, that the World should know, he generously gave the Money arising from this Grand Performance, to be equally shared by the Society for relieving Prisoners, the Charitable Infirmary, and Mercer's Hospital, for which they will ever gratefully remember his Name; and that the Gentlemen of the two Choirs, Mr Dubourg, Mrs Avolio, and Mrs Cibber, who all performed their Parts to Admiration, acted also on the same disinterested Principle, satisfied with the deserved Applause of the Publick, and the conscious Pleasure of promoting such useful, and extensive Charity. There were about 700 People in the Room, and the Sum collected for that Noble and Pious Charity amounted to about 400*l.* out of which 127*l.* goes to each of the three great and pious Charities.*

On the 20th the *Dublin Journal* followed this with a poem by Laurence White, already the bard of the New Musick Hall and of Handel, on the occasion. He approached Jennens's Scripture collection with about as much subtlety as he had approached Castle's ingenuity in solving the problems of the Fishamble Street site:

> But our *Messiah*, blessed be his Name!
> Both Heaven and Earth his *Miracles* proclaim.
> His birth, his Passion, and his Resurrection,
> With his Ascension, have a strong Connection. . . .

There remains, however, one story supposed to date from the first performance, and an important critical account which might date from the first performance but is more likely to belong to the second. The reason for hesitating to assign them to the first is that both concern clergymen, who might well have found it impossible if not imprudent to attend an oratorio in Passion Week. Nevertheless the Chancellor of St Patrick's, Patrick Delany, was not by nature a prudent man, as his friend Swift had on several occasions to remind him. (Swift was now estranged from him by his madness.) Delany may well have considered that he had a duty or right to attend a performance given by the choir of the cathedral to which, however loosely, he was attached, despite both Passion Week and the fact that he was in mourning for his wife, who had died in December. According to late eighteenth-century tradition, when Mrs Cibber sang 'He was despised' Delany, seated in one of the boxes, exclaimed, 'Woman, for this be all thy sins forgiven thee.' That this is the oratorio's return match for Mrs Fox-Lane's famous cry at the opera, 'One God, one Farinelli' makes it more rather than less likely, and Thomas Sheridan, said to have been the authority for it, was certainly a friend of Delany and himself a witness to Mrs Cibber's singing. Fourteen years later, seeking to indicate the force of 'oratorical expression' when 'conveyed to the heart with all the superadded powers and charms of music', Sheridan observed that 'No person of sensibility, who has had the good fortune to hear Mrs Cibber sing in the oratorio of the Messiah, will find it very difficult to give credit to accounts of the wonderful effects produced from so powerful

---

* The last sentence is absent in the *Dublin News-Letter* and *Dublin Gazette.*

a union.' Yet the story is first told in a life of David Garrick published in 1780 and attributed to 'a certain bishop'.

A chancellor, later a dean, might well be posthumously promoted by a theatrical biographer to a bishopric. But as it happens, a genuine bishop, Edward Synge, now of Elphin, did attend a performance or rehearsal of *Messiah*, and committed his thoughts to paper as a preamble to the outline of an oratorio, *The Penitent*, which he hoped that Handel might see his way to setting. Handel did not, but the remarks on *Messiah* are an extraordinary record of an encounter with the work when it was new:

As Mr Handel in his oratorio's greatly excells all other Composers I am acquainted with, So in the famous one, called The Messiah he seems to have excell'd himself. The whole is beyond any thing I had a notion of till I Read and heard it. It Seems to be a Species of Musick different from any other, and this is particularly remarkable of it. That tho' the Composition is very Masterly & artificial, yet the Harmony is So great and open, as to please all who have Ears & will hear, learned & unlearn'd. Without doubt this Superior Excellence is owing in some measure to the great care & exactness which M\^r Handel seems to have us'd in preparing this Piece. But Some reasons may be given why He has Succeeded better in this than perhaps He could with all his skill, fully exerted, have done in any other.

1 one is the Subject, which is the greatest & most interesting. It Seems to have inspir'd him.

2 Another is the Words, which are all Sublime, or affecting in the greatest degree.

3 a Third reason for the Superior Excellence of this piece, 'Tis this there is no Dialogue. In every Drame there must be a great deal & often broken into very Short Speeches & Answers. If these be flat, & insipid, they move laughter or Contempt. Whereas in this Piece the attention of the Audience is Engag'd from one end to the other: And the Parts Set in Recitativo, being Continu'd Sentences, & Some times adorn'd with too much applause, by the audience as the rest.–

They Seem'd indeed throughly engag'd frome one end to the other. And, to their great honour, tho' the young & gay of both Sexes were present in great numbers, their behaviour was uniformly grave & decent, which Show'd that they were not only pleas'd but affected with the performance. Many, I hope, were instructed by it, and had proper Sentiments inspir'd in a Stronger Manner on their Minds.

This puts much better some of the things that Dr Brown later tried to express about the oratorio. It is also prophetic; it predicts exactly the kind of appeal that *Messiah* has had ever since. It contains a wonderfully apt epithet for an aspect of *Messiah* that, almost of its nature, resists further analysis: the harmony that is 'So great and open'. It also introduces the dangerous word that was to dominate a century of criticism of *Messiah*: 'Sublime'. And it is the only account we have of the behaviour of the audience.

Synge's sober but unsolemn audience, many young and fashionable, was particularly fitted to respond to Susannah Cibber, and Delany's exclamation (which, as it happens, fits all we know of this impulsive, generous man, 'old and looking still older than he was', he said a year later in his proposal of marriage to Mrs Pendarves, but possessed of 'the tenderness of affection and the faith of friendship') simply dramatises what must have been a general feeling amongst those – the majority – who knew her history. In entrusting so much of the work to her, Handel was employing a singing actress, not a singer who acted. Soon after *Messiah*, Burney was to know her voice intimately, singing Palestrina's madrigals with her, Mrs Arne, Esther Young and Thomas Arne at the Arnes' home in Queen Street, and hearing her on the stage at Drury Lane where she was still singing opera songs although remaking her London career as a straight actress. Later still he stayed with her and Sloper at West Woodhay. It was, he wrote, 'but a thread', mezzo-soprano rather than true alto, but she 'captured every hearer of sensibility by her native sweetness of voice and powers of expression'. Dr Johnson maintained that as an actress her fault was 'a great sameness; though her expression was undoubtedly very fine'. She seems to have exploited her limited capacities with the utmost determination. Laetitia Hawkins, the historian's daughter, said she could make even ' "God save the King" sound like a hymn'. Handel forgave her her want of musical knowledge and became a personal friend; Garrick said that on her death 'Tragedy expired with her', but also ruefully admitted that behind the scenes, 'whatever was Cibber's object, a new part or a new dress, she was always sure to carry her point'.

Christina Maria Avoglio, by contrast, was a professional soprano who worked hard for Handel throughout his Dublin stay, taking the appropriate parts in *L'Allegro, il Penseroso ed il Moderato*, in *Alexander's Feast* and the *Ode on St Cecilia's Day*, as well as singing *Galatea, Esther*, Rosmene in *Hymen* and Michal in *Saul*. Handel would employ her extensively in his next two London oratorio seasons and in 1744 she was a popular success singing a celebrated gavotte when playing Hecate in Samuel Howard's Drury Lane pantomime *The Amorous Goddess*. It is odd that so versatile a performer should disappear without trace after a benefit concert at Salisbury in June 1746.

With the exception of James Baileys, the men soloists had unremarkable careers as vicars-choral both before *Messiah* and after it; Baileys' London venture seems never to have been repeated. The countertenor Joseph Ward, who sang 'Then shall be brought to pass', and the duet 'O death where is thy sting' with Baileys, lived until 1776, the bass John Mason until 1784.

After the end of his second subscription series and the first performance of *Messiah*, Handel's commitments in Dublin tailed off. In March a remarkable Hungarian, Mr Charles, the 'famous French horn', had arrived and in May he gave a concert at which he played, besides the horn, 'The Clarinet, the Hautbois d'Amoir and the Shalamo [chalumeaux] . . . never heard in this Kingdom before'. His programme included the overture to *Il Pastor Fido* and two Handelian medleys in which the 'Dead March' in *Saul* and selections from the *Water Music* appeared, but Handel had no part in it. His next enterprise was a performance of *Saul* on 22 May, with organ concertos, apparently by special request. It had no charitable purpose, nor did the second performance of *Messiah*, publicly rehearsed on 1 June and performed on the 3rd. As before, tickets were half a guinea, with the rehearsal *gratis*; the rehearsal was again at noon but the performance was at seven in the evening, probably because of the summer heat, since according to the advertisements, 'In order to keep the Room as cool as possible, a Pane of Glass will be removed from the Top of each of the Windows'. There was no restriction on hoops or swords, but concert-goers were informed that 'This will be the last Performance of Mr Handel's during his Stay in this Kingdom.'

So it was, though Mrs Cibber had a benefit on 31 May and Signora Avoglio on 23 June, postponed from the 16th because of the arrival from England of the actors David Garrick and Peg Woffington. On the 30th there were further visitors from London, 'the Ingenious Mr Arne, Brother to Mrs Cibber, and Composer of the Musick of Comus, together with his Wife (the celebrated Singer)'. It seems likely that information from Susannah alerted Thomas Augustine to the possibilities of Dublin. *Comus* had certainly earned itself a place in the hearts of Dublin audiences. There was a benefit for Mrs Arne at Fishamble Street on 21 July, in which her sister-in-law shared the vocal parts and the programme was about equally divided between music by Arne and Handel. After the concert was repeated the Arnes went back to London to organise their affairs and then returned to Dublin for the best part of two years, developing the market which Handel had opened up at a time when London had little to offer them.* On Friday 13 August Handel set out for London via Parkgate in a Chester trader. Before he did so, according to Mrs Pilkington's *Memoirs* which were written not more than nine years after the event, he called on Swift: 'I was told the last sensible Words he uttered, were on this Occasion. . . . The Servant was a considerable Time, e'er he could make the Dean understand him; which, when he did, he cry'd, "Oh! a *German*, and a Genius! A Prodigy! admit him." The Servant did so, just to let Mr *Handel* behold the Ruins of the greatest Wit that ever lived along the Tide of Time, where all at length are lost.' But this disconcerting visit, to the man so admired by his friend Mrs Pendarves, did not alter Handel's feelings for Ireland. Soon after he was back in Brook Street he wrote to Jennens:

London Sept. 9th *1742*

Dear S^r

   It was indeed Your humble Servant which intended You a visit in my way from Ireland to London, for I certainly could have given You a better account by word of mouth, as by writing, how well Your Messiah was received in that Country, yet as a Noble Lord, and no less then the Bishop of Elphim (a Nobleman very learned in Musick) has given his Observation in writing of this Oratorio, I send you here annexed the Contents of it in his own words. – I shall send the printed Book of the Messiah to Mr Sted for You. As for my Success in General in that generous and polite Nation, I reserve the account of it till I have the Honour to see you in London. The report that the Direction of the Opera next winter is comitted to my Care, is groundless. The gentlemen who have undertaken to middle with Harmony can not agree, and are quite in a Confusion. Whether I shall do some thing in the Oratorio way (as several of

---

* After a second visit in 1755 Arne was to return to London without his long-suffering wife, Cecilia, who preferred to stay in Dublin.

my friends desire) I can not determine as yet. Certain it is that this time 12 month I shall continue my Oratorio's in Ireland, where they are a going to make a large Subscription allready for that Purpose.

Handel's certainty was not to be fulfilled, though there can be no doubt that had he signalled his intention to return to Dublin in 1743 he would have been enthusiastically welcomed. There may have been a few dissident voices; one detects a certain asperity in the advertisement by Mr Stretch of the Puppet Theatre in Capel Street announcing the opening of his new season in November: 'and as he is no foreigner and spends what he gets in this Kingdom, he hopes to meet with due Encouragement as usual'. The absentee landlord and the artistic predator are neatly elided. Handel must have carried off a substantial sum from Dublin, but during 1742 the Charitable Musical Society had enlarged 142 debtors for an outlay of £1225. *Acis and Galatea* was given for the Society in December and the round of Dublin concerts, benefits, and assemblies continued. A local stir which brought together the elevated world of Dublin music-making and the low life of the city was the arrest, early that month, of George Hendrick, alias Crazy Crow, 'a remarkable impudent fellow, and Porter to most Bands of Musick in this Town'. The black-visaged Crow had diversified from carrying the more unwieldy instruments between the musicians' homes and the concert rooms into 'stealing dead Bodies out of graves in St Andrew's Church Yard', this being a spot familiar to him from dozens of charitable concerts. He was fined and imprisoned, but did not, so far as is known, plead too literal an understanding of 'By man came also the resurrection of the dead'. But Dublin could afford to be proprietorial when Handel's London oratorio season got under way, and the *Dublin Journal* of 15 March 1743 printed an extract from a private letter from England:

Our Friend Mr Handell is very well, and Things have taken a quite different turn here from what they did some Time past; for the Publick will be no longer imposed on by Italian Singers, and some wrong Headed Undertakers of bad Opera's, but find out the Merit of Mr Handell's Composition and English Performances: That Gentleman is more esteemed now than ever.

Samson had been performed four times to crowded houses: 'Mr Dubourg (lately arrived from Dublin) performed at the last, and

played a Solo between the Acts, and met with universal and un
common Applause from the Royal Family and the whole Audience.'

The Charitable Musical Society intended to mount *Messiah* on 1
December 1743, and with this in view obtained from Handel a tran
script of the score. It also asked the members of the two choirs to tak
part; the soloists amongst them chose and were given copies of thei
parts. But on 6 December the Society was obliged to state, through th
Dublin Journal, that, 'after preparations had been made, at considerabl
Expense, to the Surprize of the Society, several of the Members of th
said Choirs (some of whom had engaged as before mentioned) though
fit to decline performing, and returned their Parts, for Reasons tha
no way related to or concerned the said Society'. The performanc
was therefore postponed until 3 February, to the Society's manifes
disadvantage, but by then it could undertake to find 'such Performer
as will do Justice to that Sublime Composition'. A notice in a late
issue throws light on the dispute; nine musicians announce that the
will not have anything to do with any 'Society or Concert' with whic
John Church is involved, on the grounds that Church has for som
time assumed an authority at 'all Publick Performances, which he i
not entitled unto'. The signatories were all instrumentalists, several c
them members of the City Music and none of them connected wit
the choirs. Church had been prominent in Mercer's benefit concer
for several years and was a member of both choirs; he had recentl
succeeded Charles Taylor, who had died aged eighty-four, as Maste
of Song. The duties of this office appear to have been those of hea
choirman; one cannot imagine that, in his last years, Taylor was in
position to exercise them vigorously. It is reasonable to suppose tha
Church attempted to use his new position to introduce a little orde
into what must have been rather casually organised gatherings. Th
situation, in this case exacerbated by the mutual distrust of orchestra
and choirs, is not unknown in the twentieth century, and its resul
were potentially disastrous; on Christmas Eve the *Journal* publishe
verses, intended to be salutary, on the quarrel, which 'was now becom
so general, that the Charitable Musical Societies were all in danger c
being dropped, or at least suffering greatly by it'. By 3 February
chorus and orchestra had been assembled under Dubourg (signif
cantly, no mention is made of the cathedral choirs), but the perforn
ance was further delayed by Lord Netterville's trial. Ladies were agai
asked to 'put aside a Mode' (hoops), and a further performance b
the same performers, for the support of the Charitable Infirmary, wa

Taste in High Life by William Hogarth. Painted in 1742 at the request of Miss Mary Edwards, who was mocked for her old-fashioned clothes. The difficulties of negotiating a hoop in a sedan-chair are shown on the fire-screen.

given on the 27th. Henceforth it was annual, and in December 174.
Messiah was given in St Finbarry's Cathedral, Cork. It would not b«
given in an ecclesiastical building in England for another six years (th«
Foundling Hospital Chapel) or in a cathedral (Bristol) for fourteen

Matthew Dubourg continued to direct the Dublin *Messiahs* unti
1748, when John Frederick Lampe, who made a two-year visit t«
Dublin in the footsteps of his brother-in-law, Arne, conducted, an(
the composer and violinist Niccolo Pasquali led. Pasquali took ove
the direction for 1749, and the next year was succeeded by Gia«
Battista Marella, an Italian whose previous musical experience ha(
been in France. Mary Pendarves, now Mrs Delany (she had marrie(
in 1743) and an assiduous attender of Dublin concerts, had foreboding
when she first heard him: 'I am not sure I shall like his taste, till
hear him play music of *consequence*; and I believe on the whole he ha
too many tricks to please me often.' But in the event she was surprised
On 18 December 1750 she wrote to her brother, Bernard Granville
an enthusiastic Handelian from his youth, telling him that she

> was at the rehearsal and performance of The Messiah, and though
> voices and hands were wanting to do it justice, it was very tolerably
> performed, and gave me great pleasure – 'tis heavenly. Marella con-
> ducted it, and I expected would have *spoiled it*, but was agreeably
> surprised to find the contrary; he came off with great applause. I
> thought it would be impossible for his wild fancy and fingers to
> have kept within bounds; but Handel's music inspired and *awed*
> *him*.

Marella was succeeded in 1754 by Samuel Lee, the first Irishman t«
conduct *Messiah* (other notable Irish-born conductors of the work
though not in Dublin, were to be Charles Villiers Stanford and Hamil
ton Harty). In 1810 Francis Robinson, when he founded the firs
Dublin amateur choral society, named it 'The Sons of Handel'.

There is much more to say about *Messiah* in Dublin life: the improb
able number of postponements, the effects of 'boisterous weather' o«
concert-going, the possible fate of the gentleman who, in 1746, gave ;
Messiah ticket for a performance of *Esther* and was told, in the *Dubli.*
Journal, that he was 'desired to send a genuine Ticket, or the Money
or else he will be called upon'. But two matters may be considered a
specially significant. In 1852 Horatio Townsend, a Dublin barriste
and choral singer, published, following a hint from a colleague, Georg«
Finlayson, *An Account of the Visit of Handel to Dublin*, a pioneering piec

of sound documentation and good sense, which has been the foundation for all subsequent research and a model for scholarship in other areas of Handel's life besides. And *Messiah* is thoroughly embedded in Joyce's *Ulysses*. It provides the motif that heralds Boylan's entry and Bloom's exit. When Bloom is elevated as the host in the hallucinated Mass of the *Circe* episode, 'A choir of six hundred voices, conducted by Mr Vincent O'Brien, sings the Alleluia chorus, accompanied on the organ by Joseph Glynn. Bloom becomes mute, shrunken, carbonised.' In 'The Wandering Rocks' Boylan buys fruit for Molly Bloom, and Bloom, with an anticipation of both the eucharistic sacrifice and of the novel's final moment of affirmation, realises the destination and purpose of the vice-regal procession that forms the coda to the episode:

Hello, placard. Mirus bazaar. His excellency the lord lieutenant. Sixteenth today it is. In aid of funds for Mercer's Hospital. *The Messiah* was first given for that. Yes. Handel.

6: 'Bishops and other Squeamish People':

Messiah under Threat

WHEN HANDEL RETURNED TO LONDON IT WAS CERTAINLY NOT in an exultant mood, though he made, as we have seen, no secret of his obligations to Dublin. But he wrote to Jennens on 9 September with assurance: he would have nothing to do with opera; he could not determine as yet whether he would 'do something in the Oratorio way'; he intended to continue his oratorios in Ireland in a year's time. It was not a particularly creative autumn for him; he completed and tidied up *Samson* and wrote a couple of chamber duets. In London, to judge by a letter from Edward Holdsworth to Jennens written a day after Handel's, rumour had consolidated his immediate uncertainties and further intentions so that it was assumed he was returning there more or less at once. Armed with his personal knowledge, Jennens put Holdsworth right and, presuming a little on his information, expressed his 'hope to have some very agreeable Entertainments from him this Season. His Messiah is by all accounts his Masterpiece'. The last sentence, written on the basis of the Bishop of Elphin's letter and (presumably) hearsay, was hubristic; it was an opinion Jennens was to revoke and then have slowly to revise in the light of public opinion – not a dignified procedure.

By the New Year Handel had decided to venture on an oratorio season and had come to an agreement with John Rich to lease Covent Garden during Lent. But, as in Dublin, his first thought was not of *Messiah*. On 10 January 1743 he sent *Samson* to be licensed. A week later Jennens, distinctly unamused, wrote to Holdsworth, after a meeting with Handel at which he had lent him music from a box sent him by Holdsworth who, while in Rome, had managed to buy part of the collection formerly owned by Cardinal Ottoboni:

> Handel has borrow'd a dozen of the pieces & I dare say I shall catch him stealing from them; as I have formerly, both from Scarlatti & Vinci. He has compos'd an exceeding fine Oratorio, being an

alteration of Milton's Samson Agonistes, with which he is to begin Lent. His Messiah has disappointed me; being set in great haste, tho' he said he would be a year about it, & make it the best of all his Compositions. I shall put no more Sacred Words into his hands, to be thus abus'd.

Which Scarlatti Jennens meant, or even whether he was able to distinguish between father and son, is doubtful; he might well have noted the borrowings from Domenico Scarlatti in the opus VI concerti, but the Ottoboni box is more likely to have contained music by Alessandro. Jennens's annoyance, however, is not in question; Handel was offering an entertainment, by subscription on the Dublin model, and it was neither *Saul* nor *Messiah*. Worse, he had by now seen a score and word-book of *Messiah* and had taken exception both to aspects of the setting and to what he must have regarded as the subversion of his intentions so far as 'How beautiful are the feet' was concerned. Holdsworth replied in a way that suggests he had gathered that there was expectation of, and excitement about, a performance of the oratorio:

I am sorry to hear yr. friend Handel is such a jew. His negligence, to say no worse, has been a great disappointment to others as well as yr. self, for I hear there was great expectation of his composition. I hope the words, tho' murther'd, are still to be seen, yt. I shall have that pleasure when I return. And as I don't understand the musick I shall be better off than the rest of ye world.

The first performance of *Samson* was on 18 February, subscription tickets being on sale at Handel's house in Brook Street with the prices for single tickets at half a guinea for pit and boxes (the pit floored over and the two run together), five shillings for the first gallery, three shillings and sixpence for the second. Newburgh Hamilton, who had adapted Milton's poem, dedicated it to Frederick, Prince of Wales, with whom Handel's relations were volatile, and added a preface in which he contrived to puff his own adaptation of *Alexander's Feast*. It does not much add to our knowledge of Dryden or of Handel but it is something of a manifesto for the form. Hamilton had considered a theatrical adaptation:

But as Mr *Handel* had so happily introduc'd here *Oratorios*, a musical Drama, whose Subject must be Scriptural, and in which the Solemnity of Church-Musick is agreeably united with the most pleasing Airs of the Stage: it would have been an irretrievable Loss to have neglected the Opportunity of that great Master's doing Justice to this Work . . .

It is also a testimony to the forces ranged against Handel: 'it is a pity that so many mean Artifices have been lately us'd to blast all his Endeavours, and in him to ruin the Art itself . . .' But they did not blast *Samson*. It was given eight times that season, the royal family attending on 2 March. Horace Walpole, a sceptical subscriber to the Haymarket opera, observed ruefully on 24 February:

> Handel has set up an Oratorio against the Operas, and succeeds. He has hired all the goddesses from farces and the singers of *Roast Beef* from between the acts at both theatres, with a man with one note in his voice, and a girl without even an one; and so they sing, and make brave hallelujahs; and the good company encore the recitative, if it happens to have any cadence like what they call a tune.

The singers were certainly not celebrated in opera, but two of them, Mrs Cibber (Micah) and Signora Avoglio (Israelite woman and Philistine woman) are familiar to us from Dublin, and from the fourth performance were joined by Dubourg, who also played a concerto between the acts. Even Jennens, writing to Holdsworth, had to admit *Samson*'s merits, though he continued to resent the fact that Handel had chosen to start the season with it and not with *Messiah*:

> Last Friday Handel perform'd his Samson, a most exquisite Entertainment, which tho' I heard with infinite Pleasure, yet it increased my resentment for his neglect of the Messiah. You do him too much Honour to call him a Jew! a Jew would have paid more respect to the Prophets.

Earlier he had observed:

> As to the Messiah, 'tis still in his power by retouching the weak parts to make it fit for a public performance; & I have said a great deal to him on the Subject: but he is so lazy & so obstinate, that I much doubt the effect. . . . What adds to my chagrin is, that if he makes his Oratorio ever so perfect, there is a clamour about Town, said to arise from the B$^{ps.}$, against performing it. This may occasion some enlargement of the Preface.

What Jennens had in mind by way of a 'Preface' was an introduction to the 'correct' version of the word-book, which he intended to publish

James Steward his Book Docky 19

Six OVERTURES

fitted to the

HARPSICORD *or* SPINNET

Thomas viz. *Paviatt's Book*

Samson	Deidamia *Doncaster*
The Sacred Oratorio	Hymen
Saul	Pernasso in Festa

Compos'd by

Mr HANDEL.

Being all proper Pieces for the Improvement of the Hand on the Harpsicord *or* Spinnet

Eighth Collection.

London. *Printed for* I. Walsh, *in Catharine Street, in y Strand.*

Musick Just Publish'd for the Harpsicord.

Handel's 48 Overtures from all his Operas	Hasse's Comic Tunes to the Dances Perform'd at the Opera and both Theatres in 2 Vol.
2 Sets of Lessons	Hasse's 6 Organ Concertos
Voluntaries and Fugues	Burgess 6 Organ Concertos
The Celebrated Water Musick	Bononcini's Lessons
The Celebrated Aires from all his Operas in 4 Vol.	Smith's Lessons
12 Organ Concertos	Jones's Lessons
Ladies Banquet, or Dance Tunes from y Operas.	Roseingrave's Lessons and Voluntaries.

Six Overtures fitted to the Harpsicord or Spinnet (1743); the title-page refers only to *The Sacred Oratorio*.

himself if Handel did not revise the one which Jennens described as 'printed in Ireland, full of Bulls'. The reading 'B$^{ps.}$' has been contested, 'B$^{ps.}$' seems likelier than 'B$^{rs.}$', 'Brothers' (i.e. Methodists), though Jennens, as a non-juror, had no love for either. So he not only proposed to castigate Handel's unauthorised alterations to his words, but simultaneously to defend the performance of *Messiah* from its enemies, a two-pronged enterprise that, had he ever carried it out, would have been perverse even by Jennens's standards.

On 12 March a second subscription series was advertised: it began with *Samson* (announced as, though not in fact, the last performance), and continued with *L'Allegro, il Penseroso ed il Moderato* and the *Ode on St Cecilia's Day*; the third concert was announced for Wednesday 23rd as 'A New Sacred Oratorio. With a *Concerto* on the *Organ*. And a Solo on the Violin by Mr. *Dubourg*'. On the same day the *Universal Spectator*, a Tory paper, published, with a somewhat sanctimonious preamble ('I could not suppress it, as there is so well-intended a Design and pious Zeal runs through the whole, and nothing derogatory said of Mr *Handel*'s Merit') a long letter on the impropriety of oratorios in general and, by implication, of the *Sacred Oratorio* in particular, including the revelation that it had been performed in Ireland under the name of *Messiah*, which was itself an evidently opprobrious title. The writer claimed no specific knowledge of *Messiah*, but having named it retreated to his general question, as to whether '*The Place* and *Performers* are fit?'; 'An *Oratorio* either is an *Act of Religion*, or it is not; if it is one I ask if the *Playhouse* is a fit *Temple* to perform it, or a Company of *Players* fit *Ministers* of *God's Word*, for in that Case such they are made'. Philalethes, 'lover of truth', is too common an eighteenth-century pseudonym to give a clue to the author's identity, but it is quite likely that the author was himself a non-juror; Jeremy Collier, whose attack on the playhouses was the *locus classicus* for this kind of argument, was one, so too was William Law, whose saintly personality has often been allowed to obscure the rigour of his precepts in such matters as the essentially profane nature of all theatrical entertainments. The *Universal Spectator* was not a popular or, by 1743, a particularly influential paper, and it might well be questioned whether Philalethes's views remotely represented any kind of general feeling. But we have independent testimony from Jennens and from the Earl of Shaftesbury, who seventeen years later recalled that in Lent 1743 Handel

performed his Oratorio of Sampson, and it was received with

uncommon Applause. He afterwards performed The Messiah but partly from the scruples, some Persons had entertained, against carrying on such a Performance in a Play House, and partly for not entering into the genius of the Composition, this Capital Composition, was but indifferently relish'd.

It is nevertheless easy to read too much into the *Sacred Oratorio* as a substituted title; in Dublin the original announcement had promised a 'new Grand Oratorio, called the Messiah'; in London the word-book was unconditionally for '*Messiah*', and though when Walsh advertised the publication of the overture (with five others) in parts in July he described it as 'the Sacred Oratorio', the keyboard reduction, which appeared in December, was advertised as the overture from '*Messia*' (*sic*), was given on the title-page as *The Sacred Oratorio*, and appeared by the head of the piece, which led off the collection, as *Overture in Messiah*. There was no serious attempt at disguise, and as a title *The Sacred Oratorio* must have enraged those who were going to be enraged quite as much as did *Messiah*.

For the first night we have only one witness, Jennens, who the next day confirmed this point about the name:

Messiah was perform'd last night, & will be again to morrow, notwithstanding the clamour rais'd against it, which has only occasion'd it's being advertis'd without its Name; a Farce, which gives me as much offence as anything relating to the performance can give the Bs. & other squeamish People. 'Tis after all, in the main, a fine Composition, notwithstanding some weak parts, which he was too idle & too obstinate to retouch, tho' I us'd great importunity to perswade him to it.

The second performance, on Friday 25 March, was followed by a third on Tuesday 29th, which testifies to a degree of success. Only one significant retouching, besides a few verbal corrections (not resettings), can be ascribed to the influence of Jennens: the restoration of 'Their sound is gone out into all lands', originally the middle section of the cancelled da capo aria to the Romans text, now a tenor *arioso* following the duet and chorus version of 'How beautiful are the feet' which had been sung in Dublin. The other changes were dictated by the capabilities of the new line-up of singers. Handel had, as in Dublin, Signora Avoglio and Mrs Cibber. He also had Mrs Clive (in Dublin in 1741, but her visit did not coincide with Handel's), Miss Edwards, Mr Beard, Mr Lowe and Mr Reinhold.

Kitty Clive sang the Part I, section 4 Nativity sequence, in which Handel replaced the second recitative, 'And lo, the Angel of the Lord' with a continuo accompanied air, to the same words save that it began '*But lo*'. It is more overtly dramatic and illustrative than the recitative, and destroys the proportion of the section; it was used only in 1743. Mrs Clive was born Catherine Raftor, the daughter of a Kilkenny lawyer who fought for James II at the Boyne and whose property was sequestrated; he was pardoned when he married a London heiress but subsequently lost the fortune. Kitty Clive's entry into the theatre was through Colley Cibber; a friend, Jenny Johnson, was engaged to Theophilus Cibber (whose second wife, as we have seen, was Susannah Arne), and Colley, by chance hearing Kitty sing, offered to train her. She was a singing actress, excelling in comic parts and indeed, in Walpole's words, as a goddess in the farces – in 1728, when she was seventeen, she had played Venus in Pepusch's *Perseus and Andromeda*. It was her popularity as Polly in *The Beggar's Opera* that Theophilus Cibber played on when he worked up the rivalry between her and his second wife. She was also much called on as a singer between the acts, with a repertory of Purcell, Arne, Handel and Irish ballads. In 1740 she had played Emma in Arne's *Alfred* when it was given at its first performance at Cliveden, the home of the Prince of Wales; her role included one of Arne's very finest songs, 'O Peace, the fairest child of heaven' – not virtuosic, but needing exceptional control.

Evidence as to Kitty Clive's character is consistent: she was a loyal and generous ally but a spitfire enemy, 'a mixture of combustibles', said the irrepressible Yorkshire theatre manager Tate Wilkinson, from experience. Horace Walpole was to become a great friend and practical help to her, giving her in later years the use of Little Strawberry Hill, which of course he called Clive-den. Dr Johnson thought her 'a better romp than any I ever saw in nature' and told Boswell, 'Clive, Sir, is a good thing to sit by; she always understands what you say.' Her marriage to George Clive, a second cousin of Lord Clive, was short-lived, but the parting was amicable. A less clear picture emerges of her as a singer; our main informant is Burney, who thought her 'intolerable' when attempting to be 'fine', but perfect in light character pieces; he also claimed that she tended to blame the orchestra for her mistakes and that once, on coming in wrong, cried out, 'Why don't the fellows mind out what they are about?' Arne, directing, protested:

Six Overtures (1743); the first in order of appearance is plainly described as *Messiah*.

she slapped him; he put her over his knee and spanked her. Hardl
surprisingly, Arne became an enemy; but she managed to sing Delila
in *Samson*, and Handel, though he had other talent available, clearl
thought her right for that important part.

Miss Edwards had apparently been Mrs Clive's pupil; she, also
was a singing actress, and first appeared as a child in pantomime. Sh
was in Handel's Lincoln's Inn Fields company for the 1740–1 seaso
and sang in both *Deidamia* and *Imeneo*, as well as *L'Allegro*, *Acis ar*
Galatea, and *Saul*; she was taken on again in 1743, and was the secon
Israelite woman and second Philistine woman to Signora Avoglio
respective first women in *Samson*; she also performed once more i
L'Allegro, but whether she sang in *Messiah* is questionable; her nam
appears several times in the score and, most notably, against 'I kno
that my Redeemer liveth', but in every instance there is a counte
indication. The most likely thing seems to be that she stood in fo
Signora Avoglio in one of the performances, but there are sever
possibilities, of which one is that she never sang at all. Tate Wilkinso
reports that she would always blush at the hint of an indecent joke, bu
that she was unscrupulous in her private conduct and this eventuall
antagonised Mrs Clive.

The same uncertainties as to Miss Edwards's involvement recur i
the case of John Beard. Handel undoubtedly anticipated that th
versatile and popular tenor, whose career he had furthered at ever
opportunity and who had created the part of Samson with enormou
success, would sing in the London *Messiah*, and arranged things acco
dingly. But either before the first night or between the performance
as Donald Burrows has shown, he had to withdraw. So 'Their soun
is gone out', set as an *arioso* specifically with Beard in mind, wa
reallocated to Signora Avoglio, and we have no way of telling wheth
he performed it or not. Handel accordingly gave most of his music
Avoglio. But even if he was only in intention the leading tenor of th
performance Beard's later career is so bound up with *Messiah* – h
sang in every subsequent London performance until Handel's deat
except those of 1749 and 1750, and did besides much work in th
provinces – that notice should be taken of him now.

Born in 1716, John Beard sang under Bernard Gates at the Chap
Royal and as a treble was the Israelitish priest in the 1732 semi-stage
version of *Esther*. When he left the Chapel Royal in 1734 he we
straight to Handel's Covent Garden company and made his début a
Silvio in the third version of *Il Pastor Fido*. He worked continuous

with Handel until June 1739 and became established in the public mind as both the quintessential *English* voice and the predominant Handelian singer. He played a part in the canonisation of Handel which was as crucial as the patronage of three generations of royalty, the statue at Vauxhall, the association with the Foundling Hospital or the assumption that the Old Testament was the true record of the early history of the island race. Foreigners came and went; Beard sang on until deafness prompted his retirement in 1767. He was an institution, made Doctor of Music at Oxford in 1759, and a governor of the Foundling Hospital in 1760; he remained a regular attendant at Drury Lane (with his ear-trumpet) until his death.

In 1739 Beard married Lady Henrietta Herbert, the twenty-one-year-old widowed daughter of the Earl of Waldegrave. On learning of this the Earl of Egmont observed that 'there is no prudence below the girdle', and Lady Mary Wortley Montagu that she 'did not doubt that if this was broke off she would bestow her person and fortune on some hackney-coachman or chairman', and that she 'really saw no method of saving *her* from ruin, & her *family* from disgrace, but by poisoning her'. Lady Henrietta died four years later. Beard's second marriage was into his own profession, to John Rich's daughter, Charlotte. On his father-in-law's death in 1761 he became patentee of Covent Garden, but sold out when he retired from singing.

Beard was as indispensable to Boyce and Arne as to Handel, a famous Macheath in *The Beggar's Opera*, and he became the idol of the developing provincial music festivals. His art was in the use he made of his voice. Horace Walpole said that he had 'only one note' to it, yet 'did more justice to sense than any of our performers'. Charles Dibdin, who had an unhappy experience of him as a manager, but respected him nevertheless, maintained that 'he never did more than was set down for him; he never set on a quantity of barren spectators to applaud while some necessary question of the song stood still: he let his own discretion be the tutor and held the mirror up to nature'. Burney had a similar reaction: 'he constantly possessed the favour of the public by his superior conduct, knowledge of music and intelligence as an actor': 'energetic' and 'useful' he also thought appropriate epithets. No one would have applied either to Mrs Cibber, but in ascribing to Beard these downright masculine virtues he was according to him counterparts to those qualities of sweetness and sensibility which he found in her, and, however stereotyped, they suggested what was to be expected from a first-rate English singer: naturalness, sincerity

and understatement. In the title part of *Samson* Beard brought all his
qualities to the public attention. He became the type of what might
be expected from oratorio and the antithesis of mere virtuosity and
the Italianate exploitation of sound divorced from sense. He had agility
and a surprising range, but in writing for him Handel favoured the
lower part of the voice and held the rest in reserve.

Thomas Lowe afforded an obvious comparison. He was said to be
a Spitalfields weaver by birth. Burney thought that he had greater
natural gifts than Beard, but 'with the finest tenor voice I ever heard
in my life, for want of diligence and cultivation, he could never be
safely trusted with anything more than a ballad, which he constantly
learned by ear'. Dibdin agreed; this favourite of the pleasure gardens
and for songs between the acts, the man for whom Dibdin's adored
master Arne had written his Shakespeare songs, nevertheless 'lost
himself beyond the namby-pamby poetry of Vauxhall; Beard was at
home everywhere'. Lowe joined Drury Lane in 1740, the year in which
along with Kitty Clive, he performed in *Alfred* at Cliveden and sang
'Rule Britannia', which was not to be heard again in context until
1745 but was hugely popular as a solo piece. He had three minor parts
in *Samson* but sang the title-role in 1749, when Beard was unavailable
and in the previous year created the part of Joshua. But where Beard
was prudent he was spendthrift. Beard disposed of his Theatre Royal
patent for £60,000; Lowe, who leased Marylebone Gardens in 1763
was forced to sell at a depressed price six years later, and spent the
years until his death scraping a living at Sadler's Wells. The peak of
his career as a Handel singer came in the years 1748, 1749 and 1750
Precisely what he sang in *Messiah* in 1743 we do not know (it must
have been the entire tenor part in the last performance or performances), though it is clear that Handel adapted the original bass version
of 'But who may abide' for him ('*Un tono piu alto ex E* for Mr Lowe in
Tenor Cliff'); the aria was thus not exactly as he had first envisaged
it, but it was a far more satisfactory solution than the recitative substituted in Dublin.

The bass was Henry Reinhold, German by birth and popularly
believed to be an illegitimate son of the Archbishop of Dresden. He
had an easy command of two octaves from F to f', and an equally easy
command of every kind of part from the dragon in Lampe and Carey's
Dragon of Wantley to Harapha in *Samson*. As the dragon he vastly
amused the King, who kept Queen Caroline up unduly late (she was
unwell) with accounts of the comic business with which Reinhold, in

John Beard. Mezzotint after Thomas Hudson.

Carey's words, gave 'Life and Spirit' to the part. He sang for Handel
in 1736 and 1737, and from 1743 until his death in 1751 was his
principal bass. He was well liked; after his death a benefit concert
raised £101 for his widow and four children. Coached by Handel, he
became as much the model for an oratorio bass as Beard was for a
tenor, although his career did not last so long as Beard's.

Notwithstanding the ability of the cast, the success of *Messiah* was
only relative, and after three performances Handel decided, despite
having given a final airing to *Samson*, to revive it once more to round
off his second series of concerts. Contention about the propriety of
Messiah evidently continued; on 31 March, the day *Samson* was performed, a riposte to 'Philalethes' appeared in the *Daily Advertiser*:

> Cease, Zealots, cease to blame these Heavn'ly Lays,
> For Seraphs fit to sing Messiah's Praise!
> Nor, for your trivial Argument, assign
> 'The Theatre not fit for Praise Divine.'

This prompted 'Philalethes' to return to the charge in the *Universal
Spectator* of 16 April, in a medley of prose and verse, with a footnote in
his poem to make it absolutely clear that 'Not the Poetry or Musick,
the Place and Performers only, are found Fault with'. However, it
is hardly to be supposed that Philalethes was really in favour of a
performance in a sacred building by amateurs, even though this came
close to anticipating a nineteenth-century ideal. But around the time
this appeared, Handel had been stricken by what appears to have been
his old trouble of 1737. Jennens wrote to Holdsworth on 29 April that
'Handel has a return of his Paralytick Disorder, which affects his Head
and Speech. He talks of spending a year abroad, so that we are to
expect no Musick next year . . .' Horace Walpole also reported that
'Handel has had a palsy and can't compose', though his assumption
that this might affect plans for an opera season has no support. On
3 June Handel began to compose *Semele*, an opera as originally conceived by Congreve in 1706, but an oratorio, despite its highly sensual
content, as set by Handel. He followed it with the Dettingen *Te Deum*,
and went on to compose *Joseph and his Brethren*, to a text by James
Miller. He thus had two oratorios in hand for the next season, and
there were also obvious reasons for reviving *Samson*. On 15 September
Jennens gave vent to his particular vein of splenetic vanity in a letter
to Holdsworth:

I hear Handel is perfectly recover'd, & has compos'd a new Te

Deum & a new Anthem against the return of his Master from
Germany. I don't yet despair of making him retouch the Messiah,
at least he shall suffer for his negligence; nay I am inform'd that he
has suffer'd, for he told Ld. Guernsey, that a letter I wrote him
about it contributed to the bringing of his last illness upon him; &
it is reported that being a little delirious with a Fever, he said he
should be damn'd for preferring Dagon (a Gentleman he was very
complacent to in the Oratorio of Samson) before the Messiah.

Holdsworth was at his most tactfully remedial in his reply (Jennens
had also been splitting hairs about, amongst other things, Virgil's
knowledge of geography), attributing his spleen to his prolonged stay
in Leicestershire:

> It has had an ill effect upon you, and made you quarrel with your
> best friends, Virgil & Handel. You have contributed, by your own
> confession, to give poor Handel a fever and now He is pretty well
> recover'd, you seem resolv'd to attack him again; for you say you
> have not yet done with him. . . . Pray be merciful and don't you
> turn Samson, & use him like a Philistine.

Jennens denied the diagnosis:

> It is not Leic[ester]shire that has made me quarrel with Handel
> but his own Folly, (to say no worse), if that can be called a quarrel,
> where I only tell him the Truth; & he knows it to be Truth, yet is
> so obstinate, he will not submit to it.

The 1744 oratorio season was a success; the works performed were
Semele, Joseph and his Brethren, Saul and *Samson*. Dr Delany thought it
improper to go to *Semele*, the reason being that he was in orders and
it was *not* on a sacred subject – the reverse of the Philalethes position.
Mrs Delany pronounced it to be 'charming'. On 10 March she wrote
to her sister, Mrs Dewes, asking, 'How do you think *I have lately been
employed?* Why, I have made a drama for an oratorio, out of Milton's
Paradise Lost, to give Mr Handel to compose to . . .' Like Edward
Synge's *The Penitent* it remained unset, but it shows the imaginative
hold that the form had taken. She anticipated that three more oratorios
would be given in the season (assuming Handel did not start a second
subscription): *Joseph, Saul*, and, to finish, *Messiah*. But she was disappointed. 'Last night, alas! was the last night of the oratorio: it
concluded with Saul: I was in hopes of the Messiah.'

C O V E N T-G A R D E N.

By S U B S C R I P T I O N.

The Ninth Night.

AT the Theatre-Royal in Covent-Garden, Wednesday next, will be perform'd

A New Sacred O R A T O R I O.

A CONCERTO on the ORGAN,

And a Solo on the Violin by Mr. DUBOURG.

Tickets will be deliver'd to Subscribers on Tuesday next, at Mr, Handel's House in Brook-street.

Pit and Boxes to be put together, and no Person to be admitted without Tickets, which will be deliver'd that Day, at the Office in Covent-Garden Theatre, at Half a Guinea each. First Gallery 5 s. Upper Gallery 3 s. 6 d.

The Galleries will be open'd at Four o'Clock. Pit and Boxes at Five.

Announcement for the first London performance of *Messiah* from the *Daily Post*.

Handel was sufficiently encouraged to begin planning an extremely ambitious winter season. The death of James Miller, however, left him without a poet, and he had once again to have recourse to Jennens, who extracted in return a promise that he would revise *Messiah*. On 9 June he wrote to Gopsal pressing Jennens for copy and telling him that he had both taken the Haymarket opera house and engaged Francesina, Miss Robinson, Beard, Reinhold, Bernard Gates and the Chapel Royal boys and the best chorus singers from the Abbey and Cathedral choirs. He was also making special efforts to persuade Mrs Cibber to perform, which she was pleased to do provided there were no clashes with her acting commitments. Handel hoped to get John Rich to make this possible. The oratorio on which Jennens had started was *Belshazzar*. On 19 July Handel had received an act but urgently needed more and wrote accordingly. He also asked, a little perfunctorily, if Jennens would 'Be pleased to point out these passages in the Messiah which you think require altering'. This seems to have been a placatory sop; on 13 September he was impatient for the third act of *Belshazzar*, reporting that composition of the oratorio (and the phrase is revealing) 'still engages me warmly'.

The season proved to be on far too grandiose a scale. There were to be twenty-four performances from 3 November 1744, at first on

Saturdays, then on Wednesdays and Fridays throughout Lent. After six performances his losses were such that he offered to refund three-quarters of all subscription moneys received:

> As I perceived that joining good Sence and significant Words to Musick, was the best Method of recommending *this* to an English Audience . . . I have directed my Studies that way. . . . I have the Mortification to find, that my Labours to please are become ineffectual, when my Expences are considerably greater.

But many of his subscribers refused to take back their money and the machinations of a Lady Brown, who gave and encouraged parties, 'drums' and 'routs' on oratorio nights seem to have rallied rather than diverted support. Handel resolved to give as many performances as he thought the market would bear and mounted ten during Lent, those in Holy Week, on 9 and 11 April, being of *Messiah*, still announced as 'A' or 'The' *Sacred Oratorio*.

For these performances Handel made two major revisions and, to judge by a draft of a letter of 30 August 1745, this had been at Jennens's request. To an unknown friend Jennens wrote:

> I shall show you a collection I gave Handel call'd Messiah which I value highly, & he has made a fine Entertainment of it, tho' not near so good as he might & ought to have done. I have with great difficulty made him correct some of the grossest faults in the composition, but he retain'd his Overture obstinately, in which there are some passages far unworthy of Handel but much more unworthy of the Messiah.

It is clear that Handel was prepared to humour these capricious and self-serving objections, but he did once more attack the problem of the 'How beautiful are the feet'/'Why do the nations' sequence, and he reordered the rhythm of 'Rejoice greatly'.* The A section of the original da capo version of 'How beautiful are the feet' was now performed for the first time as in the autograph, and led into the new chorus which makes an astonishingly effective use of material taken over from the discarded *arioso* setting of the same (Romans) words. 'Their sound is gone out' is illustrated by a sequence of concertina'd entries which make up one of Handel's most cunning attempts to suggest that one is

---

* I am persuaded by the arguments of Donald Burrows, 'Handel's Performances of *Messiah*: the evidence of the conducting score', *Music and Letters*, vol. 56, July–October 1975, p. 329. But this is the least securely recoverable moment in the early history of *Messiah*.

hearing more of a fugue than there actually is, held together by a most ingenious and unusual bass line, with high and early pedal-points, and an eventual climax on a top e contributing a great deal to the sense of expansiveness that Handel now contrives to convey. The alteration of 'Rejoice greatly' from 12/8 gigue to common time both increases rhythmic variety in the concluding numbers of Part I and heightens the contrast of the first section with the central 'He shall speak peace'.

Whether in the event Susannah Cibber sang in *Messiah* in 1745 is unclear. She would have been free in Holy Week but until then had been exceptionally occupied. Nor was Rich's permission for her to sing any longer relevant. With the suddenness which seems to have characterised her few decisive actions she had abandoned Rich's Covent Garden and joined David Garrick at Drury Lane. There, after initial difficulties, she found her feet, and in March made a remarkable impression playing with him in an otherwise forgotten tragedy, *Tancred and Sigismunda*, by James Thomson, best known for his poem *The Seasons*. She obviously could not have created the part of Daniel in *Belshazzar* (as Handel had hoped in a letter to Jennens of 2 October 1744) because of the conflict with *Tancred*. It seems likely that, if she had sung in *Messiah*, it would have been noted, but there is no record and the conducting score is no help except that it gives La Francesina's name against 'He was despised', which again suggests that Cibber was absent.

The aria must have been sung transposed, since Francesina was a soprano, born Elizabeth Duparc in France but Italian by training (hence her stage name). Brought to England by the Royal Academy of Musick (and thus in opposition to Handel) in 1736, she was very soon being asked to sing at Kensington Palace. In 1738 she joined Handel; she sang Michal in the first performance of *Saul* and a steady run of leading parts through to the title-role in *Semele*, in which she made 'The Morning Lark' a favourite song and caused Mrs Delany to remark that 'there is something in her running divisions that is quite surprising'. Burney thought her not quite in the first rank, but praised her 'light, airy, pleasing movement'. Since Burney only noticed characterisation when popular reaction told him something was going on that he could not account for on technical grounds, he did not refer to this aspect of her skill, but she must have possessed it to have succeeded in the parts that she did.

Miss Robinson came from a musical family. Her father was organist of Westminster Abbey, and two City churches besides, a celebrated pluralist and purveyor of voluntary levities, her mother a soprano who

Mrs Clive. Mezzotint by Faber, 1734. Catherine (Kitty) Clive was one of
the sopranos in the first London *Messiah*, when her stage rival Susannah
Cibber sang alto.

had sung in Handel in the 1720s. The daughter was to have sung Cyrus in the first performance of *Belshazzar*, but took over Daniel when Mrs Cibber proved unavailable, the part having to be transposed upwards to suit her higher voice, which was evidently astonishing. She created the role of Dejanira, the tragic heroine of *Hercules*, which requires a two-octave compass, from A below middle C to high G♯, besides abundant stamina. It is the more mysterious that we know of her from this season only, after which, having been paid £210 from Handel's Bank of England account, she entirely disappears. We can be confident that, in *Messiah*, she sang 'Behold a Virgin shall conceive' and part (presumably the first) of the 'Then shall the eyes of the blind'/'He shall feed His flock' sequence. The tenor and bass were, as Handel had intended, Beard and Reinhold.

No record of critical reaction to the 1745 *Messiah* performances seems to have survived, but in May Robert Dodsley published an anonymous *Ode to Mr Handel*. It is, for once, an accomplished piece, decidedly daring in its liberal enjambement and alliteration, if a little overladen with literary allusion. It has plausibly been suggested that the poet was Joseph Wharton. Its interest for us is the way in which it celebrates *Messiah* and uses it, with precise references, as the climax:

> Him, feeder of the flock
> And leader of the lambs,
>
> The tuneful tenderness of trilling notes
> Symphonious speaks: Him pious pity paints
>   In mournful melody
>   The man of sorrows; grief
>
> Sits heavy on his soul, and bitterness
> Fills deep his deadly draught – He deigns to die –
>   The God who conquers Death,
>   When, bursting from the Grave,
>
> Mighty he mounts, and wing'd with rapid winds,
> Thro' Heav'ns wide portals opening to their Lord
>   To boundless realms return'd,
>   The King of Glory reigns.
>
> Powr's, dominations, thrones resound HE REIGNS,
> High Hallelujah's of empyreal hosts,
>   And pealing Praises join
>   The thunder of the spheres.

This is the last that we hear of *Messiah* in London (it was alive and well in Dublin) for three years. These were not devoid of incident, either personal or national. At the end of August the Reverend William Harris told his sister-in-law in Salisbury that he had 'met Handel a few days since in the street and stopped and put him in mind who I was, upon which I am sure it would have diverted you to have seen his antic motions . . . he talked much of his precarious state of health, yet he looks well enough'. Appearances were misleading, and in October the Earl of Shaftesbury was reporting to another member of the Harris clan (all, like the Granvilles, ardent Handelians), that 'Poor Handel looks something better. I hope he will entirely recover in due time, though he has been a great deal disordered in his head.'

The national circumstances worked to Handel's advantage and to Jennens's disadvantage. The Young Pretender landed at Eriksay in July 1745 and by 17 September he was in Edinburgh. Even Horace Walpole, who in his letters restricted himself on principle to matters of taste and of the town, had to write to Horace Mann about public affairs because 'The confusion I have found, and the danger we are in, prevent my talking of anything else.' Manchester was captured by, it was said, 'two and a half men'. A French invasion seemed imminent. Part of *Zadok the Priest* was played in a thunderstorm at Vauxhall, a circumstance which a resolutely Hanoverian poet saw as a good omen:

> Whilst grateful *Britons* hymn the sacred Lay,
> And, for their Sovereign, every Blessing pray;
> Consenting Jove bids awful Light'nings rise;
> And thunders his great *Fiat* from the Skies.

There were no operas or oratorios until the New Year, and Handel could do no more than write a song for the Gentlemen Volunteers of the City of London, which was sung by Mr Lowe 'with universal applause'. He planned an oratorio season for Lent 1746, and was still concerned to make up the balance of the previous year's subscription. As things worked out, he was able to give three performances only (of the outstanding eight), all of the *Occasional Oratorio*. Thereafter he never again attempted a subscription season. 'The words', the Reverend William Morris, who heard a rehearsal at Handel's house, told Mrs Thomas Harris, 'are scriptural, but taken from various parts, and are expressive of the rebel's fight and our pursuit of them.' Jennens, as might be expected, disliked everything about it, particularly Newburgh Hamilton's libretto:

'Tis an inconceivable jumble of Milton & Spencer, Chaos extracted
from Order by the most absurd of all Blockheads, who like the Devil
takes delight in defacing Beauties of Creation. The difference is,
that one does it from malice, the other from pure Stupidity . . .

It celebrated, in any case, the demise of any realistic hope of a Stuar
restoration, and it made all too clear that this could only ever have
been accomplished through French military intervention on a large
scale, something which many Jacobites were not prepared to contem
plate. Handel can hardly have improved matters by embarking, in
July, on the composition of *Judas Maccabaeus*, to a libretto by Thomas
Morell, specifically intended as a compliment to the Duke of Cumber
land on his return from the bloody victory at Culloden.

After 1745, Burney tells us, Handel was less and less seen in public
forsaking the playhouse, the opera and society, and restricting himsel
to paying his respects to the royal family and to attendance at church
But in 1747 he composed *Alexander Balus* and *Joshua*, and in 1748
Solomon and *Susanna*. His oratorio seasons were profitable, and estab
lished the pattern of twelve or thirteen performances during Lent to
which he was to conform for the rest of his life. At the end of the season
he would take his proceeds to the City to invest them; he was advised
by Mr Gael Morris, 'a broker of the first eminence', whom he would
meet at Garraway's or Batson's coffee house. For the oratorios he made
an increasing use of foreign sopranos and contraltos, without attracting
hostile comment or, apparently, objections from the opera. This is no
totally surprising, since Lord Middlesex had to call heavily on his sub
scribers to cover the losses of the 1747–8 season, and the next winter
there was no proper season at all, comic intermezzi only being given. In
fact this marks a major change in the make-up of Italian opera seasons in
London; from then on comic operas predominated and the managemen
was in the hands of professional impresarios. 1750, significantly, saw
the London premiere of Pergolesi's *La Serva Padrona*, a lively and witty
miniature with a realistic middle-class urban setting. The battle
between oratorio and serious opera had been won.

7: 'The Benevolent Design':
The Birth of an Institution

THE CONTINUOUS TRADITION OF *MESSIAH* PERFORMANCES IN England dates from 1749 when, on 23 March, Handel gave it as the twelfth and last in his Lenten season of oratorios at Covent Garden. So far as is known, it was only announced on the day of the performance, and John Watts, the publisher of the word-book, failed to get it out in time, so that it could only be bought as a souvenir. Fortunately one purchaser remembered the details of the performance clearly enough to note the performers' names beside some of the items they sang, and was sufficiently frugal to reuse the book in 1752 and 1753. We also know that this year Handel had a particularly large band of strings available, and he therefore treated those in excess of his usual forces of twelve or fourteen violins, three violas, three cellos and two double basses as ripieno instruments, literally the 'stuffing', and added them whenever an extra fullness of effect was desirable. He also subtracted them when, as in 'Why do the nations', agility was of more importance than weight of sound. He appears only to have had these augmented forces for *Messiah* in 1749, so although the senza ripieno and con ripieno directions provide a clue* to his dynamic thinking, they do not reflect his normal performance practice.

The soloists in 1749 were Frasi (soprano), 'the boy' (treble), Galli (contralto), Lowe (tenor) and Reinhold (bass). Giulia Frasi was Milanese by birth, and had come to England in 1742. Sir Joseph Hankey, a city banker and patron of music, introduced her to Charles Burney, who became her coach; it was through her that he made the acquaintance of Handel 'who used to bring an Air, or Duet, in his pocket, as soon as composed, hot from the brain, in order to give me the time & style, that I might communicate them to my scholars by repetition; for her knowledge of musical characters was very slight'. She was, Burney tells us, 'young and interesting in her person, had a clear and sweet voice, free from defects, and a smooth and chaste style

---

* It is also important to note that they are in no way analogous to the ripieno directions in a concerto grosso, which distinguish between the orchestral tuttis and the sections for soloists.

of singing; which though cold and unimpassioned, pleased natural ears, and escaped the censure of critics . . .' She began in opera, singing in works by many composers and in all kinds of roles, amongst them a male part, the giant Briareo, in Gluck's opera celebrating the defeat of the Young Pretender, *La Caduta de' Giganti*. From March 1746 she had included airs from Handel's oratorios in her concerts. When Handel took her on for the 1749 season, her first part had been the title role in *Susanna*, and she continued as his first singer until his death. According to Daniel Lysons, 'she pronounced our language in singing with a more distinct articulation' than did natives. This was important, since her strength lay in expression rather than technique. Burney reports that she was not notable for any addiction to application and diligence, and tells how Handel remarked, when she informed him that she was learning thorough-bass in order to accompany herself, 'Oh, vaat may we not expect.' In 1743 she had a daughter by Charles Churchill, the great-nephew of the Duke of Marlborough. Though she continued in oratorio after Handel's death, she got into debt as a result of her extravagance and was forced to flee to Calais where she died in 1772.

We do not know the identity of 'the boy', though he was presumably one of Bernard Gates's Chapel Royal choristers, and presumably also the one who had the taxing task of creating Daniel in *Susanna*. He is likely to have sung the nativity sequence, in which the aria version of 'And lo, the Angel of the Lord' was abandoned and replaced by the original accompanied recitative. He certainly sang 'How beautiful are the feet', which was now settled in the mould into which Handel had recast it in 1745, and he also sang 'If God is for us' in the original G minor soprano version, rather than the transposition into C minor (for alto) which had been used in Dublin and thereafter.

Caterina Galli, with Frasi, had originally been enticed to England to take part in Lord Middlesex's Haymarket season of 1742–3; she sang in operas by Galuppi and Porpora, but does not come to notice again until Handel engaged her for his 1747 Lent oratorios, during which she sang in the *Occasional Oratorio*, *Joseph and his Brethren* and *Judas Maccabaeus*. It was in this last that she gave ' 'Tis Liberty alone', not the best of the liberty arias in the oratorio, to tremendous acclaim, and she sang for all Handel's oratorio seasons until she went back to Italy in 1754. Nineteen years later she attempted to repeat her old triumphs, and returned to England, singing a *Messiah* at the New Haymarket in 1773. But in 1777 she retired and became a companion to the actress Martha Ray. It was not a long-lived arrangement. Miss Ray was the mistress of the Earl of Sandwich, as it happened an ardent Handelian who organised private performances of the oratorios. A clergyman, the Reverend Mr Hackman, became infatuated with her, and, unable to gain her affection, shot her as she was leaving Covent Garden on 7 April 1779. Galli was forced back on to the concert platform and continued to perform for another eighteen years, her voice 'cracked and trembling' according to Lord Mount-Edgecumbe, but her performance moving because of the 'animation and delight' with which she listened to the music that she had known so intimately for so long. When she died in 1804, the *Gentleman's Magazine* referred to her as 'the last of Mr Handel's scholars', and reported that in her last years she had been dependent 'on the bounty of friends, and an annual benefaction from the Royal Society of Musicians'. According to Burney she was 'less feminine' than Frasi (we should perhaps forget Frasi's appearance as a giant in Gluck), and 'there was something spirited and interesting in her manner'. Galli's survival into the nineteenth century is a striking instance of Handelian longevity, the phenomenon that makes possible those chains of inheritance such as the one that connects – amongst conductors – John Randall (himself notably long-lived), Joah Bates, Thomas Dupuis, Sir George Smart and Sir George Macfarren, and runs from Macfarren to the present. But it is impossible to believe that Galli's style was not modified by the musical revolutions through which she lived, and such pedigrees are largely of sentimental significance.

A single London performance in a year might not seem to signify a turning-point, particularly as the principal innovation, the use of a boy soloist, was repeated once only, although of course it has proved a godsend for the *Messiah*-at-Christmas industry. But 1749 was a good year for other reasons. *Messiah* was given under its proper name. It was also performed, on Friday 14 April, at Oxford, as part of the celebrations which marked the opening of Dr Radcliffe's Library (the Radcliffe Camera) and the conferring of an honorary MA on James Gibbs, the architect. On this occasion Dr William King – like Gibbs, a Jacobite – made a notably subversive Latin oration in the Sheldonian Theatre, where the public events took place, but it should be noted that the overture to the *Occasional Oratorio* and a Coronation Anthem were also performed. *Messiah* concluded three afternoons of Handel oratorio, which had begun with *Esther*, followed by *Samson*. The performances were directed by Dr William Hayes, Professor of Music and organist and master of the choristers at Magdalen College, a lifelong enthusiast for Handel both as an executant and as a pamphleteer. He owned a manuscript of *Messiah* which was copied as early as 1745.* Hayes did much to foster music-making in both university and city (the Holywell Music Room was in part a product of his efforts) and he firmly established *Messiah* in the Oxford repertoire, with performances in 1752, 1754 and 1756, and regularly thereafter. An aspect of oratorio neglected by those who persist in regarding it as somehow an inadequate substitute for music theatre (not an argument, however, which has the remotest bearing on *Messiah*), is that in the provinces, which had never known opera, oratorio represented a vast expansion of musical experience and might be re-created wherever an appropriate orchestra and choir could be assembled. Moreover, metropolitan soloists could be used in conjunction with local forces. Of course, the sneer that oratorio is 'congregational' is also a sneer at the fact that it can be participatory, but by 1754 Hayes, with soloists and instrumental leaders down from London, was operating a system which is still standard, and has played an important part in ensuring the continuing popularity of oratorio in British life.

Two other things in 1749 helped *Messiah*. After publishing the overture in 1743, Walsh had put out a version of 'He was despised' arranged for a 'German flute, Violin, or Harpsichord'; in fact a harpsichord continuo was presumed, but the transcribed vocal line could be taken by either of the instruments or by the keyboard player's right hand. In 1749 he launched an anthology of *Handel's Songs Selected from his Oratorios*, and Volume I contained 'Ev'ry valley shall be exalted' and 'O thou that tellest good tidings to Zion', the latter admittedly in an octave transposition, but at least with words. It was a start. When Volume V was published in 1759 it completed the tally of all the arias in *Messiah*. But it was only in 1763 that Walsh finally published *Songs in Messiah* (together with the overture), something made the more puzzling by the fact that it has been shown that the plates for this had been engraved at least a decade earlier, and possibly as early as 1750. No satisfactory reason has ever been advanced for this tardiness. It has been suggested that Handel and Walsh could not agree on terms, that Handel did not want the work published because he held it in special affection, and that Walsh was afraid of resentment against it

---

* Now in the Pierpont Morgan Library, Cary Ms 122. But it is puzzling that Hayes needed to borrow a *Messiah* score in 1756.

by bigots. However, Walsh and Handel agreed about the publication of everything else, Handel raising no special difficulties about providing copies of the score (though the Foundling Hospital was to misunderstand his attitude), and none of the objections raised against public performance of *Messiah* could have had any bearing on the publication of the *Songs*, which was designed to make them available for domestic performance. (It will be seen from what follows that, whatever the explanation, Handel and Walsh were in complete agreement over the matter.)

Finally, 1749 saw Handel busily involved in the kind of negotiations that would have been familiar to him from Dublin. On 4 May he was present at a special meeting of the General Committee of the Foundling Hospital. This had been founded by Royal Charter ten years before at the instigation of Thomas Coram, a sea captain and merchant, for 'the reception, maintenance, and education of exposed and deserted young children'. The Hospital, in Lamb's Conduit Fields, was begun in 1742 to the designs of Theodore Jacobsen, also a city merchant, of German descent, an amateur architect amongst whose late designs (the only one standing today) was the main quadrangle of Trinity College, Dublin. A number of artists had associated themselves with Coram's scheme, notably William Hogarth, who decorated the Court Room with a grand 'scripture-piece' of *Moses Brought to Pharaoh's Daughter*. Another governor, elected in 1748, and a donor to the tune of the conventional £50, was John Walsh. He seems likely to have been the immediate cause of Handel's involvement. At this meeting Handel 'generously and charitably offered a performance of vocal and instrumental musick to be held at this Hospital, and that the money arising therefrom should be applied to the finishing the chapel of the Hospital'. The Committee accepted, fixed a date, appointed an executive subcommittee, and resolved to recommend that Handel be elected a governor of the Hospital. There was a problem about royalty and the date, the windows had to be 'sashed' (that is, filled with temporary paper panels as there were insufficient funds to glaze them), and Handel demurred at being a governor, but was elected the next year nevertheless, thus joining Hogarth and having had paid him a (not disinterested) compliment comparable to that which another charity, St Bartholomew's, had paid James Gibbs.

The concert was finally held on 27 May in the presence of the Prince and Princess of Wales, the young princes and princesses, and a 'prodigious Concourse of the Nobility and Gentry'; over a thousand people were present, and tickets were half a guinea each. The music consisted of the pieces for the Royal Fire-Works, which had gone all but unheard on that farcical occasion (which ended with the artificer of the fire-works drawing his sword on the Comptroller of the Ordnance), the Dettingen Anthem with new words appropriate to the peace of Aix-la-Chapelle, selections from *Solomon,* and the newly put-together *Foundling Hospital Anthem,* a partial composite which concluded with the Hallelujah chorus. The alto soloist was Signor Guadagni, shortly to become a name to conjure with in the history of *Messiah.* But the real importance of the occasion was the link it forged between Handel, the Foundling Hospital and, almost a year later, the oratorio. At some time in July Handel made a contract with Jonathan Morse of Barnet for building an organ, a gift towards the furnishing of the chapel.

In 1750 Handel again ended his oratorio season with *Messiah.* He had revived *Saul, Judas Maccabaeus,* and *Samson* and introduced a new work, *Theodora.* Gaetano Guadagni had sung in these last two, creating the part of Didimus in *Theodora.* He was born at Lodi, had sung opera in Venice, and came to England for the 1748–9 comedy season; he was then in his late twenties. Frasi suggested that Burney should coach him and, like her, Guadagni became as proficient and admired in English as in Italian. He also greatly admired Garrick's acting, and Garrick enjoyed giving him lessons in the art. He clearly had a winning personality; Handel went to great trouble on his behalf. He also had uncommon intelligence and determination, with the result that it is not easy to recapture his qualities as they manifested themselves during his first stay in England, which lasted until 1753, since his later impact was so marked and so different. He then went to Paris, Venice, Vienna and Frankfurt, and in 1762 created the male title role in Gluck's *Orfeo ed Euridice.* He revisited London in 1769, by which time his voice was soprano rather than contralto, with a greatly extended range, but a much less rich and concentrated tone. Burney says that 'though his manner of singing was perfectly delicate, polished and refined, his voice seemed, at first, to disappoint every hearer. Those who remembered it when he was in England before, found it comparatively thin and feeble.' Indeed, Burney himself was so fascinated by the phenomenon of the later, post-*Orfeo* Guadagni, with his artful manner of diminishing the tones of his voice like the dying notes of an 'Aeolian harp', that he was apt to forget that he had once been 'very young, wild, and idle, with a very fine counter-tenor voice of only six or seven

The Foundling Hospital. Engraved after a drawing by Thomas Shepherd in 1829, this is a more accurate representation than the idealised contemporary prints, which disguise the stringent economy with which it was built.

notes compass, performed the serious man's part in these burlettas
and was but little noticed by the public; till Handel, pleased with hi
clear, sweet and full voice, engaged him to sing, in Samson and the
Messiah, the fine airs which he had composed for Mrs. Cibber's swee
and affecting voice of low pitch'.

Only the airs in *Samson* had been composed for Susannah Cibber
and when Burney had attempted to explain why she was so effective
in 'Return, O God of Hosts' he put the effect down, not to vocal power
but to 'her intelligence of the words and native feeling'. In other words
when he wanted to describe Mrs Cibber's singing he came close to
saying what he said of the later Guadagni: 'his voice seemed, at first
to disappoint every hearer'. This suggests that he may have exagger
ated the difference between Guadagni's earlier and later manner, and
perhaps confused a difference of two styles, Handel and the baroque
Gluck and the neoclassic, with a change of voice. Handel modified an
existing idiom to cope with Guadagni's (and Cibber's) strengths and
weaknesses; Gluck created in his reform operas (of which *Orfeo* wa.
the first) a new idiom which emphasised simplicity and refinement a
every point. Guadagni could be made to sound natural by Handel
artificial by Gluck. The voice had changed less than Burney imagined
circumstances rather more. For Guadagni Handel wrote the new ver
sions of 'But who may abide the day of His coming', and 'Thou ar
gone up on high'. Both have become the 'standard' versions, though
the once prevalent custom, for which there is no authority, of having
'But who may abide' in the Guadagni version transposed down for a
bass still seems to have left an interpretative taint, and the fioritura to
lack the lightness with which the accounts (admittedly confusing) o
his voice suggest that he would have had to tackle it. The revision o
'Thou art gone up on high' does not alter the character of the aria in
the same way; the changes are slight but felicitous.

Guadagni's connection with *Messiah*, however, was shortlived. He
sang in the vitally important performance which followed three week.
after that of Maundy Thursday 1750; he probably sang in the Found
ling Hospital performances of 1751; he was in Ireland that winter and
the following spring (a racehorse named for him ran at Bellewstown
one fears it was a gelding) and consequently unavailable for *Messia*
in 1752; he sang in 1753 and then went abroad. He did attempt the
soprano part on his next visit but there is no record of this potentially
fascinating event. Guadagni's retirement at Padua was marked by
extravagant generosity and infatuation with his *fantocini*, the puppets

in his private marionette theatre who would re-create *Orfeo ed Euridice* while he sang his most famous part. But he preserved another loyalty, and once, when the young Irish tenor, Michael Kelly, Mozart's first Basilio, had been singing with him, said:

Follow me up stairs, Sir, and I will introduce you to one, whom, all my life, I have made my study, and endeavoured to imitate. I followed him into his bedroom, and, opposite to the head of the bed, saw a full-length picture of Handel, in a rich frame. There, Sir, said he, is the portrait of the inspired master of our art; when I open my eyes in the morning, I look upon him with reverential awe, and acknowledge him as such, and the highest praise is due to your country for having distinguished and cherished his gigantic genius.

The second performance in 1750 was on 1 May, and its success accidentally engendered a third. The governors of the Foundling Hospital had been pressing on with the completion of the chapel, and by February had foreseen a grand formal opening with a sermon by the Archbishop of Canterbury. For this occasion they appointed 3 May. But within a fortnight they had reconsidered this over-ambitious plan, postponed the formal opening, and decided to ask Handel if he would give a concert on 1 May. The revised occasion for this would be the opening of the new organ which Handel had presented to the Hospital. That too went wrong. Jonathan Morse failed to make organ-building history by completing his work on time, but the date was left unchanged and Handel offered a performance of *Messiah*. Tickets were available at the Hospital, and at Arthur's, Batson's and Tom's Coffee Houses. They cost half a guinea, the performance was at noon, and the 'no swords and hoops' request was made, as at Fishamble Street. But the stewards were not as fortunate as those in Dublin. William Stukeley, the antiquary, reported 'an infinite crowd of coaches' at his end of the town, and more people arrived than the chapel could accommodate; hence the need for another performance on 15 May.* The whole exercise netted almost £1000 after expenses. In the absence of other evidence it is reasonable to assume that Handel used the same soloists as he had at Covent Garden, with the exception of Frasi, whose absence at one or both performances would explain a tangle of

* The official figures were 1386 tickets sold for 1 May, 599 for the 15th.

reallocations in the conducting score; Bernard Gates provided the Chapel Royal choristers. Before the end of the year the Committee was mooting another performance of sacred music for the following February, but Handel refused and seems to have made a counter-proposal, since the successful scheme of performing *Messiah* twice was repeated, on 18 April and 16 May 1751. That Lent Handel's oratorio season had been curtailed by the death of Frederick, Prince of Wales, and the consequent closure of the theatres. At some time in the spring the Foundling Hospital organ was finally completed (it was not a success, and had to be replaced in 1769), and at the 1751 *Messiah* performances Handel was able to give a concerto on it.

The last eight years of Handel's life were shadowed by the onset of blindness. On 13 February 1751 he had to stop work on the second part of a new oratorio, *Jephtha*, because of a serious weakening of his left eye; he was in the middle of setting the chorus 'How dark, O Lord, are Thy decrees'. He resumed composition when sight and circumstances allowed, but *Jephtha* was not completed until the end of August. Neither a visit to Bath and Cheltenham nor a consultation with Samuel Sharp, a surgeon at Guy's Hospital, did anything to improve matters; by the end of the year Mrs Delany, in Ireland, had heard that 'poor Handel has lost the sight of one of his eyes'. Nevertheless he gave his usual oratorio season in 1752, concluding with two performances of *Messiah*, the soloists being Frasi, Galli, John Beard (now back with Handel for good) and a new bass, Robert Wass, a gentleman of the Chapel Royal since 1744, and a member of the St Paul's and Westminster Abbey choirs; it is therefore likely that Handel had originally spotted his ability in the chorus. Having sung Caleb in *Joshua* and Zebul in the first performance of *Jephtha*, Wass went on to do most of the major bass roles, filling the gap left by the death of Reinhold before the more talented Champness came into the ascendant in 1757, after which he concentrated on the increasingly busy provincial circuit until his death in 1764. He was clearly competent, but not inspired. *Messiah* was repeated at the Foundling Hospital on 9 April.

Later in 1752 Handel was afflicted 'with a Paralytick Disorder in his Head, which has deprived him of Sight'. In November he was operated on by a Mr Bromfield of the St George's and the Lock Hospitals; there was a short-term improvement followed, in January 1753, by a complete loss of sight. His oratorio season proceeded as usual, but Lady Shaftesbury, having been to *Alexander's Feast*, reported that:

The chapel of the Foundling Hospital. Engraved by John Sanders, 1774. The organ replaces the one given by Handel.

it was such a melancholy pleasure, as drew tears of sorrow to see the great though unhappy Handel, dejected, wan, and dark, sitting by, not playing on the harpsichord, and to think how his light had been spent by *being overplied in music's cause*. I was sorry to find the audience so insipid and tasteless (I may add unkind) not to give the poor man the comfort of applause; but affectation and conceit cannot discern or attend to merit.

Some accounts suggest, however, that it was sympathy and embarrassment that inhibited audiences. In 1753 there was one *Messiah* at the end of the oratorio season, and two more for the Foundling Hospital a few weeks later; the cast was as before, with the substitution of Guadagni for Galli. Incessant practice enabled Handel still to play organ concerti, but he composed no significant work after *Jephtha*. When the Hospital chapel was finally dedicated in April 1753, the music that he provided had all done service before. The only new work that he contemplated testifies to his state of mind; the *London Evening Post* believed him to be 'composing a Funeral Anthem for himself, to be performed (when it shall please God to take him hence) in the [Foundling Hospital] Chapel, for the Benefit of the Charity'.

Messiah concluded the oratorio season in 1754, but we have to deduce the soloists from the Foundling Hospital performance of 15 May, about which we are exceptionally well informed. There Handel employed two sopranos, Frasi and Signora Passerini, along with Galli, Beard and Wass. Christina Passerini had been recommended to Handel by Telemann, and he had met her briefly at The Hague in 1750. She and her violinist–composer husband Giuseppe were en route for Scotland, where they intended to stay about six months and she hoped to perfect her English. In fact they stayed for at least two years, and both were taken on for the 1753–4 Haymarket opera season; in March 1754 Christina played Trasimede in a revival of *Admeto*, the last for over a hundred years of any Handel opera.* Handel cannot have disapproved, although this production had nothing to do with him, since he engaged her for the entire oratorio season, and relations with the Haymarket management must have been reasonable, because the times within which the performances were held overlapped. She sang for him in *Alexander Balus*, *Deborah*, *Saul* and *Samson*, as well as *Messiah*. She also sang in the 1755 season,

---

* That is, if we exclude the *Giulio Cesare* of 1787: 'The music entirely by Handel, and selected from various operas . . . under the direction of Dr Arnold'.

but by then had, with her husband, become heavily involved in oratorio outside London, particularly the festival at Bath, for which Giuseppe Passerini acted both as leader and treasurer. They were a team
who could operate most successfully outside London and its existing
professional monopolies; in 1763 they found a happy solution to this
problem by settling in Dublin where, John O'Keefe recalled, the excellencies of Christina's voice, and of his directing and composing,
ensured their popularity and considerable affluence. In 1754 she sang
the original version of 'If God be for us' and transposed versions of
the 1750 recomposed 'Guadagni' versions of 'But who may abide' and
'Thou art gone up on high' – one major aria in each Part. Watkins
Shaw comments on the excitement of hearing 'But who may abide' up
a fifth in A minor, and on the 'brilliant, ringing' character of her voice
which this disposition of materials suggests. Frasi was thus left with
the ordinary soprano part (with nothing diverted to a boy treble),
including the original version of 'He shall feed His flock' and a recitative and aria first conceived for tenor, 'He was cut off out of the land
of the living' and 'But Thou didst not leave His soul in Hell'. Galli
and Beard sang the alto and tenor parts minus the numbers transferred
to Frasi and Passerini, and Wass a straightforward run of the bass
solos. In general the soprano voice was favoured, and Frasi's exploited
to the utmost; she was given a fee of 6 guineas – the highest – for her
1754 Foundling Hospital performance, as opposed to Passerini and
Galli's 4½, and Wass's 1½ guineas. John Beard declined his fee.

Beyond this we learn that there were fifteen violins, five violas, three
cellos, two double basses, four bassoons, four oboes, two trumpets,
two horns, and drums. Many of the players were well known: the
celebrated pair of oboists Thomas Vincent (a founder of the Royal
Society of Musicians) and Redmond Simpson (Matthew Dubourg's
son-in-law); the cellists John Hebden (an equally adept bassoonist)
and the younger Gillier, both composers; the bassoonist Samuel Christian Baumgarten, who was to survive to be a leader in the 1784 Westminster Abbey Commemoration. One of the horn-players, Trowa, has
a Hungarian name, which reminds us how regionally-based this skill
remained; there are, of course, no horns in Handel's scores and these
must have doubled the trumpets at the octave in the choruses. The
chorus consisted of six boys from the Chapel Royal and thirteen men,
amongst whom one notes Samuel Champness, soon to be promoted to
singing the bass solos; Thomas Dupuis, a future director of the Handel
Commemoration and influential in Handelian matters; and the

brothers Joseph and Thomas Baildon, notable all-round musicians and minor composers. The soloists also sang in the choruses (and could be commended for their excellence in this department).

Our knowledge of the 1754 Foundling Hospital performance derives from the accounts, which also tell us that Handel's servant, Peter Le Blond, received a guinea (as much as Abraham Brown, the leader), as did the music porters, and that the organ blowers were given 4 shillings.* They do not tell us precisely what part Handel played in all this, though their existence indicates that the practical organisation was now out of his hands and in those of John Christopher Smith the younger (he also played the organ for which he received no fee, but was 'presented' with 5 guineas). Earlier in the year there had been a distinctly awkward passage in the composer's relations with the Hospital. How it began is not known, but it may have started with the Committee's concern when they learned from the newspaper reports that he was contemplating an anthem for his own funeral, but also for their benefit. They had hastened to communicate their desire for the 'Continuance of his Life, who has been and is so great and generous a Benefactor'. He was certainly of enormous value alive (roughly £600 per annum). Perhaps at this point he had mentioned to the Treasurer his wish to see that this income did not cease at his death, and a possible way of securing it.

By 2 January 1754 the Treasurer certainly believed he understood Handel's wishes because he reported to the Committee his 'kind intention to this Charity, of securing his Oratorio of Messiah to the Hospital, and that it should be performed nowhere else, excepting for his own Benefit'. Handel was worried, the Treasurer further reported, because another body had obtained a copy of *Messiah* from Dublin, intending to perform it for their own benefit. This may have been a confused understanding of a letter Handel had had within the last month from the Edinburgh Musical Society, saying that they had all the recitatives and songs in *Messiah* except 'How beautiful are the feet', and were anxious to obtain that and the choruses; Niccolo Pasquali had recently moved there from Dublin. The Committee therefore resolved to thank Handel for his generosity, and to apply for an Act of Parliament to secure the benefaction 'to the sole use & benefit of this Hospital'. A credible story has it that he was enraged by the

---

* A low-paid and unsung occupation of great importance; on modern baroque organs the effect of hand-blowing can now be electrically simulated.

JOHN CHRISTOPHER SMITH.

From an Original Picture Painted by Zoffany.

Published May 1.1799. by Cadell & Davies Strand

John Christopher Smith the younger. Engraved by Harding after Zoffany.
Essential to Handel as an amanuensis, he played a vital part in the direction
of Handel's last oratorio seasons.

prospect of his music 'going to the Parliament'. Whatever he had said
he had not envisaged that, and his physical incapacities, together wit
his financial dependence on his work, must have made it an alarming
prospect. The Hospital retreated gracefully, and the performance of
15 May demonstrates that no lasting harm was done. (It has been
surmised that this contretemps may have accounted for Walsh
failure to issue the *Songs in Messiah*, but the hypothesis leaves
good deal unanswered.) Both the Hospital's mistaken move and
Handel's reaction to it seem extremely natural; any further threat
however remote, to his independence must have seemed intolerable
When the Hospital had taken in the accounts of the May perform
ance they returned to the matter much more tactfully, and decided
to consult Handel as to how 'proper Regulations' might be devised
Handel told their emissary that his health prevented him 'giving
any further instructions relating to the Performances', but that he
approved of Mr Smith's being appointed organist to the chapel, in
order to conduct his compositions.

In 1755, when *Messiah* was performed at the Foundling Hospital
having been given twice at Covent Garden before Easter, Handel
name was not mentioned, although he may well have been present
Smith conducted. The same pattern obtained in 1756. The oratorio
seasons were not uniformly well attended; Mrs Delany, who had been
in London for the Hospital *Messiah* in the preceding year when she
thought the music '*too fine*, I never heard it so well performed', was
now again in London in March and found the oratorio season
'miserably thin; the Italian opera is in high vogue, and always full
though one song of the least worthy of Mr Handel's music is worth all
their frothy compositions'. But an editorial in the *London Daily Adver
tiser*, which tactlessly commented on Handel's physical decline and
recent surge in the popularity of Arne, nevertheless depicted him as
'the composer of the Messiah, rewarded by the universal voice', and
in 1756 Catharine Talbot, writing rather self-consciously to the arch
blue-stocking, Mrs Carter, said that she gathered the success of two
Messiah nights of the oratorio season had 'made amends for the solitude
of his other oratorios'. Handel was now being identified with *Messiah*
and Miss Talbot's letter helps explain why. She had gone to the play
house although it was 'an unfit place for such a solemn performance
but her social engagements precluded attendance at the Foundling
Hospital 'where the benevolent design and the attendance of the little
boys and girls adds a peculiar beauty even unto this noblest compo

sition'. Charity has now become a moral alibi, rather than, as in Dublin, a practical one.

Catharine Talbot's letter also tells us not only that the 'Morocco Ambassador' was present (the music, she thought, spoke for itself to any feeling heart, though she had doubts as to the interpreter's capacity to cope with the divine words), but also that the audience stood for the 'grand choruses' – presumably the 'Hallelujah' and 'Worthy is the Lamb', if she really meant the plural. This is the first reference to the practice of standing, also adopted for the 'Dead March' in *Saul* and for 'God Save the King'. According to a letter written by James Beattie thirty-seven years after the event with which it dealt, the custom had been initiated at the first London performance of *Messiah* (in 1743). George II 'happened to be present'; he and the rest of the audience 'started up' on 'For the Lord God Omnipotent Reigneth', and the practice was observed thereafter. This James Beattie had from Lord Kinoull, who also recounted that a few days after the first performance Handel paid a call and, on being complimented on the 'noble entertainment' he had given the town, replied, 'My lord, I should be sorry if I only entertained them, I wish to make them better.' It is a comment that would have pleased Beattie, a poet and philosopher much concerned with the unity of truth, nature and beauty, and of course it delighted the nineteenth century, but it does not sound much like Handel, whose piety seems to have been profound but private. It could have been a witty observation on the attempts to discredit *Messiah* on the grounds of religious propriety, and if heard as ironical is much more natural. Neither the King nor any member of the royal family is recorded as having attended *Messiah* in Handel's lifetime. However, Burney tells a story of Lord Chesterfield, when he was in waiting on the King, having been encountered by an acquaintance emerging from Covent Garden improbably early: ' "What! my lord, are you dismissed? Is there no Oratorio to-night?" "Yes," says his lordship, "they are now performing; but I thought it best to retire, lest I should disturb the King in his *privacies*." '* The story is suggestive in several ways – of urbane aristocratic scepticism at odds with the domesticity of Hanoverian devotion, of a director of the Opera putting down a subscriber whose tastes had led him elsewhere – but it implies incognito visits and its tone confirms a general impression that George

---

* A preferable form of the anecdote, which I regret I am unable to find a source for, has 'lest I should disturb my monarch at his devotions'.

was a more frequent attender at oratorios than surviving records suggest. It is reasonable to suppose that he established the precedent,
but to question the Beattie/Kinoull version as to when. It is at least
satisfactory to know that it took place in Handel's lifetime.*

In 1757 *Messiah* was given twice at Covent Garden and as usual at
the Foundling Hospital; Handel's health continued to decline although
the Hospital performance was reported as being under his direction,
and in a third codicil to his will (originally drawn up in 1750), he
bequeathed 'a fair copy of the Score and all Parts of my Oratorio
called The Messiah to the Foundling Hospital'. He also left two paint-
ings, heads of an old man and an old woman by Baltasar Denner (who
had painted noteworthy portraits of Handel himself), to Jennens. The
popularity of *Messiah* is attested by the three performances with which
he concluded the 1758 Covent Garden season. The Foundling Hospital
performance was given on Thursday 27 April; the soloists were Frasi,
Miss Frederick and Miss Young (alto), Beard, and Samuel Champness
(bass). Cassandra Frederick had made her début playing a Handel
concerto on the harpsichord at the New Theatre in the Haymarket
for her own benefit, aged 'Five Years and a Half': Lord Shaftesbury
thought she was eight. Her master for keyboard and singing was Domenico Paradisi, whose cuckoo toccata shows he did not lack a sense of
humour; Handel may have taken an interest even at that stage. He
certainly did by the end of 1757, when he adapted five arias from the
operas for Miss Frederick to sing in the final revision of *The Triumph
of Time and Truth*. Lord Shaftesbury was once more *au courant*, and
said that Handel had 'great expectations' of her. He allotted her a
permanent role in the season, with parts in five oratorios. It opened
with *The Triumph of Time and Truth*, and Mrs Delany was there with
her god-daughter, Sally Chapone. Mrs Delany was out of sorts and
reluctant to judge, but described the 'new woman' as being '*so* fright
ened that I cannot say whether she sings well, or ill'.

The range of Miss Frederick's parts suggests that today we would
class her as a mezzo-soprano rather than a contralto. She was not re-
employed in 1759 and thereafter appears as both a keyboard player and
a singer, eventually marrying Thomas Wynne, a Welsh landowner.
She was paid four guineas to Miss Young's three, but it was Isabella
Young who was retained in 1759. Curiously, like Miss Frederick

---

* Standing for the 'Dead March' appears to have been a consequence of its use at funerals
from c. 1750; standing for the National Anthem not to have begun until George III'
madness and the Regency crisis of 1788.

Mrs Mary Delany, formerly Mrs Pendarves. Engraving after J. Opie.
The lifelong friend of Handel and admirer of *Messiah* in her old age.

she was an accomplished organist as well as singer, and had also
made her début as something of a prodigy (though not in Frederick's
class), at the New Theatre, Haymarket, in 1751. She was Mrs Arne's
niece, and her father was a clerk in the Treasury. In 1757 she
married the Hon. John Scott, brother of the 4th Earl Deloraine, and
most surprisingly continued singing – something that Richard Sheridan lacked the confidence to allow his wife Elizabeth Linley to do,
thus depriving the English concert platform of one of its finest voices
despite (or because of) the fact that they were both born in the profession. Isabella Young went on to perform at the Three Choirs Festival and at Ranelagh, and deserves attention for her ruthless way with
fees; asked to sing in *Acis and Galatea* at the Holywell Music Room in
1766, she requested 'Two and forty guineas for one Night's Attendance
in a Private Room' (as it was subsequently put, not without point) and
even Oxford jibbed. Champness, from an equally confusing though far
less significant musical family, came up (as we have seen) from the
chorus, but had also done solo work in oratorio under Thomas Chilcot
of Bath in 1755. He sang Time in the 1757 *Triumph of Time and Truth*
and was in five of the oratorios in the 1758 season. His subsequent
career took him into the provinces during the 1760s and back to Coven
Garden in oratorio in the 1770s, and he sang in the Handel Commemoration of 1784. It is interesting, incidentally, that the soloist
assembled by Handel in his last years were all (except for Beard) in
the earlier rather than later stages of their careers.

    In August 1758 Handel went with Thomas Morell (the librettist of
Alexander Balus, Judas Maccabaeus, Theodora, Jephtha and *The Triumph of
Time and Truth*) to Tunbridge Wells. There he was operated on by the
itinerant oculist John Taylor, who nine years earlier had couched J. S.
Bach without success; Handel's treatment was also a failure.* He
opened his last oratorio season on 2 March 1759; there were two
performances of *Solomon*, one of *Susanna*, three of *Samson*, two of *Judas
Maccabaeus* and, finally, three of *Messiah*. The *Whitehall Evening Post*
recorded this and the 'great Encouragement' they had received and
went on to observe: 'And this Day Mr Handel proposed setting out
for Bath, to try the Benefit of the Waters, having been for some Time
past in a bad State of Health.' But he did not go. On the 11th he added

---

* Taylor's services were risky, and he could be out-charlataned. He restored the sight of Sir
William Smyth, a close kinsman of Dr King of Oxford. Sir William, congenitally avaricious,
pretended the operation had been only marginally successful, and persuaded Taylor to
reduce his fee from 60 to 20 guineas.

a last codicil to his will, adding, amongst other particular bequests, one of which was to Dubourg, £1000 to the Society for the Support of Decayed Musicians and a request that he might be buried in Westminster Abbey, with provision for a monument to be erected to him there, and a limit of £600 on its cost. This was presumably an attempt to keep matters in his own hands; having had a structure erected to him in his lifetime he can hardly have doubted that he would be in some way commemorated, and by arranging for it to be done in the Abbey in stone himself, the only option he left others was, ultimately, to attempt the same thing in sound. James Gibbs, whose career, as we have seen, offers points of comparison with Handel's, and who had died in 1754, left instructions that he was to be buried in his parish church of Marylebone (very modest compared to Philip Hardwick's church, which still stands), that his funeral was not to cost more than £120, and that a monument, already commissioned, was to be set up. The church was near the Cavendish–Harley estate, for which he had been resident architect. Like Handel, Gibbs died unmarried and childless. His monument, as the tablet reminds us, was in his buildings and his printed books. It is a more modest gesture than Handel's, partly because Gibbs was a Jacobite. But it demonstrates the naturalness of Handel's instructions.

On returning from the final performance of *Messiah*, the *Whitehall Evening Post* tells us, Handel took to his bed, and on the morning of the Saturday in Holy Week – the 14th – he died. His death was widely noted. He had wished to be buried as privately as possible, but three thousand people attended the funeral in the Abbey on the evening of Friday 20 April and the gentlemen of the Chapel Royal combined with the choirs of St Paul's and the Abbey to sing Croft's funeral service, which incorporated Purcell's 'Man that is born of woman'. *Messiah* had been planned for 3 May at the Foundling Hospital and went ahead as usual, the singers being Frasi, Mrs Scott (Miss Young), Beard, Champness and Signor Ricciarelli. Ricciarelli is said to have been a soprano, but his name appears in the conducting score beside 'But who may abide' and 'Thou art gone up on high' (in the Guadagni versions), which suggests that he was an alto and took over Miss Frederick's part. On the 24th a memorial concert was given at the Hospital. The *Whitehall Evening Post* warned people not to expect the much talked-about funeral piece; what was given was the Foundling Hospital Anthem together with the four Coronation Anthems.

Whether or not Handel had given any informal directions as to the nature of his monument in the Abbey we do not know. The sculptor chosen was Roubiliac, who had executed the Vauxhall statue; it proved to be his last work and, according to Sir John Hawkins, 'the composer's most perfect resemblance'. The birthdate is wrongly given as 1684 and there is no epitaph. Handel is in the process of writing (Roubiliac's triumph is that one never questions the totally implausible mechanics of this) 'I know that my Redeemer liveth'.

8: 'The Universal Song': The Apogee of *Messiah*

HANDEL'S DEATH WAS NOT UNEXPECTED. AT LEAST FIVE papers published the news two days before it took place; the eulogists were ready. A sonnet printed in the *Gazeteer* on 17 April 1759, which evidently caught the public mood since it was widely reprinted and copied in manuscript, made the obvious connection in its factual title ('On George Frederick Handel, Esq., who performed in his celebrated Oratorio of *Messiah*, on the 6th, and dyed the 14th Instant') and its fanciful text:

> Ah! when he late attun'd Messiah's praise,
> With sounds celestial, with melodious lays;
> A last farewel his languid looks exprest,
> And thus methinks th'enraptur'd crowd addrest:
> 'Joint sons of sacred harmony, adieu!
> 'Apollo, whisp'ring, prompts me to retire,
> 'And bids me join the bright seraphic choir!
> 'O for Elijah's car,' great Handel cry'd;
> Messiah heard his voice – and Handel dy'd.

John Lockman, the poet and librettist who had been on the fringes of the musical world for a quarter of a century, wrote an elegy most inappropriately addressed to 'the Manes' of Mr Handel – inappropriately because the point of the poem was that classical invocations were out of order in the case of a Christian musician who would go to heaven and there be greeted both by the sight of the Messiah, and by cherubs singing the anthems and hallelujahs that he himself had written on earth. Less than a year after Handel's death John Mainwaring, Fellow of St John's College, Cambridge, and Rector of Church Stretton, Shropshire, published anonymously his *Memoirs of the life of the late G. F. Handel*. This consisted of a biography, for which Mainwaring's main source of information was John Christopher Smith's memories of Handel and his anecdotes, a catalogue of the works, compiled by James Harris, a gentleman classicist who was the main force behind the strongly Handelian festival at Salisbury, and concluding observations on the music, to which Robert Price, a painter who had lived in Italy, contributed a section on Handel and Italian musical taste. It has the distinction of being the first book-length biography of a composer in any language, and extracts appeared in several English journals; there was also a translation into German with annotations from personal knowledge by Johann Mattheson (1761), and an abridgement into French (1768).

It is customary to be kind to Mainwaring, and to excuse the innumerable deficiencies of his account by alleging the absence of any eighteenth-century tradition of investigative biography or by blaming his lapses on a rambling Smith and a senile Handel. This is absurd; if either Horace Walpole or Samuel Johnson had felt inclined they could have done a decent job, but Walpole was indifferent to music and Johnson affected to be hostile. In questions of fact Mainwaring lacked a critical mind, and is unreliable even in matters he could easily have checked. Despite this, there is no doubt that, in making *Messiah* the agent of Handel's return to popularity, the 'favourite Oratorio', the salvation of the Foundling Hospital, Mainwaring, although he exaggerated badly, identified a current of opinion and swelled it in doing so. 'The very successful application of this wonderful production of his genius to so beneficent a purpose, reflected equal honour on the Artist and the Art'. The 'magic of his name' and the 'universal character of his sacred Drama' coalesced.

Whether Handel himself regarded *Messiah* as his masterpiece has sometimes been questioned, generally on the basis of the observation by Thomas Morell, the librettist, that Handel valued *Theodora* 'more than any Performance of the kind; and when I once ask'd him, whether he did not look upon the Grand Chorus in the Messiah as his Master Piece? "*No*", says he, "I think *the Chorus at the end of the 2nd part in Theodora far beyond it.*" ' Whether Handel would have regarded *Messiah* as an oratorio comparable in kind to *Theodora* is questionable (it is too easy to take 'The Sacred Oratorio' as merely an alias for, rather than a description of, *Messiah*); the chorus 'He saw the lovely youth' is of remarkable dramatic subtlety and complexity: ending an act which must for formal reasons be concluded chorally, but has just reached its dramatic climax, it resolves the problem by reflecting on what has happened in narrative form (it tells the Gospel story of the widow's son of Nain, which becomes an analogue for the miracle which alone can save the imprisoned Theodora, condemned to serve in a military brothel). It is totally successful, a stroke of genius on both librettis

and composer's part, and technically undoubtedly a greater feat than
the Hallelujah chorus. But the comparison is not of like to like, the
context is quite different. Handel persevered with *Messiah* when it
aroused controversy, modified it with great care to make the best of
changed circumstances of performance, made the performance of it
and not of any other oratorio his annual gift to the Foundling Hospital,
and for it alone made a special provision in his will. Handel was not
the first composer to have music on his monument (Corelli's charmingly has him holding the *giga* from his violin sonata opus V no. 5)
and we do not know that the choice of 'I know that my Redeemer
liveth' was his, but it sufficiently indicates the strength of the association in the popular mind: Handel and *Messiah* could easily be taken
as synonyms.

Messiah had, in any case, assumed a life of its own from the moment
that Handel had furnished Mercer's Hospital with a score for their
proposed performance in 1743. It had reached Oxford, as we have
seen, by 1749; James Harris and his friends mounted it, with over
thirty performers (just enough for *Messiah*, but a large number for a
small city) in the Assembly Hall at Salisbury; in 1752 parts of it,
described as 'anthems', were actually given, framed by a Te Deum
and 'God Save the King' from *Zadok the Priest*, in the Cathedral, and
the forces were much enlarged. On 17 May 1755 Dr Hayes directed
it at Bath, in Wiltshire's Rooms on the Walk; Christina Passerini sang,
Guiseppe Passerini led. In January 1756 it was the work with which the
New Musick Room was opened at Bristol, with vocal and instrumental
performers from 'London, Oxford, Salisbury, Gloucester, Wells, Bath,
&c'. It was repeated in 1757 when an organ was installed, and in
August 1758 was performed, complete, in the Cathedral. Amongst
those present was John Wesley, who recorded in his Journal:

> I went to the cathedral to hear Mr Handel's *Messiah*. I doubt if that
> congregation was ever so serious at a sermon as they were during
> this performance. In many places, especially several of the choruses,
> it exceeded my expectation.

Wesley was from a musical family, and he did not, as it happened,
admire *Messiah* to idolatry (four years later he thought the music in
Exeter Cathedral 'exceeded the *Messiah* itself'), but Methodists were
to take to the oratorio with particular warmth, and it was welcomed
in their chapels.

The Three Choirs Festival had been held at Gloucester, Hereford and Worcester in annual succession since at least 1719; in 1757 *Messiah* closed the six days of intensive music-making at Gloucester. It was given in the Booth Hall, once more under Hayes, with Frasi, Beard and Wass, an impressive London line-up. It then became a regular part of the festival, being performed in College Hall at Worcester in 1758 and in Hereford Cathedral in 1759. In that year it was also given for the first time at Cambridge, in James Gibbs's Senate House. The director, John Randall, was organist of King's College, Professor of Music, and had sung in Bernard Gates's 1734 production of *Esther* at the Crown and Anchor. *Messiah* had already been performed at Winchester; it reached Halifax in 1766 where it was given to inaugurate a new organ in the parish church, directed by Joah Bates, the son of the vicar, and led by William Herschel, the future discoverer of Uranus. In the same year it was heard in Liverpool, and, in aid of the General Hospital, in Birmingham in 1768. It had established its own life north of the border in Edinburgh, and its London life, independent of Handel, in the hands of the Academy of Ancient Music, continued in 1758. It would be interesting to know if the score owned by Henry Needler, the Academy's leader, represented what they did in 1758 as well as in 1744 and 1747. If so, these performances, in common with provincial ones for which details survive, represent forms of *Messiah* uninfluenced by Handel's changes after 1745. This situation would prevail until in 1767 Messrs Randall and Abell, successors to John Walsh, at last published a full score.

One music festival deserves special mention because it so clearly indicates a direction *Messiah* would take in the future, which would cause it to be both loved and loathed. The Reverend William Hanbury was the incumbent of a disproportionately large and fine church in a small Leicestershire village. He was an enthusiast, and as much an individualist as Jennens (who lived at the other end of the county). But he had far less money. He therefore set about making two of his enthusiasms, music and gardening, pay for a third – gothic architecture. What he had in mind was a collegiate foundation dominated by a vast church several times larger than the existing one, with a tower and lantern like Ely's, but taller than Salisbury spire. The college would house a 'Temple of Religion and Virtue', library, observatory, music school, printing office, physic garden, county hospital and other *necessaria*. To this end he started horticultural nurseries and a music festival, the plans for which were extended, on the news of Handel's death, to include *Messiah*, which was given on 27 September 1759.

MEMOIRS

OF THE

LIFE

OF THE LATE

GEORGE FREDERIC HANDEL.

To which is added,

A CATALOGUE of his WORKS,

AND

OBSERVATIONS upon them.

by J. Mainwaring [S.T. B.] Coll. Cath. Camb.

Εἴρηθ᾽ ὅ ἐστιν ἐλεῖν, ὥς τι οἱ θεσπέσιαι μεγίσται ὕσεων πυκνα καθεῖφαι. Τὸ γάρ τι ὡστι ὑπερκὺ, χωρίς τῆς γνώ-μεσδἀς. LONGINUS.

Untwisting all the Chains that tie
The hidden Soul of Harmony.
MILTON.

Anno ætat.56.

LONDON:

Printed for R. and J. DODSLEY, in *Pall-Mall.*
M. DCC. LX.

Title-page of John Mainwaring's *Memoirs of the Life of George Frederic Handel* (1760).

Church Langton had been provided with a new organ for the event, built, as it happened, by Abraham Adcock, who played first trumpet in the Foundling Hospital *Messiahs*. The weather was fine, and Mr Hanbury was a good publicist: 'the foot-roads from every quarter were lined with common people, and the quality and gentry in their different carriages rattled in from every part.' More than two hundred coaches, chariots, landaus and post-chaises were counted. The performance was directed by the ubiquitous Dr Hayes, and 'the music, on so solemn a subject, by so good a band, was most affecting'; so much so that concealment of the emotion it engendered was impossible: 'Tears then with unconcern were seen trickling down the faces of many; and then indeed, it was extremely moving to see the pity, compassion, and devotion, that had possessed the greater part present.' When the oratorio was over and the company out, 'the doors were set wide open, and part of it performed again for the entertainment of the common-people'. But the crush was too great, 'and such outcries were made by the fatter part of this rabble, that few could attend to what the band was doing; it pleased them however . . .'

It was *Messiah* that people (many of whom had never heard an oratorio) came for; when, in 1761, *Judas Maccabaeus* was tried as well, Church Langton was almost empty, but *Messiah* was again thronged. There was no discouragement of hoops, and Hanbury was openly disappointed that, presumably for comfort in travelling, 'some of the ladies made a point of coming in an undress or dishabille. This was indeed more convenient, but the brilliancy of the appearance was thereby eclipsed.' It is to be lamented that the sale of cuttings of

> The red Mezerion and Syringa white,
> The dusky Bay, and Laurustinus bright . . .

and the takings of the music festival did not suffice to raise a church in the best vein of gothick, and greater than any cathedral of the land, in southern Leicestershire. Though the doors were not more than ajar to the masses, in scale, overt emotionalism, and the mixture of artistic, religious and charitable motives which prompted it, *Messiah* at Church Langton looked to the future. It seems to have been a vastly enjoyable experience for all involved, the 'rabble' being able to rent any spare space and to sell provisions at inflated prices, as well as having an unprecedented topic of conversation.

In London the Lenten oratorio season continued under J. C. Smith

Dr Charles Burney. Engraved by Bartolozzi after Joshua Reynolds.

the younger, as did the annual Foundling Hospital *Messiah*, and the practice began of using, when possible, the same soloists for *Messiah* in each venture. Smith was assisted, in both enterprises, by the blind organist and composer John Stanley, whose playing at the Temple Church Handel, when he was still active in society, had frequently gone to hear. In Lent Smith both revived oratorios and gave new ones, either pasticcios of Handel or compositions of his own. This continued until he retired to Bath in 1774. He gave up the direction of the Foundling Hospital performances earlier, in 1769, as a result of an affront by the Committee, who had asked the violinist Felice Giardini to lead the orchestra for a performance of *Messiah* given to mark the opening of the new organ which replaced the one built by Morse of Barnet. Smith learned of this through a newspaper advertisement. In any case he had no liking for Giardini, whose magnificent musicianship was matched by a personal malevolence that induced Burney to write of him: 'His disposition is so truly diabolical, that, preferring the evil principle of the Manicheans to the good of the Christians, if it is a matter of indifference to his interest, whether he shall serve or injure an individual, he would always chuse the latter.' He would 'rather gain half a crown by superior subtilty and cunning, than a guinea by usual and fair means'. Despite John Stanley's involvement (he was elected a governor in 1770) the annual performances never recovered, and finally came to an end in 1778 for no better reason than the unavailability of a soloist on a particular date. The Lent seasons, under the management of Stanley, assisted by Thomas Linley, lasted until 1785.

Before John Christopher Smith the elder died in 1763 he made a fresh copy of the conducting score of *Messiah* for his son, which gives an indication of the standard form after 1760. 'Rejoice greatly' was in 4/4, 'He shall feed His flock' divided between alto and soprano, 'But who may abide' and 'Thou art gone up on high' were as sung by Guadagni, the 'Pastoral Symphony' was in its short form, as too was 'Why do the nations', with the alternative ending. The main changes made by Smith seem to have been transpositions to suit new singers and their relative ranges and stamina. Of these the most remarkable was the male soprano, Guarducci, who had studied at Bologna and became a protégé of Farinelli. He was in England from 1766 to 1768, and was engaged by Smith for the 1767 season, being paid £600 for twelve oratorios, the highest fee hitherto given outside opera. Burney reports him as tall and awkward in figure, inanimate as an actor, and in countenance ill-favoured and morbid; but with all these disadvantages, he was a man of great probity and worth in his private character, and one of the most correct singers I ever heard. . . . He soon discovered that a singer could not captivate the English by tricks or instrumental execution, and told me some years after that the gravity of our taste had been of great use to him . . .

Guarducci was nothing if not polite; he might have observed that a couple of seasons in Vienna with Gluck had helped, too. But when Burney visited him after he had retired to his birthplace, Montefiascone, in 1770, he found his house fitted up in the English manner, and was able to listen to him with particular attention, finding him 'a very chaste performer, and adds but few notes; those few notes however, are so well chosen that they produce great effect, and leave the ear thoroughly satisfied'. He seems to have been, in this respect, not unlike his house: an Italian singer in the English taste. Smith gave him 'Comfort ye', 'Ev'ry valley', the soprano section of 'He shall feed His flock', the soprano transposition of 'He was despised', 'Thy rebuke hath broken His heart', 'Behold and see' and 'I know that my Redeemer liveth'. The soprano and alto were Frasi and Mrs Scott (which must have made 'He shall feed His flock' something of a record as an expensive aria), and since the bass part stayed unaltered, the tenor, one Hayes, was left with nothing more than 'He that dwelleth in heaven', 'Thou shalt break them', and his part in 'O death, where is thy sting?' Here Smith went far beyond anything for which Handel's practice gave warrant, though it is true that Handel's practice implies he was less interested in the pitch of a part than the quality of voice that took it, and all accounts of Guarducci suggest that his possessed the masculinity which, paradoxically, distinguished the great male sopranos.

Guarducci's success does honour both to his intelligence and to the catholicity of the London public, but Elizabeth Ann Linley's did not involve doing violence to the disposition of parts in the oratorio. Her father, Thomas Linley, of whom more later, was from Bath, where he made his career directing concerts and as a singing teacher; of his twelve children eight were remarkable musicians – a 'nest of nightingales' as Burney said. Elizabeth Ann, always known as Cecilia, was born in 1754, first appeared in London oratorio in 1769, sang *Messiah* at Worcester in 1770 and preferred it to all other works. Extraordinarily beautiful, she was painted by both Gainsborough and Reynolds not once but several times. At Gloucester in 1772 she divided the soprano part with her younger sister Mary who had first sung in *Messiah* in London in 1770, at the age of eleven, and the pair, aged eighteen and fourteen, did the same at Covent Garden and went on to save the Foundling Hospital performances for a few years by their success in 1773. Her voice had, Burney says, a 'crystalline clarity'. She last sang in public at Worcester, just after her clandestine marriage to Sheridan, in 1773; the work was *Messiah*, in the Three Choirs Festival. Her younger sister Maria (not to be confused with Mary) also made a reputation in oratorio. All three sisters died young, Maria – as yet another sibling, Alicia, reports – singing 'I know that my Redeemer liveth' on her deathbed, a feat which finally exhausted her. Their brother Thomas, an exceptionally gifted composer, died in a boating accident aged twenty-one. The Linleys became part of the mythology of *Messiah*, and reveal the extent to which it had become the standard work within which vocal and interpretative ability could be gauged. Yet this proposed special terms; descriptions of Elizabeth Linley's voice do not convince one that this 'exquisite and darling' singer from a doomed family had a universal technique or, indeed, a power of characterisation that would have commended her in opera, though her hand in the libretto of her husband's *Duenna* shows that she had an understanding of what was involved.

These are considerations that take us to the Commemoration of Handel in Westminster Abbey in 1784. For better or for worse, it set the seal on the estimation of *Messiah* for the next century and a half. The Commemoration consummated English feeling about Handel, but it also reflected the peculiar circumstances of English music in the four decades of the eighteenth century after Handel's death. Enthusiasm for Handel in general, and *Messiah* in particular, was not, needless to say, universal. Samuel Johnson, notoriously, claimed he did not care for music. Mrs Thrale, who had, at the expense of considerable effort and guile, made him her friend and the chief lion in her drawing-room of celebrities, supposed that even he could not be impervious to the sublimities of the oratorio. She took him with her to hear it on 8 March 1770. He was normally a liability, even at a play, being given to gestures, involuntary twitches, and overt demonstrations of boredom. This time, she says, in one of her several, not wholly consistent, accounts of what was clearly a memorable experience, 'he sat surprisingly quiet, and I flattered myself that he was listening to the music'.

He was not; he was writing a Latin poem, beginning 'Tertii verso
quater orbe lustri', which he repeated to her when they got home to
Southwark. The point of the poem was that he was wholly unmoved
by the proceedings, to the extent that he seems not to have noticed that
he was at an oratorio, not an opera; the second stanza, as translated by
Mrs Thrale, who added the specific references to the singers, runs:

> The scholar's Pride can Brent disarm?
> His heart can soft Guadagni warm?
> Or scenes with sweet delusion charm
>   The climacteric Eye?

He would, he goes on to say, have been happier amongst friends or in
his study.

Another literary man, William Shenstone, who had created at the
Leasowes, near Halesowen, a landscape in miniature that prompted
a new taste in gardening, had reported of the performance at the Three
Choirs Festival in Worcester in 1758, that he had found the audience
'dazzling enough', and as for the music, 'I presume, nothing in the
way of harmony can possibly go further. . . . It seems the best
composer's best composition. Yet I fancied I could observe *some parts*
in it, wherein Handel's judgement failed him; where the music was
not equal, or was even *opposite*, to what the words required.' This is a
reasonable comment on those moments where local illustration pre-
dominates, as in 'All we like sheep', over the general sentiment of the
passage. But Shenstone was equally interested in defining the elusive
essence of Lady Coventry's beauty, and when *Messiah* came round to
Worcester again in 1761 he made it clear that he went to hear it as
much for the company as the music. For Shenstone, in rural Shropshire, *Messiah* was a valuable social amenity.

It became a social amenity on a larger scale when, in 1768, Samuel
Arnold, who eighteen years later was to launch the first attempt at a
collected edition of Handel, took the risk of performing oratorios at
playhouse prices, thus opening them to a public who could never have
contemplated going to them in Handel's lifetime. The publication of
the full score in 1767 with its appendix of alternative settings subsequent to 1745, meant that any sufficiently determined musical
society throughout the country had access to *Messiah*, and could devise
a version suited to the soloists it was able to engage. But even in
London soloists were a problem, and in 1775 Mrs James Harris could

M.ʳˢ Stanley, Organist

Jaˢ McArdell fecit

John Stanley. Mezzotint after a portrait by James McArdell. Stanley, who took on the Foundling Hospital performances after Smith withdrew, was blinded in a childhood accident.

not say much of them, though she believed that 'the instrumental parts and the choruses went as well as in the days of Handel'.

London in the late eighteenth century was the largest and richest city in the world. It attracted musicians from all over Europe but offered precious little music of its own. Charles Burney was no poet, but he summed up matters better in verse than anywhere in his prose when he welcomed Haydn to England in 1791:

> Our *Tallis*, *Bird* and matchless *Purcell*, still
> Each sacred dome with sounds seraphic fill;
> But grace and elegance, to them unknown,
> (Of which elsewhere, no seeds had yet been sown)
> With strains impassion'd for the lyric scene,
> From foreign fields we are ever forc'd to glean. . . .

Opera was a commercial speculation, and there was no substantial tradition of native opera. None of the problems considered in Chapter 1 had been resolved. When Lieutenant General John Burgoyne, more successful as a librettist of English opera than he was as an exponent of English arms at Saratoga, came to write a preface to his well-liked *The Lord of the Manor* (1780), an opera with spoken dialogue and good airs by William Jackson of Exeter, he took as read all those objections to recitative in English raised by Addison in his *Spectator* papers of seventy years before:

> Very few serious pieces, except Artaxerxes, can be recollected upon our Theatre where it has not entirely failed, even when assisted by action: in Oratorios it is, with a few exceptions, and those sustained by accompaniment, a soporific that even the thunder of Handel's choruses are hardly enough to overcome.

Alexander's Feast, Burgoyne suggests, would be preferable if all recitative were removed and a good actress allowed to speak the lines instead, with 'emphatic Elocution'. It is hard to listen to the interminable discussion on military engineering between Gobrias and Cyrus in Act 1 Scene II of *Belshazzar* without agreeing; and that kind of thing is, of course, exactly what does not happen in *Messiah*. English opera, where spoken dialogue replaces recitative, was a compromise form, and the uneasiness that engendered it permeated productions of any kind of opera in England. Tampering was endemic. J. C. Bach, who was as guilty as most, also attempted to establish a rival oratorio season, catering for a more 'advanced' taste that might applaud

Jommelli and Pergolesi. It did not succeed and, when Bach played an organ concerto to conform to Handelian custom, the boys in the chorus sniggered and the audience hissed him.

Yet as a composer of instrumental music and, away from the hallowed context of oratorio, as an executant, Bach enjoyed great popularity; his operas were admired as was his lighter vocal music – Elizabeth Linley made her début in his operetta *The Fairy Favour*, and many of his songs were given at Vauxhall. The concerts that he promoted with the viola da gamba player, Carl Friedrich Abel, did much to consolidate such entertainments as a regular and fashionable part of London life, and enabled Bach to introduce a good deal of recent German and Italian music. He popularised both the forte-piano and the *galant* style. His career as an impresario left him deeply in debt, and there was a falling-off in the popularity of his music before his death on New Year's Day, 1782, but without his initiatives in both areas it is doubtful whether Salomon could have brought Haydn to England for his immensely creative series of visits between 1791 and 1795. It is only necessary to think of Haydn's last twelve symphonies to realise the distance that music had travelled since the composition of *Theodora*; and though J. C. Bach and Haydn are convenient points of reference that throw things into relief, it is also worth considering the work of John Stanley, who lived from 1712 to 1786 and was so intimately involved in the world of Handel. Mutual admiration and loyal service by Stanley in the cause of Handel's music did not prevent his style from changing so markedly over the years that by the end of his life his concerti are far nearer to J. C. Bach's than to the Handelian models from which he began, and the influence of the forte-piano on his keyboard writing is unmistakable.

Such were the forces of innovation that in 1776 the Earl of Sandwich together with friends amongst the aristocracy, founded a society to resist them. At the time he was First Lord of the Admiralty, and notorious in both public and private life. It was during his tenure of office that the corruption and mismanagement of naval affairs contributed so much to the American victory in the War of Independence. For his treacherous behaviour towards John Wilkes, a fellow member of the Medmenham Hellfire Club, he was widely known as 'Jemmy Twitcher', after the character in *The Beggar's Opera* of whom Macheath says: 'That Jemmy Twitcher should peach me, I own surprised me. He was famous for his lack of physical coordination; on leaving Paris as a young man he asked his French dancing master if there was any

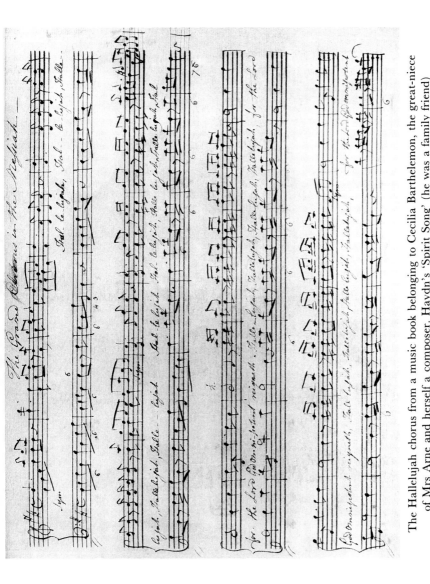

The Hallelujah chorus from a music book belonging to Cecilia Barthelemon, the great-niece of Mrs Arne and herself a composer. Haydn's 'Spirit Song' (he was a family friend) is the next item in the book.

service he could perform for him in London and received the reply: 'I should take it as a particular kindness if your Lordship would never tell anyone in London of whom you learned to dance.' His *amours* were celebrated long before the murder of Martha Ray (see Chapter 7) drew his private life to public attention. He was a passionate musician, a leading spirit in the Catch Club, and he could muster a local orchestra at his Huntingdonshire home, Hinchingbrooke Hall. His enthusiasm had been shared (some said nurtured) by Martha Ray – hence her choice of Caterina Galli as a companion. Sandwich's son had gone to King's College, Cambridge, where he had for his tutor Joah Bates, the musical son of the Vicar of Halifax, who became Sandwich's secretary and, eventually, Commissioner of the Victualling Office. He was also, from its inception, the conductor of Sandwich's society, the 'Noblemen's Concert of Antient Music', the principal rule of which was that nothing should be performed at it which had been written less than twenty years previously. (Coleridge, in 1794, was to see 'their resistance to *Novelty*' as characteristic of 'the vulgar Aristocrats', though he was thinking in general, not musical terms.)

The Antient Concert was an immediate artistic and social success, and early in 1784 it was Bates who, with his friends Viscount Fitzwilliam and Sir Watkin Williams Wynn, Bt, laid, at his house at the Victualling Office on Tower Hill, plans to commemorate the centenary of Handel. They had got the date wrong, but in this they merely followed Mainwaring and the monument in Westminster Abbey. They had to an extent lifted an idea from David Garrick, whose Stratford Jubilee of 1769 marked the opening of a new theatre rather than any anniversary and was more remarkable for the publicity that surrounded it than for artistic achievement, but did much to advance the cult of Shakespeare. It also happened to be a very musical affair, opening with Arne's oratorio *Judith* and including Arne's *Dedication Ode*, with *spoken* recitative declaimed by Garrick who stood at a desk in a pose irresistibly reminiscent of that of Handel as sculpted by Roubiliac on his monument in Westminster Abbey. Bates and his friends saw not just an occasion to mark, thoroughly congenial to the principles of the Antient Concert', they also noted that 'the number of eminent musical performers of all kinds, both vocal and instrumental, with which London abounded, was far greater than in any other city of Europe'. They therefore conceived an event that would be remarkable for the scale on which it was carried out, drew the other directors of the Antient Concert into the scheme, and used their influ-

ence to acquire Royal patronage and permission for the use of Westminster Abbey. Assistant directors, professional musicians, were
appointed; they included Samuel Arnold, Benjamin Cooke, and T. S.
Dupuis; Charles Burney was extensively consulted and eventually
became 'the Historian of the transaction'. The whole affair was to be
in aid of the Society for Decayed Musicians and the Westminster
Infirmary.

Three concerts were planned, two sacred, one secular. The sacred
concerts were to be held in Westminster Abbey, the secular one in the
Pantheon, Oxford Street. The Abbey was essential for the success of
the Commemoration. It could be made to take a large number of
performers and a big audience if it was properly fitted up; it had been
the scene of the enormously famous and successful Coronation music;
it was Handel's burial place; it had a unique historical and symbolic
significance. The surveyor, James Wyatt, whose task it would be to
arrange the nave in a suitable manner, was also the architect of the
Pantheon, a 'winter Ranelagh' which Horace Walpole called 'the most
beautiful edifice in England'. It was Wyatt's fate as an architect to
build temporary structures which looked permanent and 'permanent'
structures which proved temporary. His galleries, platforms and decor-
ations in the Abbey, with the Royal Box at the east end and the vast
stepped tribune for the performers which had built into it an organ by
Green of Islington destined for Canterbury Cathedral at the west, 'so
wonderfully corresponded with the style of architecture of this venerable and beautiful structure, that there was nothing visible, either for
use or ornament, that did not harmonize with the principal tone of
the building'. It was so arranged that all the performers were in full
view of Bates and of his assistants – an important consideration as
there was a chorus of 257 and an orchestra of 250. The choir consisted
of fifty-three trebles, forty-five altos, eighty tenors and seventy-nine
basses; all the altos were men and all but six of the trebles boys. In
the orchestra there were forty-eight first violins, forty-seven seconds,
twenty-six violas, twenty-one cellos, fifteen double basses, twenty-six
oboes, twenty-six bassoons, twelve trumpets, four timpanists, six
flutes, twelve horns, six trombones and a double bassoon. It is hard
to imagine exactly how the mere six flutes were used (perhaps they
played or doubled the two top parts in the *pifa*), but there is every
reason to suppose that all other instruments were employed, at least
in the second performance, for at the request of the King and Queen
two of the concerts, the last being *Messiah*, were repeated in the sub-

sequent week, and two experiments were then attempted. At the first performance 'Lift up your heads, O ye gates' had been sung, as Handel intended, with the alternate question-and-answer semi-choruses performed by all the voices singing each part. But on this occasion they were taken by just the principal singers, the full chorus not entering until the end of bar 33, with 'He is the king of glory', which, Burney says, 'brought tears into the eyes of several of the performers' and, apparently, of many of the audience as well. Handel himself had already doubled the trumpets with horns; now (again in the second performance), trombones were introduced in the Hallelujah chorus and in 'Worthy is the Lamb', voted by Burney another 'new and grand effect'. They must have doubled the bass and perhaps vocal bass and tenor parts.

The Commemoration performances were to give a licence for almost any kind of maltreatment of *Messiah* in the future. No one called on them as an alibi, but they mark the advent of a new attitude; the question being asked is not 'What can we do *within Messiah*?' but 'What can we do *with Messiah*?' Before considering how harmful this licence was to prove, it is important to remember how natural it must then have seemed. The Commemoration performance was textually conservative; *Messiah* was given uncut, in a version that followed the Foundling Hospital pattern. In that respect it was closer than Smith's Guarducci version to anything that Handel had done. As for the vastly augmented forces, they were in the first place a cause, a consequence of the instigators' sense of untapped resources, but once the Abbey had presented itself as the natural venue, they were also an effect. The Abbey with Covent Garden forces might have been a possibility, but only if Wyatt had been instructed to arrange seating in the nave for an audience of two thousand rather than four thousand. Size, however, soon became an end in itself. In his *Account* Burney was at pains to demonstrate that this was 'the most numerous band that ever was assembled in modern times'. The late Georgians were as keen on such claims as their nineteenth-century descendants and it is curiously apt that Wyatt should have played so important a part in these proceedings. The Pantheon was renowned for its size, its magnificence, its cost. Wyatt's later career was to be notable for the grandiosity and ruthlessness of his schemes: at Magdalen College, Oxford, at Durham Cathedral, at the Houses of Parliament and elsewhere he had the same idea – to tear down ancient Gothic and replace it with 'improved' modern gothic. It was what both he and his clients wanted. Similarly

Ticket for *Messiah*, Westminster Abbey Commemoration of Handel, 29 May
1784. Engraved by Haward after R. Smirke.

the Concerts of Antient Music looked to, in Burney's words, 'the new effects produced from such old and venerable productions of great masters of harmony'.

The number of performers was dictated not by the size of the Abbey but by the presence of so many spectators and an uncritical admiration for statistics. Burney says of Harriet Abrams, who sang 'But thou didst not leave His soul in hell' in the soprano transposition which Handel had occasionally used, that she did not really have a 'theatrical' voice but a *voce da camera*; nevertheless, as a result of the 'happy construction of Westminster Abbey for cherishing and preserving musical tones, by a gentle augmentation without echo or repetition', her voice was more audible than it had ever been in any London concert room. The scale of the performance was prompted by psychology and salesmanship rather than physical necessity. Indeed neither the Directors of the Commemoration nor their successors could have known anything about the real effect of additional numbers, since the crucial question of the relationship between phons (units of loudness generated) and sones (units of loudness perceived) defeated even so sophisticated a contemporary acoustician as Ernst Chladni, and can only be answered tentatively today. What is clear is that the larger the numbers involved the larger the numbers required to make any significant increase in the volume: to double the sound produced by one trombone three more must be added, and so on to the power of the cube root of the number in question. The Westminster Abbey Handel anniversary concerts after 1784 employed still larger forces, but the fact that there were almost twice as many singers and players in 1791 did not mean that they sounded significantly louder to the audience. The effect was in the statistics, which commanded awed attention.

Of the three sopranos, the most notable was Gertrud Elisabeth Mara, a German who had started her career as an infant prodigy on the violin, been brought to England when she was nine and after a stay of six years returned to Germany in 1765. She spent the 1770s in Berlin, but though her singing delighted Frederick the Great she disliked the rigid discipline he imposed on his court musicians and was twice under arrest for attempting to decamp from Prussia. When she was at last permitted to leave she came to England via Munich, Vienna, and Paris; her performance in the Commemoration launched her London career, which included Cleopatra in the much mangled version of *Giulio Cesare* that was staged to please the King. She was not a natural actress, and was marked by childhood rickets, but she

View of the ORCHESTRA and Performers in Westminster Abbey, during the Commemoration of HANDEL.

The Handel Commemoration in Westminster Abbey. From an engraving by Edward Burney from Charles Burney's *Account of the . . . Commemoration of Handel.*

brought an operatic voice to oratorio, and was a sensational success at the Commemoration. There was a contrary streak in her, however: at a later *Messiah* in the Abbey she was hissed for failing to stand in the Hallelujah chorus, and having separated from her drunken cellist husband she left London in 1802 with the young flautist and composer Charles Florio whose reputation she hoped to make; they eventually separated in Russia, where she was to suffer in the French invasion.

Harriet Abrams's part in the proceedings is noteworthy not only because, as Burney suggests, her type of voice involved a risk, but also because she was Jewish: a few years earlier a fellow Jew, the tenor Michael Leoni, had upset other members of his community by singing in *Messiah*; perhaps as a consequence, he had subsequently left London for Dublin. The third soprano, Miss Cantelo, from Bath, was well known on what was now a recognisable oratorio circuit, as were the two tenors, Harrison and Norris. The alto part was taken by a castrato Bartolini, and the bass was also an Italian, Tasca. It is noteworthy that three of the singers were foreigners, and that Burney should have paid a special tribute to Mara's enunciation.

The Commemoration was widely considered an unqualified success. But there were dissenting voices. John Newton, the slaver captain turned clergyman, preached and published his fifty sermons on the scriptural passages used in *Messiah*. His intimate friend William Cowper, expressed his distaste in *The Task*:

> Remember Handel? Who that was not born
> Deaf as the dead to harmony, forgets,
> Or can, the more than Homer of his age?
> Yes – we remember him; and while we praise
> A talent so divine, remember too
> That His most holy book from whom it came
> Was never meant, was never used before,
> To buckram out the memory of a man.

It was the Philalethes position, forty years on, and the only surprising thing about it is that it should have been Cowper who voiced it. The most interesting reservations, however, were expressed privately by the eulogist of the celebrations himself.

Charles Burney's advice had been sought by the directors when they were planning the Commemoration – at least in theory. In practice at the 'five or six dinners' he had attended he could not get a word in edgeways, and thought the organisers self-important and incompetent

To his surprise he was so moved by the actual concerts that he decided to write an account of them, and published a 'plan' of it to warn off competitors. He showed this to Lord Sandwich who had it to hand when, in the Royal Box, the King observed that some suitable person should write a history of the event. From that moment everything went wrong. The account itself took on a momentum of its own. Burney had envisaged a pamphlet, but in attempting to sketch Handel's life became aware of the deficiencies of Mainwaring's account and found himself embarked on a book. He then made the mistake of reading over some of what he had written to Lord Sandwich and the other directors of the Antient Concert. The King granted permission. Lord Sandwich, in front of his colleagues, said: 'You intend giving the profits of this account to the Fund [for Decayed Musicians], don't you?' Burney had no such intention. It had been a bad year for the musical profession and his teaching practice had suffered from the bankruptcies of schools; moreover, the Commemoration had already passed £6000 to the Fund. But Sandwich persisted: 'His Majesty expects it. You would not, I dare say, be the only one who benefited by the Commemoration?'

Burney was caught. He was obliged to Sandwich for his patronage of his eldest son James, who was in the navy, and he had hopes of both a royal musical appointment for himself, and of a court position for his unmarried novelist daughter Fanny. With great reluctance ('I fretted afterwards, & grumbled in the gizzard') he decided he had no choice but to fall in with Sandwich's suggestion. He also found himself subject to criticism both from the directors and, in detail, from the King. He was fortunate in persuading Dr Johnson to compose the dedication for him. But the book could not be the candid history he had intended. Only twenty years later did he reveal, in Rees's *Cyclopaedia*, what he thought about the special instruments which Sandwich, as befitted an enthusiastic player of the kettle-drums, had ordered: 'the double drums, double curtals, tromboni &c. augmented his lordship's pleasure in proportion to the din and stentorophonic screams of these truly savage instruments'. In a note-book he had jotted down an even darker reflection: 'I dare not say what I have long thought. That it is our reverence for old authors and bigotry to Handel, that has prevented us from keeping pace with the rest of Europe in the cultivation of Music.'

For all that, the admiration expressed in the *Account* was genuine, and remained true to the occasion. The proceedings were given an almost religious significance by the setting, the constant attendance of the royal family (at the second performance of *Messiah* it was the King who, with a gentle motion of his right hand, holding the printed word-book, signalled for the Hallelujah chorus to be repeated) and the pomp. A medal was struck to mark the event. And it was *Messiah* that was the culmination. It was the absentees, such as the Bishop-Earl of Bristol, who reflected: 'What a Crash!' Those who were present generally seem to have shared the impression recorded in her diary by Mary Hamilton, who, with Boswell, Burney and Sir Joshua Reynolds, was at the performance of *Messiah* on 5 June:

> I was so delighted that I thought myself in the heavenly regions. 513 Performers, the Harmony so unbroken that it was like the fall of Waters from one source, imperceptibly blended. The Spectacle too was sublime, So universal a silence, So great a number of People.

9: *Messiah* Improved?

THE WESTMINSTER ABBEY COMMEMORATION HAS ABOUT IT SO obvious a monumental quality that it is easy to forget that it confirmed feelings that already existed. It is just as significant that in 1759 Burney, then working in comparative obscurity at King's Lynn, should have advised an acquaintance that 'He was despised' ought to form part of the repertoire of his new barrel-organ, or that from the 1770s onward the Hallelujah chorus is to be found in any number of the manuscript music books in which young ladies were accustomed to record their repertoire. On the barrels of mechanical organs, and in those oblong quarto books, 'He shall feed His flock' can be found alongside 'The March of the Coldstream Guards', and the Hallelujah chorus next to anything from Haydn's 'Spirit Song', 'Mamma Mia', 'as sung by Signor Viganoni', or Linley's 'Young Lubin'. The chorus might equally well occur in the volumes of engraved music, where favourite items were collected and given a binding for greater permanence; one such containing sonatas by Sterkel and quartettos by Davaux (suitably adapted), ends with 'Handel's Hallelujah in the Messiah and Grand Coronation Anthem to which are prefixed two new fugues. The whole composed and adapted for 2 performers on one organ or harpsichord by J. March Esqur.'. The owner was Miss Jane Austen.

When Colonel John Byng (later Lord Torrington), an indefatigable tourist, visited the small town (but with a large church) of Dronfield, Derbyshire, in 1789, he was told by the parish clerk's wife that 'There would be a *Rory Tory* in a few days, and the Sheffield men to sing it'. It caused him to reflect that 'since the fame of the abbey musick, the country has gone wild in its imitations'. That fame spread far beyond the British Isles. A translation of Burney's *Account* into German was published in Berlin and Stettin and in 1786, more surprisingly, given the extent of the royal involvement and the prominence accorded to it by Burney, Alexander Reinagle, newly arrived in New York, advertised arias from *Messiah* as from 'Handel's Sacred Music, as performed in Westminster Abbey'.

The history of the reception of *Messiah* in North America makes an intriguing contrast with its reception in German-speaking Europe; in both it was enthusiastically but differently embraced. On 16 January 1770 a concert was given in George Burns's Music Room in the New York City Tavern on Broadway for the benefit of William Tuckey, formerly choir-master of Trinity Church, tickets to be had of Mr Tuckey at 8 shillings each. It was performed by a mixture of amateurs and professionals; the first part consisted of instrumental music chosen by the performers, of which the most notable item was a concerto on the French horn by a gentleman just arrived from Dublin. The second part was described as:

> A Sacred Oratorio, on the Prophecies concerning Christ, and his coming; being an Extract from the late Mr. Handel's Grand Oratorio, called the Messiah, consisting of the Overture, and sixteen other Pieces, viz. Airs, Recitatives and Choruses. Never performed in America.

What is impressive about this is the firm theological grasp apparent in the advertisement, and the fearless assumption that this element in *Messiah* would actually attract an audience to the New York City Tavern. If one believes – and the case has been argued in Chapter 3 – that *Messiah* embodies a serious and not altogether easy argument then it is an awkward fact that on the whole this argument has been disregarded. When John Mainwaring chose a motto from Longinus's *On the Sublime* for the title-page of his biography he pointed a direction that criticism of the oratorio would follow in Britain and, particularly in Germany. When this notion no longer commanded acceptance it was replaced by the proposition that *Messiah* was pantheistic or humanistic. This is not to say that there were no informed and orthodox listeners east of the Atlantic. But only in North America do we find so positive a reaction to the work as conceived by the compiler of the word-book. Mr Tuckey, as it happened, offered a word-book, free to the ladies and gentlemen who patronised the concert, and to others for 6 pence. What the sixteen pieces were we do not know.

On 3 October 1770 part of *Messiah* was given at Trinity Church itself when the rector, Dr Samuel Auchmuty, preached a charity sermon for 'The Corporation for the Relief of the Widows and Children of Clergymen in the Communion of the Church of England in America' this performance was to the organ, while the New York Tavern performance appears to have been orchestrally accompanied. In Lent 1772 part of 'the sacred Oratorio, called the Messiah, on the *Passion Crucifixion*, *Resurrection*, and triumphant Ascension of Jesus Christ' was again given at Trinity Church. Tuckey was a teacher of music, and had sung in the choir of Bristol Cathedral (his claim that he was a vicar-choral cannot be substantiated); if he had emigrated in 1753, as seems likely, he could not have sung in *Messiah* there, but he could well have had first-hand experience of Handel's oratorios. In 1772 it was again a benefit for the widows and children of Church of England clergymen that prompted a performance of the Hallelujah chorus in Christ Church, Philadelphia. While in England, the chorus attained a separate existence as an obligatory party piece, in North America it rounded off concerts, though even when used in this way it could be described as 'The Hallelujah Chorus: on the extent and duration of Christ's Government', with the emphasis once again on what it was actually about. Philadelphia eventually heard selections from the oratorio in 1801. There had in fact been, in 1786 at the Reformed German Church in Rae Street, an attempt to emulate the Westminster Abbey Commemoration, but the buildings were hardly commensurable and, though a choir of 230 and band of fifty was impressive in the circumstances, the programme was miscellaneous and the only item from *Messiah*, the Hallelujah chorus, was introduced for its aptness as a finale.

It was also the chorus which introduced *Messiah* to Boston, at a concert on 22 September 1773 which marked the anniversary of the coronation of George III. This was for the benefit of William Selby, a musician whose concerts frequently involved items from *Messiah*. He appears to have been a Loyalist, but neither Handel nor *Messiah* can have had strong Hanoverian connotations since, during George Washington's visit to the city in 1789, a celebratory concert was put on at Stone Chapel (the King's Chapel), with which Selby was associated; though described as an 'oratorio' it was a medley of sacred music, including the 'favourite air', 'Comfort ye'. What seems to have slowed up the acceptance of *Messiah* in the United States was not politics, but the effect of the War of Independence, and subsequently of the Napoleonic wars, on the willingness of experienced performers to explore the possibilities of America. Reinagle was an exception, as was his soprano, Maria Storer, who sang 'Comfort ye', 'Ev'ry valley', and 'I know that my Redeemer liveth' in his 1786 concert; she had performed in oratorio at Bath and Salisbury. But on the whole the infant republic was thrown on its own resources.

As a result there was what appears to have been a more or less complete *Messiah* in India, over thirty years before this was achieved

in the United States. Mrs Cargill, formerly Miss Brown, had a career
as a singer almost as filled with incident, though much shorter, as that
of Susannah Cibber. It was Mrs Cargill who made a popular success
of Thomas Linley's 'Young Lubin was a Shepherd Boy' from the 1781
Drury Lane opera, *The Carnival at Venice*. Her father, a coal-merchant,
was so strongly opposed to her appearance as Polly in *The Beggar's
Opera* at Covent Garden that he hired bruisers to abduct her; this
was only thwarted when 'the theatrical garrison sallied out in great
numbers', Macheath's gang armed with their appropriate weapons.
Her marriage to Mr Cargill proving unsatisfactory, she bolted with an
army officer to Calcutta, where she was an instant success in both
Messiah and opera, cleared a great deal of money, but returning to
England in the packet *Nancy*, was shipwrecked, and 'found on the rocks
of Scilly floating in her shift, an infant in her arms'. She was under
thirty. Intriguingly, Jamaica also heard at least part of *Messiah* in the
1780s.

Though *Messiah* had reached the tropics well before the end of the
eighteenth century, in the United States it was still performed only in
selections. Some of these, at Charleston in 1796 and Norfolk, Virginia
in 1797, were ambitious, but the difficulty was in assembling both an
adequate chorus and adequate singers. Mrs A. M. Pownall could
offer arias (several transposed) in Charleston, while the Moravians in
Bethlehem, Pennsylvania, had an accomplished chorus; but geography
and communications prevented them from performing together. Scores
were available: the Bethlehem Collegium Musicale had a manuscript
full score which could have been made as early as 1780, and a vocal
score was published by Sage & Clough in New York in 1803; the
problem was one of organisation and determination. It might be
thought that the foundation in 1807 of the Massachusetts Musical
Society for the practice and performance of choral works by Handel
and Haydn would have clinched matters, but it failed to do so, and it
was not until Gottlieb Graupner, Thomas Smith Webb and Asa Pea-
body took a fresh initiative in 1815 and founded the Handel and Haydn
Society of Boston that things got moving. It is not surprising that this
should have coincided with the end of the Napoleonic wars and the
re-establishment of diplomatic relations with Britain after the war of
1812. Even so, it was not until 1817 that *Messiah* was given complete,
and then it was on three evenings, 1, 4 and 6 April, one part of *Messiah*
and the corresponding part of *The Creation* being given on each. This,
it was hoped, would provide an opportunity for judging between the

Dighton del.

The LADY of the LAKE.

"The maiden paus'd, as if again,
 She thought to catch the distant strain,
 With head upraisd, and look intent,
 And eye and ear attentive bent,
 And locks flung back, and lips apart,
 Like monument of Grecian art"   Walter Scott's Poem

Pub. by Dighton, Spring Gardens

Mrs Billington. Caricature by Robert Deighton the younger, 1810. As a singer in *Messiah* she was commended for the reticence of her ornamentation. Lord Mount-Edgecumbe said 'the blind must have been delighted by Mrs Billington'.

comparative merits of the oratorios, a question about which there was 'a diversity of opinion'. The reluctance to contemplate *Messiah* entire and on a single evening seems bizarre; it was only on Christmas Day 1818, at Boylston Hall, Boston, that this – as it would seem – so obviously desirable object was achieved. The performance, the first of any oratorio entire in North America, was a success, and the occasion became annual. It is scarcely believable that the experiment was not ventured in New York for another thirteen years when, on 18 November 1831 the Sacred Music Society gave it with seventy-four voices and thirty-eight instruments, conducted by Uriah Corelli Hill in St Paul's Chapel.

The success of the Handel and Haydn Society's *Messiah* should not be taken as a comment on the quality of performance. The violins were so wavering as to put the chorus off their stride more than once – a remarkable feat given that there were 160 singers to just sixteen players. The soloists were also lacking in confidence. All this must have been painfully apparent to Graupner, who had played the oboe in London orchestras. Fortunately the excellent English tenor Charles Incledon, who had had almost thirty years' experience of the London oratorio season, was touring the United States at the time. He had fallen out with the management of Covent Garden and his best days were over, but this vigorous, stocky ex-sailor with seven rings on his fingers, five seals on his watch-ribbon, and a gold snuff-box, had qualities which endeared him to Americans. His only rival as a *Messiah* tenor had been Samuel Harrison, who sang in the Commemoration, but where Harrison had sweetness Incledon had purity, strength and an unexpected falsetto. Though he had sung in Exeter Cathedral choir as a boy, by shipping in the Royal Navy he had forgone any chance of further training, and critics were at a loss to know quite how he had come by so disciplined a voice. In 1818 he was asked to sing for the Society; he was also encouraged to impart what he knew 'by tradition'. This he did and, taking 'For unto us a Child is born', 'bluntly remarked, the choir knew nothing about the grand and peculiar characteristics of that chorus . . . and proceeding to drill the singers insisted on the unexcited progress of the semi-chorus portions till the climax was reached with the words, "Wonderful!" "Counsellor," etc, which should burst upon the ear with the square and solid stroke of vast explosion'. This lesson was well taken and the Handel and Haydn Society's performances set standards for the Continent. New York once more lagged behind Boston in establishing an annual *Messiah*

Charles Incledon. Engraving. The celebrated London tenor who coached the Handel and Haydn Society of Boston in their second performance of *Messiah* in 1818.

this began only in 1850 when Jenny Lind inaugurated the first cor
of the Harmonic Society, and again, as had Incledon, exemplifiec
best that Europe had to offer.

The specifically theological interest which *Messiah* evoked wh
was first brought to America did not last. Just as in Britain *éclat*
term frequently used of early performances of *Messiah* (and acc
well with the reaction in Dublin, 'a most finished piece of Mus
only to be smothered by assertions of sublimity and solemnity, s
the United States perceptions began to alter. Emerson heard *M*
in Boston on Christmas Day, 1843, and involuntarily recordec
transition:

> I walked in the bright paths of sound, and liked it best when
> long continuance of a chorus had made the ear insensible to
> music, made it as if there was none; then I was quite solitary a
> at ease in the melodious uproar. Once or twice in the solos, w
> well sung, I could play tricks, as I like to do, with my eyes, – dar
> the whole house and brighten and transfigure the central sin
> and enjoy the enchantment.
>
> This wonderful piece of music carried us into the rich, histor
> past. It is full of the Roman Church and its hierarchy and
> architecture. Then, further, it rests on and requires so deep a f.
> in Christianity that it seems bereft of half and more than hal
> power when sung to-day in this unbelieving city.

The value of a diary entry is often in the fact that it is unconsid
Emerson's reactions are as impressionistic as his deliberate distc
of his physical vision. The past he evokes for *Messiah* is totally ina
priate. The question as to whether it is bereft of power 'when
to-day in this unbelieving city' is both unreal and vague. Does he
that it is bereft of power because it cannot be heard with convictio
because what it conveys carries no conviction, in which case v
does he stand? That is surely the crucial issue. Of course he s
both in and out of it, and in a more self-conscious reflection o
experience, in the essay 'Nominalist and Realist', proclaims that
genius of nature was paramount at the oratorio.' It is a convictior
offered for him, however much it might sound like an evasion,
resolution of his tangled and nostalgic state of mind. 'I walked i
bright paths of sound' is his best and truest phrase.

*

In Germany and Austria Emerson's transcendentalist approach had
been anticipated by sixty years. *Messiah* was introduced by Thomas
Arne's son Michael at a private concert in Hamburg in 1772.
Only selections were performed, and they were in English. It was repeated
a few weeks later, twice the following year, and eventually given in
full by C. P. E. Bach in December 1775, with German words by
Klopstock. The choice of adapter could hardly have been more apt.
From 1748 to 1773 Klopstock, a formative figure in the literary life of
emergent Germany, had been engaged on a twenty-canto epic, written
in emulation of *Paradise Lost*, called *Der Messias*. It recounted the passion and redemption of Our Lord, and was memorably described by
C. P. Moritz, in his autobiographical *Anton Reiser*, as the kind of poem
all German youth was bored by, but none dared admit was boring. For
all that, Klopstock could achieve greatness, and inspired memorable
settings by Gluck of his odes, and by C. P. E. Bach of his songs.

In 1780 Klopstock's admirer, the philosopher and poet J. G. Herder,
who was then, through the influence of his friend Goethe, employed
at Weimar, arranged for a private performance of *Messiah* in the Court
Theatre there. Goethe attended, and was seized by that admiration
which repeatedly drew him back to the work during the rest of his
long life; forty years later his enthusiasm was sufficiently well known
for his friends to arrange for a performance of part of it at his own
house, and he was to claim it as the work which 'led me to the most
serious in musical art'. In 1781 it was again given at Weimar, this
time with Herder's own translation of the text, something that he was
uniquely equipped to provide, since his particular interests included
the structure of Hebrew poetry, the relation of words to music in
folk-song, and even that not-so-remote ancestor of *Messiah*, the English
Cecilian ode. He had published, or was to publish in the near future,
on all these subjects, since in Germany at that time there was a general
fascination with the affinities of words and music. He soon extended
the scope of the topic by writing on *Messiah*.

This fuelled interest when, in 1783, *Messiah* was given before the
Crown Prince of Prussia at Potsdam. We know of this from the auto-
biography of Goethe's friend, the composer and teacher Carl Friedrich
Zelter; he had close links with Potsdam through his father, who had
worked on the palace as a stone-mason. Though an ardent musician,
Zelter had followed his father in this trade, and it was on hearing this
Messiah that he realised he must ultimately abandon his craft for music;
he had known the texts from his mother's knee, and found that the

music so perfectly expressed their inner meaning that he could not refrain from expressing his joy in 'loud, indeed in painful exclamations'. He was assumed to be unwell and the Crown Prince sent to ask what the matter was. 'I slipped out ashamed, went through the night on foot to Berlin, and shed tears of emotion on the lonely road.' In due course he was to become Berlin's most influential music teacher; his pupils included Mendelssohn and Meyerbeer. In 1786 he led the violins in an event directly inspired by the Westminster Commemoration and the German translation of Burney: Johann Adam Hiller's performance with 302 performers in the Berlin Domkirche. Hiller was, besides being an extremely effective musical catalyst and organiser, a prolific composer and businesslike writer on music, so that his venture of 19 May was soon written up by his own hand. Berlin could not run to London forces, though it did very well for so much smaller a city, but Hiller took the line that merit was not to be found merely in numbers. What he could offer was 'improvements . . . by the employment of the wind instruments according to the fashion of the present day'. Accordingly he added flutes, trombones, horns, oboes and bassoons, treating them entirely as a composer of the 1780s might have done and not (in the case of horns, oboes and bassoons, which Handel had – though Hiller did not know this – used) as doubling instruments. The translation was into Italian. Hiller repeated his version, with forces larger than he had employed in Berlin, in Breslau. In 1789 he was appointed Kantor of the Thomaskirche in Leipzig and continued to give large-scale performances of *Messiah* there until his death in 1804.

In 1789, at the request of Baron Gottfried van Swieten, Mozart, by all accounts a profound admirer of Handel, also re-orchestrated *Messiah*. In this case the scale of the performance had nothing to do with it, since van Swieten's Sunday concerts in the Hall of the Imperial Library used small forces. It is often said that the object of the re-orchestration was to compensate for the absence of an organ in the hall, but this is not borne out by what Mozart does, which seems more of a translation into terms suggested by the ordinary forces for these concerts; these included flutes, oboes, clarinets, bassoons, horns and trombones. The trumpets were demoted from melodic to harmonic instruments. 'The trumpet shall sound' and 'If God be for us', which van Swieten called the 'cold aria', were rewritten, the latter as a recitative. The Baron was pleased, telling Mozart that

He who can clothe Handel so solemnly and so tastefully that he pleases the modish fop on the one hand and on the other still shows himself in his sublimity, has felt his worth, has understood him, has penetrated to the well spring of his expression, from which he can and will draw confidently.

When Mozart's version was eventually published in 1803 it was further modified and touched up by Hiller. This score soon reached Britain, where it was performed at Covent Garden in 1805, and the United States, where it was used in many of the concerts of selections from *Messiah*; in all cases what were known as 'Mozart's additional accompaniments' bore little resemblance to what he wrote.

Yet despite the intense interest in *Messiah* shown by Goethe and his circle, which included Zelter and the pioneering popular music critic and historian J. F. Rochlitz, Mozart's *Requiem*, Haydn's *Creation* and, of Handel's oratorios, *Israel in Egypt* and *Joshua* enjoyed greater popularity in the German lands. In the United States, as we have seen, it took a remarkably long time for *Messiah* to achieve a complete performance, but it was always the archetypical oratorio. In Germany it was given a complete performance very soon after its introduction, but was soon seen as atypical – which, if Handel's output is taken as a whole, it undeniably is. Moreover, the circumstances that initially favoured it soon disappeared. The great literary, artistic and social movement at the end of the eighteenth century had been the *Sturm und Drang*. This anticipated both romanticism and realism, but it always had the sublime as a vital if necessarily undefinable component. Schiller described this as 'the statutes of pure spirit'; 'the beautiful is valuable only with reference to the *human being*, but the sublime with reference to the *pure daemon*'. The *Sturm und Drang* was marked by its anxiety to preserve a core of religious apprehension while rejecting revealed religion, and by its tendency to relocate revelation, finding it not in scripture but in poetry, of which scripture was simply the highest and most socially important manifestation. But this apprehension could be popularised only to a limited extent (because, popularised, the notion that religion is a metaphor emerges as the message that religion is a confidence trick); and in any case after 1797 the important factor in much of Germany became war and the surge of nationalism in the face of French occupation. Handel's narrative oratorios had an obvious appeal here, and interest in the sublime was largely replaced by an exaltation of nature – hence the popularity of *The Creation*. But *Messiah* was neither neglected nor without its

The interior of St Paul's Chapel, New York, where *Messiah* received its first performance in the city in 1831.

devoted admirers – Beethoven in particular. He used the fuga theme from the Hallelujah chorus in the *Agnus Dei* of the *Missa Solemnis*. And after playing through for the first time Graun's oratorio *Der Tod Jesu*, which was performed annually in Berlin, and not being impressed, he picked up *Messiah*, saying, 'Here's a different fellow.' He regarded Handel as 'the master of us all', with *Messiah* as his greatest work.

The 1784 Commemoration inspired performances in Copenhagen and Stockholm in 1786, and *Messiah* was to enjoy a steady popularity in Denmark. But the picture was very different in the Latin countries. In 1784 Lord Mount-Edgecumbe heard Madame Mara at a *concert spirituel* in Paris: 'Amongst other things, she sung "I know that my Redeemer liveth", which was announced in the bills as being, musique de Handel, paroles du *Milton*. The French had not the taste to like it.' In 1817 Alexandre Choron founded a 'Conservatoire de Musique Classique et Religieuse' to train choristers for Church and opera house and also gave historical concerts. In 1827 he gave Part I of *Messiah*

with Latin words and Mozart's additional accompaniments at
l'Opéra Comique, and this was succeeded by performances of extracts
which were well received. But no French score appeared before 1840
and the first complete performance did not occur until 19 December
1873 when Charles Lamoureux conducted La Société de l'Harmonie
sacrée. This ensured its subsequent popularity, but France was never
without a lobby of anti-Handelian music critics who found in *Messiah*
the easiest substantiation of their charges that Handel was grandiose,
bourgeois and, worst of all, German. They needed only to take their
cue from the sharply expressed views of Berlioz, whose natural antipa-
thy to the contrapuntally portentous was aggravated by what he saw
as the polarity between Handel and his idol, Gluck. Momentarily
suppressing his own scepticism, he maintained that the final 'Amen'
in *Messiah* was a blasphemous appendage and, borrowing a phrase of
Liszt's, derided 'la lourde face emperruqué de ce tonneau de porc et
de bière qu'on appelle Haendel'.

When the musicologist and Nobel prize-winning novelist Romain
Rolland published *La vie de Haendel* in 1906 he deliberately steered
clear of *Messiah* and stressed the smaller-scale works because he was
anxious both to avoid exacerbating existing prejudices and to reveal
a composer more easily assimilated to the classical tradition of French
taste. All this is particularly remarkable because one of the two greatest
Handel scholars of the nineteenth century, Victor Schoelcher (the
other being Friedrich Chrysander) was French, and in 1873 gave to
the Conservatoire the extensive collection of books, scores and manuscripts which he had made during the compilation of his *Haendel et
on temps*, of which the first edition, in English translation, had been
published in 1857. The reason why Schoelcher was able to investigate
his subject in such detail was that Napoleon III had banished him
from France for his extreme republicanism; ironically, much of his
exile was spent amongst the Handel scores in the Royal Music Library,
then still housed (inadequately, he thought) in Buckingham Palace.

Messiah did not reach Italy until 1879, and this was in emulation of
the French experiments. Despite fairly frequent performances since
then, it is reasonable to say that the process of what Lorenzo Bianconi
has called the fetishisation, *la feticizzazione*, of *Messiah* has passed Italy
by; it is probably more popular there in 1992 than it has been at any
time.

In England, the Victorian cult of Handel can only be characterised,
physically as well as morally, as a case of sustained enormity. The

1784 celebrations may have let loose the virus, but when they a
considered in the light of the 1859 First Great Handel Festival in th
Crystal Palace at Sydenham, there is a refreshing innocence abou
them. They seemed to threaten to turn a cathedral into a concert ha
(in the event they did not, to the scarcely concealed surprise of th
sceptics), but at least they did not turn a palace of commerce an
industry into a cathedral. The rot, or so some English Handelians wh
might be taken as reliable witnesses claimed, set in from abroa
but it attacked a vulnerable, because oversize, organism. Mozart
additional accompaniments were introduced at Covent Garden in 18c
and moved *The Sun* and other papers to protest: the original scorin
had 'obtained the sanction of time and of the best musical judge
There is an *integrity* in the productions of this great Master, the resu
of the most powerful talents in his art.' James Bartleman, the intell
gent and gentlemanly bass who was a mainstay of the Three Choi
Festival for a quarter of a century and the great reviver of Purcell
bass parts, refused to sing if the additional accompaniments were
be used. Apart from anything else, they deprived the singer of th
opportunity to decorate cadential points. In 1812 George Smart, f
this reason, and because he felt not all of the additions were 'suitab
to the accustomed *English* ear', omitted some of the additional accom
paniments. This guarded admission that Mozart's improvemen
might not be exactly that provoked an extremely sardonic essay fro
John Carter in *The Gentleman's Magazine*. This was quite unsparing
Smart, a little unfairly since he had already begun to see the error
his ways:

> Since Handel's compositions [Carter wrote] in these *enlightened* time
> are found to be *incorrect* and *puerile*, why condescend to meliorat
> and bestow on them a modern polish? Rather throw his *disorganise*
> masses on the shelf, and let oblivion be their fate, than thus violat
> the memory of an exalted name, whose soul anticipated in his bliss
> ful strains, that eternity of joy, known only in the realms above.

Carter, although he composed music, was an architect by professio
and his other contributions to *The Gentleman's Magazine* are viole
attacks on James Wyatt for his refurbishment of Gothic architectu
– so violent that he has been described as gripped by a 'pathologic
frenzy'. His identity is worth elucidating because he demonstrates th
the modernisation of *Messiah* was indicative of a cast of mind th
extended far beyond musical matters, and that it was perfectly pos

View of the Great Handel Festival at The Crystal Palace, Sydenham, in 1859. The conductor was Sir Michael Costa.

ible, in 1813, to see the absurdity of simultaneously deifying and reconstructing Handel. It had been the fate, as Thomas Campbell pointed
out in 1834, of England's greatest poet: 'Verily, if Shakespeare be the
idol of England, he must be called our molten idol; – we allow him to
be cast into so many shapes, and to be adulterated with such base
alloy.' The comparison was all too apparent to the German literary
and musical scholar, Georg Gottfried Gervinus, who in 1868 published
a study of *Haendel und Shakespeare*. It was a potent eulogy of a surprisingly romantic Handel, but Gervinus was also an impassioned enemy
of the pruning of the composer, of the imposition of increasingly drastic
cuts, that perversely went hand in hand with his 'improvement'.
    The moral enormity of the cult of Handel in Victorian England has
only indirectly to do with the misrepresentation of *Messiah*. There is
nothing wicked about that, provided that what is being done is understood and explained. What was self-deceiving was the elevation of
Handel to divine status, while at the same time accepting all kinds of
drastic modifications of what he wrote. *The Edinburgh Review* in 1857
spoke of *Messiah* as 'a creation of mortal imagining, which has almost
won the reality of an article of belief'; J. Cuthbert Hadden in 1888
considered that 'anything like a criticism of a work so well-known as
the *Messiah* would be both unnecessary and impertinent. Besides we
do not criticise the *Messiah*: a hearing of it is always felt to be something
like an act of worship . . .'; in 1909 R. A. Streatfeild, who as a biographer was concerned to demythologise Handel, claimed, nevertheless,
that 'you can no more call the *Messiah* a work of art than you can call
the *Book of Common Prayer* popular as a masterpiece of literature'. Yet
no one had much hesitation about remaking the image of this idol.
    The difficulty was finding a temple in which to worship it. The last
celebration in Westminster Abbey was in 1834; but this prompted a
question by the Duke of Newcastle in the House of Lords which effectively prevented its further use for secular performances. Though the
Duke's arguments were religious, what really worried him was that
lower prices had begun to attract a different class of person. *Messiah*
was increasingly the property of the artisan and lower middle classes:
city clerks, Lancashire mill-workers, employees of Mr Clay's printing
works at Bungay whose singing so delighted the poet Edward Fitzgerald. When the Crystal Palace was opened on 1 May 1851 the
Queen, performing the ceremony, was greeted by the National
Anthem, in which the onlookers were led by a choir of a thousand
voices and an organ. After the Prince Consort had read the address of

the Commissioners of the Great Exhibition, the Queen had replied, and the Archbishop of Canterbury had said a prayer, the choir and organ 'burst forth once more in the Hallelujah Chorus'. The exhibition over, the Palace could no longer remain in Hyde Park and was rebuilt at Sydenham. The private company which had taken it over at once approached the Sacred Harmonic Society with a view to testing its possibilities as a venue for a centenary celebration of Handel's death. A trial festival was mounted in 1857, and attracted 48,114 listeners to the public rehearsal and three subsequent oratorios, the first of these being *Messiah*. The centenary festival in June 1859 consisted of a rehearsal, *Messiah*, a concert of selections and *Israel in Egypt*. Sir Michael Costa conducted 2765 choral and 460 instrumental performers. There was a total audience of 81,319. The festival became a regular event and finally expired in 1926, after which Paxton's glass masterpiece was abandoned to flower-shows, dog-shows, baby-shows, revivalist meetings and organ recitals, until consumed by fire on 30 November 1936.

Of those festivals *Messiah* had become the lynch-pin, as it had of all the other celebrations of Handel throughout Britain. In 1853 a twenty-two-year-old girl, Elizabeth Sara Sheppard, published a novel, dedicated to Benjamin Disraeli, entitled *Charles Auchester*. Its hero was Mendelssohn, its characters all recognisable figures from the musical world. It had a considerable success, and was eventually reprinted in Everyman's Library. It remains remarkable for its evocations of music and for the social detail which is, in its precision, so totally at odds with the spirit of fervent rapture in which the book is conceived – 'half-crazy', as the music critic Henry Chorley put it. The course of the novel is strange and extravagant, but it starts when the youthful Auchester becomes caught up in the performance of *Messiah* at a music festival in a Midlands town, and the telling thing is the centrality of 'this oratorio . . . the most beloved of any by children and child-like souls', which is treated as universal in its appeal: 'How strangely in it all spirits take a part.' *Charles Auchester* is a flawed novel, but highly unusual in its subject and in the force with which it presents musical experience; it allows one the vicarious thrill of participating in a Victorian *Messiah*, and leaves one wondering about the wavering boundaries of music, eroticism and religion.

Nothing could be further from the raptures of Miss Sheppard than the austere outlook of Samuel Butler, the author of *The Way of All Flesh*. But he was steeped in Handel, to the point that he illustrates

Alps and Sanctuaries, his account of holidays walking in north-western Italy and Switzerland, not only with his own drawings, but with those passages of the Master which spectacles of particular grandeur evoke. Looking over a churchyard near Faido, he sees the purple mountains of Biasca and hears the 'subdued but ceaseless roar of the Ticino', two thousand feet below. Involuntarily he recalls, high on a lonely Swiss hillside on a June evening, bars 123 onwards of 'I know that my Redeemer liveth'. What gives the music particular poignancy, apart from the combination of image, words and music, is the undisclosed fact that in *The Fair Haven* Butler has launched a sardonic attack on the concept of the Resurrection. The music (and it is significant that he does not print the vocal underlay) is all that is left for him. He does not need to preserve the kind of ambiguity that clouds Emerson's account.

The converse of Butler's attitude is to be found in Jane Welsh Carlyle's account of going to *Messiah* at Exeter Hall in 1856 with her friend Geraldine Jewsbury, neither of them believers:

> Singing about Him with *shakes* and white gloves and all that sort of thing, quite shocked my religious feelings, – tho' I have no religion. Geraldine did a lot of *emotional weeping* at my side; and it was all that I could do to keep myself from shaking her and saying, 'Come out of *that.*'

But Mrs Carlyle made no pretensions to having musical feelings either.

It is worth remembering that some of the excitements of the Victorian *Messiah* are unrecapturable. When the great composer of hymn tunes, John Bacchus Dykes, went to the Three Choirs Festival in 1869, his behaviour would not have endeared him to a modern audience:

> Sat next to Hullah, during the whole of the first part. His intelligent remarks on the music much enhanced my pleasure. At the beginning of the second part of 'the Messiah' went round with Randegger into the Lady Chapel; joined there by Oakeley, Cattley, and Madame Patey.
>
> Stood in the Pulpit and heard wonderfully distinctly. At 'Thou shalt dash them', came round, heard the 'Hallelujah' and 'I know that my Redeemer' under the organ; then went to my old place for 'Worthy is the Lamb'.
>
> Stood up with Hullah, exactly in the middle – the best place. Glorious!

The idea of all these distinguished musicians perambulating around blocks of sound is, at least, disconcerting. But in the later nineteenth century we should be prepared for anything with *Messiah*. Its editors, for example, cut it ruthlessly in their efforts to make it a solidly choral affair, a sort of follow-up to *Israel in Egypt*. Nor should it be assumed they did not know what they were doing. Sir George Macfarren, at different times in his life:

1. praised Mozart's additional accompaniments but said that they only worked because he was an original genius and that he should therefore not be imitated;
2. revealed in a discussion at the Royal Musical Association that he fully understood the eighteenth century practice of orchestral doubling;
3. argued against turning secco recitatives into accompanied recitatives;
4. forcefully defended the survival in England of slide trumpets because he believed valves denatured the instrument and destroyed the composer's intentions;
5. produced an edition of *Messiah* which added to the already swollen orchestra a military band.

But what was happening was the manipulation of an icon, attempted from the inside, which is an awkward place from which to manipulate anything successfully. It needed a Dublin man, George Bernard Shaw, to see the situation, in 1891, as it really was:

I have long since recognised the impossibility of obtaining justice for [Messiah] in a Christian country. Import a choir of heathens, restrained by no considerations of propriety from attacking the choruses with unembarrassed sincerity of dramatic expression, and I would hasten to the performance if only to witness the delight of the public and the discomfiture of the critics. That is, if anything so indecent would be allowed here. We have all had our Handelian training in church, and the perfect church-going mood is one of pure abstract relevance. A mood of active intelligence would be scandalous. Thus we get broken in to the custom of singing Handel as if he meant nothing; and as it happens that he meant a good deal, and was tremendously in earnest about it, we know rather less about him than they do in the Andaman Islands, since the Andamans are only unconscious of him, whereas we are

misconscious. . . . . Why, instead of wasting huge sums on the multi-
tudinous dullness of a Handel Festival does not somebody set up a
thoroughly rehearsed and exhaustively studied performance of the
Messiah in St James Hall with a chorus of twenty capable artists?
Most of us would be glad to hear the work seriously performed once
before we die.

10: *Messiah* Restored?

NOTHING, IT MIGHT BE THOUGHT, COULD HAVE BEEN EASIER than to implement the Shavian scheme for the redemption of *Messiah*. As it happened, three years after it was propounded, Dr A. H. Mann put on a performance not far removed from what Shaw had in mind, though Mann needed no prompting from a London music critic, and in important respects he went, and indeed had to go, further than Shaw envisaged. What Shaw did not realise was just how tangled the textual questions were. He was absolutely correct in assuming that his 'favourite oratorio' required to be freed from the elephantine bulk which weighed so heavily on it. But which *Messiah*? The unperformed oratorio of the autograph score? The Dublin *Messiah*? *The Sacred Oratorio* of 1743? The first Foundling Hospital *Messiah*? The Guadagni *Messiah*? For Handel the work had been a living entity, to be adapted, but also to be re-created, as the occasion demanded. His luck in encountering Mrs Cibber involved him in minor changes, his good fortune in the availability of Guadagni in 1750 in greater ones. He conceded a few points – not many, but important – to Jennens; he learned from the reception of the work about other things that needed to be done to it. Shakespeare appears to have treated *Hamlet* in just the same way, but we have neither fair nor foul papers, only the evidence of a bungled editorial resolution and two imperfect witnesses to earlier states. It is a happy situation, absolving us all. But *Messiah* can be reconstituted at most of its successive states. This leaves the performer with what can easily seem a problem.

The difficulty is implicit in the title of the first full score, published by Randall and Abell in 1767. They described it as:

> Messiah / an Oratorio / in Score / As it was Originally Perform'd.
> / Composed by Mr Handel / To which are added /
> His additional Alterations.

This incipiently tautological announcement has aroused indignation in the twentieth century. It is true that it enabled Randall and Abell to use the plates, which had become their property, from John Walsh's *Songs in Messiah*; it is also true that the Appendix, while it claims to contain revised settings, in fact contains some original versions which ante-date those printed in the main text. But it is not a mere 'piece of commercialism'; short of employing a scholarly editor of a type that barely existed in England or anywhere else in Europe at that time, it does almost everything that such a publication could be expected to do. It is an altogether more responsible effort than, in its different field, Mainwaring's *Life*. If Randall and Abell were unsure as to what might have constituted a definitive edition, they were only in the position of modern editors who, however opinionated, cannot do without their appendices of alternative versions.

It is a mistake to underestimate nineteenth-century awareness of the difficulties involved, though it is also fair to say that a sense of them encouraged many musicians to avert their gaze. Much can be learned from an engagingly cranky vocal score (the choruses are set out with the alto part on the top stave) published by James Peck in 1813. A great deal more can be learned from the study of the manuscripts by Sir William Cusins which appeared in 1874. The Sacred Harmonic Society used the new technique of photo-lithography to produce a facsimile in 1868, and Chrysander prepared another in 1892, though this has a number of confusing features. But neither his critical edition, nor its rival by Ebenezer Prout, appeared until 1902. Mann, however, was a scholar with a markedly independent mind. His detailed investigations into eighteenth- and early nineteenth-century music in East Anglia, with particular attention to performances of Handel, are still a mine of unpublished information, and use sources, especially newspapers, the value of which has really only been appreciated (save by Horatio Townsend) in this century. A chorister at Norwich Cathedral, he became organist at King's College, Cambridge; the modern reputation of its choir owes much to his reforms. It was with a performance at King's in mind that he set about making his own performing edition, and as a consequence of this that the Foundling Hospital parts once more saw the light of day. The details are debatable, but what seems to have happened is that Mann, aware of the codicil of the will, made the obvious inquiry, and the organist of the Hospital was suddenly alerted to what he had in his custody. As a result Dr Mann was able to mount a performance which conformed very closely to a possible Handelian model both in scale and in content, and such performances were continued by his successors. The remarkable thing is that, despite their local popularity, they should have had so little national impact.

For an explanation of this we have to look at those social factors

that affected *Messiah* above all other musical works, at least in Britain
and in North America. Even if Shaw's prescription had been applied
in London it is reasonable to doubt whether it would have had a
lasting effect. The position, in outline, is that from about 1900 there
was a considerable reaction against Handel amongst precisely those
educated musicians who might have been capable of improving the
editions and the manner of performance, and that those musicians who
were concerned to defend his reputation ostentatiously disregarded
Messiah. This was partly because they found the popular cult of the
oratorio an embarrassment, and partly because a sound strategy for
the defence of Handel was to concentrate on those extensive tracts in
his works that were totally unfamiliar.

The great antagonist was Ernest Walker, whose combatively and
pungently written *A History of English Music* was published in 1907.
The heart of Walker's contention is that

> Handel himself . . . took originally to oratorio-writing simply as an
> experiment towards recapturing the favour of his patrons among
> the gentry and nobility who had grown tired of Italian opera; but
> the experiment, risky as it was, secured alike the virtual extinction
> of original English music for more than a hundred years, and the
> artistic canonisation of the experimenter.

Messiah was the villain-in-chief because it remained 'a part of the
average Englishman's religion, and he criticises its music no more than
he criticises its words'. Walker did not deny Handel's genius, but he
did all that he could to qualify it: 'no-one, it is true, is always at his
best, but the pity is that Handel is so very often at his worst'. He 'kept
an unnecessarily steady finger on the pulse of his visible public, and,
so far as a man of genius could, wrote for the taste of the moment in
the spirit of the mere impresario'. By and large Walker was no intellectual snob, but his loathing of Handel turned him into one, and, as his
fellow historian of English music, Henry Davey, pointed out, his sneers
at Handel ensured that no foreign musician was likely to take his
praise of English music seriously. They also ensured that no one would
attend to his sensible remarks about performance. Walker was an
influential figure in Oxford until the Second World War; the still more
influential figure at Cambridge was Edward Dent. He was an inspired
recoverer of neglected music, a tireless proponent of new music, an
incisive critic and, simultaneously, a great populariser. It is hard to
think of anyone with comparable attainments who has had so much

faith in the public's capacity to be educated. Yet even he could exhibit impatience with *Messiah*, though in his case this was not because he blamed the cult of Handel for the neglect of English music but because he blamed the cult of *Messiah* for the neglect of Handel. Besides, his labours for the propagation of the best in music did not oblige him to exert himself on behalf of what was already recognised. To this can be added that, being a King's man, he took for granted those advances that had already been made within its walls.

Dent, with the conductor Cyril Rootham and the producer Mrs Camille Prior, was also behind that (in England) predominantly Cambridge phenomenon, the staging of oratorio. Appropriately enough the germ of this seems to have been a comment of John Mainwaring's (a graduate of St John's College), ill-judged even by his standards One undergraduate of King's to be fired with enthusiasm by the experiment was Winton Dean, in due course to become the Bentley of Handelian scholarship. His enormously influential work has done much for the cause of Handel generally, but its benefits for *Messiah* have been incidental, a continuing legacy of the reverse discrimination that has been described.

In Germany and North America, despite Chrysander's advocacy of a *Messiah* with the original forces, or at least proportions, even less was accomplished than in Britain. It is hardly to be expected that in France and Italy, where the oratorio was comparatively new, anything in the way of a revisionist interpretation could be attempted. But a performance in Paris at the Trocadéro on 23 April 1910 deserves mention because it attempted something which was undeniably part of Handel's practice, but does not otherwise seem to have been revived the performance of organ concertos between each part. They were played by Alexandre Guilmant; Vincent d'Indy was one of the timpanists. But a promising annual tradition was broken by the First World War. Later, the advent of the National Socialist Party also disrupted the career of the oratorio in Germany, though *Messiah*, unlike *Judas Maccabaeus*, was never Aryanised.

Intellectuals who were not primarily musicians seem very widely to have shared the same opinions, which was natural enough, but particularly so in this case, when the matter was not primarily aesthetic. Ezra Pound, a fervent admirer of Vivaldi and enthusiast for original performance practices, swallowed whole Walker's view of Handel's effect on native English music and expanded it with the insight that 'Heer Haendel and boiled potatoes' were a by-product of 'the cancer of usury'. A single 'Recit. from the Messiah' could provoke an explosion in 1919. It was:

a bore in the manner long since shelved and parodied in the Oratorio 'Blessed is the man that sitteth . . . etc. . . . . blessed is the man that sitteth . . . etc. . . . on a red hot stove (bis.ter. et quatuor) for he shall RISE again.' This solemn manner is just a musical bluff. Sterne's definition of gravity . . . fits the matter. Gravity is a mysterious carriage of the body to conceal the defects of the mind. Samuel Butler tried to vamp us some interest in Handel's harmony, but it would require a greater genius than Butler to put interest into Handel's melodic faculty.

A comprehensive statement of the position comes from a surprising source, Compton Mackenzie writing in the *Gramophone* in 1934:

It is the early Handel I like best. . . . There is no doubt that he expressed the musical ideals of the English nation in *The Messiah*, and though I wouldn't walk five yards to hear *The Messiah* (indeed, I would walk five miles not to hear it) I recognise the kind of brassy inspiration which it gave to English emotion. It is the kind of music which I feel the butcher Cumberland could enjoy. It is the music of port wine and apoplexy. . . . If Income Tax collectors ever indulge in community singing, I have no doubt that they sing the choruses from *The Messiah*, for *The Messiah* is the first great anthem of man's enslavement by materialism.

It is a pity to have to take the edge off this tirade by reporting that the piece of 'early Handel' which prompted it was the C major sonata for viola da gamba and harpsichord, now attributed to J. M. Leffloth. But it is interesting that Mackenzie, whose musical interests had been latent until awakened by Arnold Dolmetsch, had been listening to a recording of the sonata on original instruments, and reasonable to suppose that he might have had different feelings about *Messiah* had he heard it treated in a similar spirit. When he wrote, the first recording of *Messiah* which came anywhere near to being complete was still two years in the future. This was by the BBC Choir and the London Philharmonic Orchestra under Sir Thomas Beecham, and although the limitations of recording techniques prevented it from being a very large-scale account it is certainly conceived in that tradition.

There have been subtler detractors of *Messiah* than Pound and Mackenzie, and they have wisely not allowed the fact that Handel bought deferred annuities, or indirectly celebrated the battle of Culloden, to colour their criticisms. Their objection, most influentially advanced by Winton Dean, is that 'Handel was not a religious composer (which is not to say he was not a devout man)'. *Messiah*, Dean claims, 'owes its unique reputation, not so much to its musical excellence – Handel wrote half a dozen oratorios as fine or finer – as to the chance that it sums up to perfection and with the greatest eloquence the religious faith, ethical, congregational, and utterly unmystical, of the average Englishman'. For Dean Edward Fitzgerald's remark that Handel was 'a grand old pagan at heart' contains a profound truth. 'Inspired more by ethical humanism than by the doctrine of any church, *Messiah* draws its unity from the fervour of Handel's personal faith', but this faith is not Christianity, in which he 'found little inspiration'; rather it is the pantheism most explicitly realised in *L'Allegro*, which Winton Dean and Professor Wilfrid Mellers are at one in supposing to be the closest that Handel ever came to religious experience. For a real musical adumbration of Christianity, both Dean and Mellers agree, we have to look to the works of J. S. Bach.

A reproach that one might be mistaking false religion for true religion is particularly unnerving; it has about it something of the unanswerable quality of the taunt that one does not know what love is, and is the more effective for being, in the twentieth century, less commonplace. In any case, debating about the meaning of 'religion' in a secular age (at least, a secular age so far as those who can use the word in this way are concerned) is a sterile activity. 'Mystical' is probably more to the point, since there is widespread agreement that mystical experience is an element which is a factor common to a variety of religions. Here the contrast between Bach and Handel becomes more explicable, which it is not when, for example, the charge of being 'congregational' is levelled against Handel: there is nothing as literally congregational in Handel as Bach's use of the chorale, whether the worshippers took part or not. That Bach is more *mysterious* than Handel is undeniable. An everyday instance (though it has a relevance for *Messiah*) is in his treatment of fugue. To simplify drastically: a fugue involves a subject and an answer. In classical practice this answer could be 'real' or it could be 'tonal'. 'Real' answers do not alter the key of the subject; they reply at the fifth above or the fourth below and stay there. 'Tonal' answers modify or 'mutate' the key of the subject. They sound more abstruse, but they make the development of the fugue easier. Bach was the master of the tonal answer, making the most of every possibility mutation offered; Handel surprisingly often contrived to use real answers; they sound straightforward but involve great judgement. So too do Bach's mutated answers, with all that they postulate about what is to come; the difference is that they admit us to complexity in a way that Handel's do not. From a technical point of view both composers had an absolute freedom; Bach could have provided all the real answers in the world, and Handel all the tonal answers; but they had their predilections.

This does not make Handel incapable of conveying the mystic, though to be knowing about this seems presumptuous in all kinds of ways. But if one can accept that some extraordinary experience is conveyed in two works written in Rome during the spring and summer of 1707, the antiphon *Salve Regina* and the motet *Saeviat Tellus* (I am thinking specifically of the section which begins 'O nox dulcis', though this is dependent on its context), then one has at least admitted the possibility that profound religious experience was not unknown to Handel. If these passages come as a surprise, it is largely because of their comparative unfamiliarity. They were written for performance in a confession to which Handel did not adhere, but that is irrelevant; they are both prayers which distil the essence of prayer. *Messiah* has no place for prayer in an invocatory sense; it is a meditation on revelation. Yet this does not mean that 'He was despised' and 'I know that my Redeemer liveth' are not infused with the same spirit. And should the asides of men who we have no reason to suppose are religious weigh more than the words of Dean Edward Ramsay of Edinburgh, who in his *Two Lectures on the Genius of Handel* was prepared to say that to him the words and music of 'He was despised' seemed indissoluble and that 'I suppose I should so connect them were I hearing them on the bed of death'? This was not a statement for a churchman, particularly an easily assailable Anglican, unconsideringly to publish in Edinburgh in 1862.

There is more than a little arrogance in the denial that true religion is to be found in Handel, because it impugns the religious feelings of, at least, the majority of its early admirers. In a sense *Messiah* was, as Dean suggests, 'an entertainment designed to recall the audience to their obligations as members of a Christian Society', but it did not set out to achieve this by being an exercise in dogmatics and dialectic. It carried conviction, and to deny the reality of this is to reveal a prejudice as comprehensive as that of M. S. Briggs, the first Englishman to write a study of baroque architecture, who in it found it necessary to say of his subject that 'There is no humility and no genuine piety in its composition.' The denial of religious feeling to Handel is in large measure an extension of the impulse to belittle *Messiah* for social reasons: that is to say, it is a form of snobbery. However, the objects of snobbish disdain are usually happily oblivious of it, and if the metamorphoses of *Messiah* since 1950 have not been without their more emotional moments, the work itself, or at least the concept of the work itself, has buoyantly weathered the storms.

It must also be admitted that the provocations to, if not a snobbish at least an aloof, attitude were formidable. The most monstrous of these was Newman Flower's *George Frideric Handel: His Personality and Times.* First published in 1923, it had reached a third edition by 1959. It would not have mattered that it was a third-rate costume melodrama but for the fact that it contained some important new information and that, in part because of Flower's position as an influential publisher, it was widely read. Most of the new information derived from Flower's ownership of much of what had been the Earl of Aylesford's collection, which originally derived from Charles Jennens; and Flower refused to allow scholars who had cavilled at his book to use this. All in all Flower's work is thoroughly dislikeable, a classic example of a book which actively underestimated the intelligence of its potential readers. Its tone is such that the few sensible observations it contains, such as those on the proper balance of choral and orchestral forces, are buried in its mawkishly sentimental distortions.

The significant change in attitude was signalled in 1946, when John Tobin was appointed conductor of the London Choral Society. A performance of *Messiah* was mooted, and Tobin was sufficiently dissatisfied with the editions at his disposal to undertake research with the object of making his own. Although he continued to work on *Messiah* for some years afterwards, he was able, on 18 March 1950, to perform his version in St Paul's Cathedral. It was, in his words, 'presented swept free of textual errors, garnished by the conventions of eighteenth-century performance, and in the chamber music style which was an essential part of Handel's conception of the work'. Reviewing it, Robert Donnington wrote that:

> *Messiah* has been cleaned like the pictures in the National Gallery and with equally startling results. Shorn of subsequent accretions, and still better of the overgrown choir and orchestra which usually stifles it, given a certain amount of free ornamental embellishment

in the 18th century tradition, it glows in fresh colours and moves us anew. Tobin is not a substantial enough conductor in either technique or inspiration to achieve impressive results; moreover the free ornamentation sounded rather artificial plastered on a general style of playing not in the least Handelian but nondescript modern, while the smaller but more important bread and butter ornaments remained largely incorrect. But which of the great conductors has ever attempted so salutary a reform?

Certainly not Malcolm Sargent, who recorded the oratorio with the Huddersfield Choral Society and the Liverpool Philharmonic Orchestra in 1946, nor Beecham, who finally managed the complete work in 1947. Beecham's 1947 recording was the first to be transferred on to long-playing records. Of course the record-player won new audiences for this type of performance just as, on the concert platform, it had begun to be undermined. It has to be said that, in his greatest moments, Beecham makes the size of his forces seem irrelevant, but also that this is a matter of moments. It has also to be ruefully acknowledged that Eugene Goossens reorchestrated Beecham's last *Messiah*. To contrast the report of the St Paul's concert (amply substantiated by what Tobin was doing fifteen years later) with Beecham's recording is to encounter the problem that dogged *Messiah* for many years afterwards; valuable experiments were being made, directed towards a more convincingly 'Handelian' performance, and much first-rate musical talent was expended in performances of a more traditional kind, but there seemed no sustainable point of contact. At that time the tensions between exponents of 'early music' and of performers on the routine professional circuits, still present today, were strong, particularly because the musicianship of some of the newcomers left a good deal to be desired. Even those at whom this charge could not be levelled suffered; it was at a performance of *Messiah* that the counter-tenor Alfred Deller heard the leader of the orchestra remark, to an eminent conductor, 'I see we have the bearded lady with us tonight', and it was Dame Joan Sutherland's addition of extravagant coloratura embellishments that prompted another conductor to refer to her 'mad scenes in *Messiah*'.

John Tobin had the right personality to create enthusiasm for his ideas and to make his performers willing co-experimenters; he also attracted a loyal audience. His full score in the Hallé Handel Edition was published in 1965 and the vocal score in 1967. The forces he

LONDON CHORAL SOCIETY

PAULINE BROCKLESS

NANCY EVANS   GRAYSTON BURGESS

RICHARD LEWIS   JOHN HOLMES

HANDEL'S

MESSIAH

in its entirety with the original accompaniments

THURSTON DART   JOHN DYKES BOWER
(Harpsichord Continuo)   (Organ Continuo)

A Section of the

LONDON PHILHARMONIC ORCHESTRA

Leader Henry Datyner

Conductor

JOHN TOBIN

SATURDAY 15 MARCH 1958 AT 6PM

ROYAL FESTIVAL HALL

General Manager T. E. Bean

Edited by JOHN TOBIN

The Airs, Choruses and Orchestral Music
edited afresh from Handel's Manuscripts
in a desire to recapture the colour and
style of the early performances under
Handel's own direction

TICKETS :

12 6,   10 -,   7 6,   5 -

Available from 15 February

ROYAL FESTIVAL HALL BOX OFFICE
(WAT 3191) and usual Agents

Members of the LONDON CHORAL
SOCIETY may obtain tickets immediately
from the Hon. Secretary,
to whom applications for vocal and
associate membership should be addressed

Poster for *Messiah* in the Festival Hall, 1958, conducted by John Tobin.

customarily used in his performances were probably slightly larger than those employed by Handel in 1749, which seems to have been the year in which they were at their most numerous, and Tobin's balance favoured the choir where Handel's favoured the orchestra. It is hard to see how this could have been avoided; in provincial musical societies, where the choir was an integral part of a local community, to prune it to Foundling Hospital dimensions would have been (and often still is) both impractical and unnatural. A certain wryness can be discerned in the programme note which Basil Lam, the distinguished radio producer and himself the editor of a fairly radical performing edition, wrote for a broadcast in 1975:

> Tolstoy said that Art should bring about an end to violence by conveying the spirit of peace and fraternal love to all members of the community. . . . He seems not to have known what is, perhaps, the only great work able to meet his demand. . . . Messiah stands alone for sublimity of theme and perfection of design. These qualities, instinctively recognised by those who would find them impossible to design, have given it a central place in the English choral tradition, itself happily untouched by social change.

A corollary of this is that tampering with *Messiah* is a form of social experiment that like most forms of social experiment, involves unpredictable risks and stirs unguessed-at passions. Childhood memories, religious and national certainties are at stake. Professor Nicholas Temperley, who is happy to accept *Messiah* as an accretive phenomenon, has, without a trace of irony, compared it to the *Odyssey*, a medieval cathedral, or, indeed, the British Empire, and does not hesitate to say that 'the greatness of *The Messiah* in the 19th century far transcends even that of Handel's score' and sees 'no reason in principle why greatness should not be the work of many hands'. The last point, of course, is incontestable.

1957 saw the publication of a work of fundamental importance to the study of *Messiah*, Professor Jens Peter Larsen's *Handel's Messiah: origins, composition, sources*. This had had its origins in a series of lectures given in the University of Copenhagen to mark the two-hundredth anniversary of the first performance. It subjected the sources to a far more detailed and scientific scrutiny than that of Tobin, although it did not seriously upset his findings. It did, however, introduce a new scale of precision, and explained logically much that Tobin had deduced from rather shaky reasoning. In 1959 Dr Harold Watkins Shaw produced a performing edition based on many years of research and covering much of the same ground, but with a more practical emphasis. His *Textual and Historical Companion to Handel's Messiah* (and to the making of his edition) appeared in 1965.

Almost simultaneously the shape of Handelian scholarship in general had been transformed by the appearance of O. E. Deutsch's *Documentary Biography* in 1955, of Winton Dean's *Handel's Dramatic Oratorios and Masques* in 1959, and William C. Smith's *Descriptive Catalogue of the Early Editions* in 1960. No amount of quarrelling with one particular tendency of Dean's book can diminish its importance as a source of information and incisive commentary on its subject, and on much else besides. Deutsch and Smith are quiet miracles of erudition. Without the information provided by the historical record, above all of who sang in a given work at a particular time and place, the evidence of the manuscripts would often be quite meaningless. For those who prefer, in constructing a *Messiah*, to perform from the available historical options, the information is essential. For those who simply want to establish a frame of mind in which to approach the oratorio it is equally important.

Putting on *Messiah* in the 1990s is not an easy task for absolutists.

Not only has the effect of scholarship been to multiply the number of possible *Messiahs* textually, but it has also complicated rather than simplified the questions that condition its actual manner of performance. It is, as ever, necessary to hang on to Hans Keller's answer to the question: 'What is the proper finale for Beethoven's Op. 130?' – 'As if there were only one performance, in which case the question would make sense.'

The question of editions still remains a problem. Of the two best, those of Shaw and Burrows, only the vocal scores are readily available. Shaw's suffers from having editorial embellishments fully written out on the stave, a procedure which has psychological consequences for singers, since it becomes very difficult, even with specialist knowledge, to treat these intrusions properly as ornaments, and the whole point of the convention of ornamentation is lost. Burrows's vocal score is blameless in this respect, and invaluable for its appendix of variants and of specimens of cadenzas and contemporary ornamented versions, but the publishers have skimped by retaining a keyboard accompaniment which dates from 1939 and is not always idiomatic; nor is there any figuring for the recitatives and the numbers with solo obbligati. For a study score the miniature version of Tobin's edition remains serviceable from a scholarly point of view and is unusually well printed and laid-out. Despite these snags anyone who wants to satisfy themselves as to what Handel actually wrote will be far better served than they would have been in 1958.

In the meantime virtually every aspect of baroque music has been challenged: instruments and their construction, pitch, intonation, rhythmic alteration, ornamentation, continuo realisation. 'Authenticity' itself, that banner beneath which so many bright-eyed zealots marched out in the late 1960s and 1970s (in a long tradition, it is true, but it was convenient to forget this), has been called in question. Innocents who merely thought they were trying to decorate a vocal line or play an oboe as these things would have been done in Handel's time now find themselves tangled in the net of intentionalism and speared by the trident of tradition, anxiety and the musical scene.

Sceptical musicologists (some of whom may never, in any case, have been much interested in how music actually sounds), conventional performers, part of whose repertoire has been cut out by the light cavalry of the early music movement, and the kind of conservative thinkers whose ultimate stimulus is nursery food have made common cause against these incursions. They have done so rather late in the

Saturday 25 June at 2.00 p.m.

CHURCH OF
SS. GREGORY AND MARTIN,
WYE

HANDEL'S MESSIAH

Michael Deason Barrow	Treble
Sally le Sage	Soprano
Alfred Deller	Counter Tenor
Mark Deller	Counter Tenor
Max Worthley	Tenor
Maurice Bevan	Baritone
Harry Gabb	Organ

CONCENTUS MUSICUS from Vienna
The Festival Choir
Conductor Alfred Deller

Drawings by John Ward, RA, to accompany the performance of *Messiah* given as part of the Stour Music Festival on 25 June 1966 at Wye, Kent. Alfred Deller conducted Concentus Musicus in what was the first performance in Britain using original instruments.

day. The consequences of the movement for *Messiah* have already been profound and irreversible.

Just when, from a social and religious point of view, *Messiah* might have been thought a dinosaur, ripe for extinction or neglect, or at least for the derision of an irreverent and satirical age, it became the work which, because it was the most familiar, could be the most drastically remodelled by the almost exclusively youthful singers and players who had taken up the cause of authenticity. Consequently it received a major infusion of new blood which was also a salutary shock to the system. It is understandable that Liszt disliked *Messiah*, though it is surprising to discover how often he had to conduct it; and this was to be equally true of many conductors of conventional symphony orchestras in the three decades after 1950. But the effect of the change in musical climate was to make them far less willing to undertake it as a routine chore, and at last they had a reason for not doing so.

It had an equally drastic effect on singers. Dame Joan Sutherland, demure and ornament-free under Sir Adrian Boult, was – as we have seen – transformed under Richard Bonynge, even if she was closer to the nineteenth-century Mara or Catalani than to Frasi. And Hell hath no fury like a contralto discarded in favour of a counter-tenor, unless it is a conventionally trained soprano rejected in favour of one noted for her vibratoless 'white' tone; but when blood pressure has returned to normal the point tends to sink in. Alfred Deller, gifted with a counter-tenor voice for which he worked to find a context, and thus one of the elder brethren of the movement, had never heard a clarino trumpet until he gave *Messiah* with Concentus Musicus in 1966. In an interview he recalled the consequences for the interpretation he directed. 'This is what Handel meant! "The trumpet shall sound" – not the martial sound of the military trumpet, on a human level of calling the forces together, but as a heavenly trumpet from afar, the still, small trumpet in the ear.' Historically this is not quite right (an eighteenth-century military trumpet would have sounded comparatively dulcet) but in metaphoric terms could not be better as an illustration of the new world of sound that even seasoned explorers were entering. John Eliot Gardiner, a late convert to early instruments, has described how: 'The light yet penetrating sonority of baroque instruments, when played idiomatically, allows phrase lengths to emerge as clauses, with appropriate "commas", forming intelligible sentences, as opposed to the smoothed-out legato of their modern counterparts'. But the modern counterparts are not incapable of learn-

ing, as indeed players for Gardiner were demonstrating before he
seceded to the cause.

The happy result of all this has been that much of the old solemnity
that enshrouded *Messiah* has been dispersed. A consequence of the
impulse to translate scholarly findings into practice has been the discovery that the small numbers involved cost less to record. Beyond
this, smaller forces and lower costs mean more competition. The result
is a multiplication of recorded *Messiahs*. Even for those who have
restricted access to them, or prefer any *Messiah* live to a *Messiah* on
disc, they are powerful indirect influences. There are still lost opportu-
nities; so far only Christopher Hogwood has troubled scrupulously to
recreate one specific performance – that at the Foundling Hospital
in 1754. I have yet to hear 'The trumpet shall sound' with a quaver
on the second half of the second beat given its full value; to clip it
is, I suspect, a pseudo-archaism, of a 'Ye Olde Tea-Shoppe' kind. But
I do not anticipate general agreement with this, nor with the proposition (clear enough to my ears) that Nikolaus Harnoncourt offers the
most romantic interpretation available on whatever kind of instruments. This kind of speculation and provocation is only possible
because *Messiah* does not merely survive: it thrives. It seems to me, at
best, to do so in a form and spirit that would have gratified those three
passionate early enthusiasts, Edward Synge, Patrick Delany and Mrs
Pendarves.

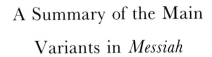

A Summary of the Main
Variants in *Messiah*

(This is intended merely as an outline map of a confusing subject. Minor changes are not noted, nor straightforward transpositions. 'Dublin' signifies Dublin, 1742; 'London' signifies one of the London performances in 1743 and does not attempt to discriminate between them; 'Guadagni' signifies an alto aria composed or recomposed in 1750. No additional number in later versions of *Messiah*, except for recitatives and the aria version of 'And lo, the angel of the Lord', is made up of wholly new material.)

But who may abide: bass aria, MS; bass secco recitative, Dublin; aria, Guadagni; soprano aria, 1754.

Pifa: 11 bars, MS; extended for Dublin; shortened version of Dublin thereafter.

And lo, the angel of the Lord: soprano accompanied recitative, MS; as MS, Dublin; soprano arioso beginning 'But lo', London; Handel reverts to original ?1745.

Rejoice greatly: soprano da capo aria, MS; emended, Dublin; repeated London; further emended version in 4/4 rather than 12/8 thereafter.

He shall feed His flock: alto aria, MS; revised for Dublin; alto and soprano duet London.

Thou art gone up on high: bass aria, MS; as MS, Dublin; revised for soprano, London; Guadagni; further soprano version, 1754.

How beautiful are the feet: soprano aria MS; two sopranos and chorus, Dublin; soprano aria MS shortened for London; Guadagni.

Their sound is gone out: originally middle section of *How beautiful*; omitted Dublin; independent tenor arioso, London; chorus thereafter.

Why do the nations: bass aria, MS; emended and shortened, Dublin; as emended thereafter.

Thou shalt break them: tenor aria, MS; bass recitative Dublin and London; original subsequently restored.

If God be for us: soprano aria, MS; Guadagni.

Bibliography

This is not a comprehensive bibliography of *Messiah*, but a list of works directly drawn on in the text.

ABBREVIATIONS

ML   *Music and Letters*
PRMA   *Proceedings of the Royal Musical Association*
The place of publication is London unless otherwise indicated.

Abraham, Gerald, ed. *Handel: a Symposium.* 1954
Arnold, Denis. 'Charity Music in Eighteenth-Century Dublin'. *Galpin Society Journal*, xxi (1968), 162
Arnold, Denis and Elsie. *The Oratorio in Venice.* 1957
Arundell, Dennis. *The Critic at the Opera.* 1957
Avison, Charles. *An Essay on Musical Expression, with Alterations and large Additions*, 3rd edn. 1775
Bairstow, E. C. *Handel's Oratorio 'The Messiah'.* Oxford, 1928
Banister, Henry C. *George Alexander Macfarren: his Life, Works and Influence* 1891
Bayly, Anselm. *The Alliance of Musick, Poetry and Oratory.* 1789
Beckett, R. B. *Hogarth.* 1949
Black, Cecilia. *The Linleys of Bath.* 2nd edn, 1926
Boswell, James. *Life of Johnson*, ed. G. Birkbeck Hill. 6 vols. 1887
Boydell, Brian. *A Dublin Musical Calendar 1700–1760.* Blackrock, 1988
Breffny, Brian de and Ffolliott, Rosemary. *Houses of Ireland.* 1975
Brown, John. *A Dissertation on the Rise, Union, Power, the Progressions, Separations, and Corruptions of Poetry and Music.* 1763
Brownlow, John. *The History and Design of the Foundling Hospital.* 1858
Buelow, George J. and Marx, H. J., eds. *New Mattheson Studies.* Cambridge 1983
Burney, Charles. *An Account of the Musical Performances in Westminster Abbey and the Pantheon in Commemoration of Handel.* 1785
   A General History of Music. 4 vols. 1776–89
   Memoirs, ed. S. Klima, G. Bowers and K. S. Grant. 1988
Burrows, Donald. 'Handel's Performances of *Messiah*: the evidence of the conducting score'. ML, lvi (1975), 319
   'Handel and the Foundling Hospital'. ML, lviii (1977), 269

'Sources for Oxford Handel Performances in the First Half of the Eighteenth Century'. ML, lxi (1980), 177

'The Autographs and Early Copies of Messiah: Some Further Thoughts'. ML, lxvi (1985), 201

Butler, Charles. Reminiscences. 2 vols. 1824

Butler, Samuel. Alps & Sanctuaries of Piedmont and the Canton Ticino (1881). 1913

Byrom, John. The Private Journal and Literary Remains, ed. A. W. Ward. 4 vols. Manchester, 1894–95

Campbell, Thomas. The Life of Mrs. Siddons. 2 vols. 1835

Cannon, Beekman C. Johann Mattheson: Spectator in Music. New Haven, 1947

Carey, Henry. The Poems, ed. F. T. Wood. 1830

Carter, John). 'Thoughts on the Music of Handel'. Gentleman's Magazine, lxxxiii (1813), 220

Chrysander, Friedrich. G. F. Händel. 3 vols. Leipzig, 1858–67

Clifford, James L. Hester Lynch Piozzi. Oxford, 1942

Cowper, William. The Poems, ed. H. S. Milford. 4th edn. 1934

Coxe, W.). Anecdotes of George Frederick Handel and John Christopher Smith. 1799

Craig, Maurice. Dublin 1660–1860. Dublin (1952), 1980

Crowdy, John. A Short Commentary . . . on 'The Messiah'. 1875

Cudworth, Charles. 'Mythistorica Handeliana'. Festskrift Jens Peter Larsen. Copenhagen, 1972, 161

Cullen, L. M. The Emergence of Modern Ireland 1600–1900. 1981

Culwick, J. C. Handel's Messiah: the discovery of the original wordbook . . . with some notes. Dublin, 1893

Cusins, W. G. Handel's Messiah: an examination of the original and of some contemporary MSS. 1874

Davey, Henry. History of English Music. 2nd edn. 1921

Dean, Winton. Handel's Dramatic Oratorios and Masques. 1959

'Charles Jennens's Marginalia to Mainwaring's Life of Handel'. ML, lv (1972), 160

Dean, Winton and Knapp, J. Merrill. Handel's Operas 1704–26. Oxford, 1987

Delany, Mary. Autobiography and Correspondence of Mary Granville, Mrs. Delany, ed. Lady Llanover. 6 vols. 1861–62

Dent, Edward J. Handel. 1934

'English Influences on Handel'. Monthly Musical Record, lxi (1931), 225

Deutsch, Otto Erich. Handel: a Documentary Biography. 1955

Mozart: a Documentary Biography (1965). 1966

Devonshire, The Duchess of. The House: A Portrait of Chatsworth. 1982

Dibdin, Charles. The Professional Life of Mr. Dibdin. 4 vols. 1803

Dorris, George E. *Paolo Rolli and the Italian Circle in London*. The Hague 1967

East, John. *Christmas Eve: A Dream, or, a Review of the Oratorio of 'The Messiah'*. 1836

Emerson, R. W. *Works*. 5 vols. 1906

Fiske, Roger. *English Theatre Music in the Eighteenth Century*. 1973

Fitzgerald, Percy. *The Life of Mrs. Catherine Clive . . . together with her Correspondence*. 1888

Fleischmann, Aloys (ed.). *Music in Ireland*. Cork, 1951

Flower, Newman. *George Frideric Handel: His Personality and His Times*. 192

Fothergill, Brian. *The Mitred Earl: an Eighteenth-Century Eccentric*. 1974

Fowler, J. T. *Life and Letters of John Bacchus Dykes*. 1897

Fraser, A. C. *Life and Letters of Bishop Berkeley*. 4 vols. 1871

Friedman, Terry. *James Gibbs*. 1984

Fuller-Maitland, J. A. and Mann, A. H. *Catalogue of the Music in the Fitzwilliam Museum*. 1893

Gervinus, G. G. *Händel und Shakespeare: zur Ästhetik der Tonkunst*. Leipzig 1868

Gilbert, J. T. *A History of the City of Dublin*. 3 vols. Dublin, 1854–59

Girdlestone, Cuthbert. *Jean-Philippe Rameau: his Life and Work*. New York (1957), 1969

Goldsmith, Oliver. *The Present State of Polite Learning*. 1759

Grassineau, James. *A Musical Dictionary*. 1740

Gray, Thomas. *Correspondence*, ed. Paget Toynbee and L. Whibley. 3 vols. Oxford, 1935

Guinness, Desmond. *Georgian Dublin*. 1979

Hamilton, Phyllis. 'Handel in the papers of the Edinburgh Musical Society (1728–1798). *Brio*, i (1964), 19

Hanbury, William. *The History of the Rise and Progress of the Charitable Foundations at Church-Langton*. 1767

Hanslick, Eduard. *Hanslick's Musical Criticisms*, trans. and ed. Henry Pleasants. New York, 1988

Hardwick, Michael and Mollie. *Alfred Deller: A Singularity of Voice*. 1968

Harrison, Frank Ll. 'Music, Poetry and Polity in the Age of Swift' *Eighteenth-Century Ireland*, i (1986), 56

Haweis, H. R. *Music and Morals*. 16th edn. 1892

Hawkins, John. *An Account of the Institution and Progress of the Academy of Ancient Music*. 1770

A General History of the Science and Practice of Music. 5 vols. 1776

(Hayes, William). *Remarks on Mr. Avison's Essay on Musical Expression*. 175

Hayes, William. *Anecdotes of the Five Music Meetings at Church Langton*. Oxford, 1768

Heartz, Daniel. 'From Garrick to Gluck: the Reform of Theatre and Opera in the mid-Eighteenth Century'. *PRMA*, xciv (1967–8), 111

Hemlow, Joyce. *History of Fanny Burney*. Oxford, 1958

Herder, J. G. *Sämtliche Werke*, ed. B. Suphan. 33 vols. Berlin, 1877–1913

Heriot, Angus. *The Castrati in Opera*. 1956

Hervey, Lord John. *Memoirs*, ed. Romney Sedgwick. 1952

Hobhouse, Christopher. *1851 and the Crystal Palace*, rev. edn. 1950

Hogwood, Christopher and Luckett, Richard (eds.). *Music in Eighteenth-Century England*. Cambridge, 1983

Husk, W. H. *An Account of the Musical Celebrations of St. Cecilia's Day*. 1857

Hutchings, A. J. B. *The Baroque Concerto*. 2nd edn. 1963

Ilchester, The Earl of (ed.). *Lord Hervey and his Friends* (1726–38). 1950

Jacobi, Peter. *The Messiah Book: the Life and Times of G. F. Handel's Greatest Hit*. New York, 1983

Johnson, David. *Music and Society in Lowland Scotland in the Eighteenth Century*. 1972

Johnson, Samuel. *Lives of the Poets*, ed. G. Birkbeck Hill. 3 vols. 1905

Keates, Jonathan. *Handel: the Man and his Music*. 1985

Keller, Hans. *Criticism*, ed. Julian Hogg. 1987

Kelly, Michael. *Reminiscences*. 2 vols. 1826

Kerslake, John. 'The Likeness of Handel' in *Handel and the Fitzwilliam*. Cambridge, 1974

Kivy, Peter. 'Mainwaring's *Handel*: its relation to English aesthetics', *Journal of the American Musicological Society*, xvii (1964), 170

Landon, H. C. Robbins. *Haydn in England 1791–1795*. 1976

Lang, Paul Henry. *George Frideric Handel*. New York, 1966

Larsen, Jens Peter. *Handel's Messiah: origins, composition, sources*. 1957

Le Huray, Peter and Day, James. *Music and Aesthetics in the Eighteenth and Early-Nineteenth Centuries*. Cambridge, 1981

Little, Bryan. *The Life and Work of James Gibbs*. 1955

Lockman, John. *Rosalinda, a Musical Drama . . . to which is prefixed, an enquiry into the rise and progress of operas and oratorios . . .* 1740

Lonsdale, Roger. *Dr. Charles Burney: a literary biography*. 1965

Lysons, Daniel. *History of the Origin and Progress of the Meeting of the Three Choirs of Gloucester, Worcester, and Hereford*. Gloucester, 1812

Mackenzie, Compton. *My Record of Music*. 1955

(Mainwaring, John). *Memoirs of the Life of the Late George Frederick Handel*. 1760

Memorie, ed. Lorenzo Bianconi. Torino, 1985

Mason, William. *Essays, Historical and Critical, of English Church Music*. 1782

Maxwell, Constantia. *Country and Town Life in Ireland under the Georges*. Dundalk, 1949

Dublin under the Georges 1714–1830. rev. edn. 1956

Mee, J. H. *The Oldest Music Room in Europe*. 1911

Mellers, Wilfrid. *Harmonious Meeting: a Study of Music, Poetry and Drama in England 1600–1900*. 1965

Montagu, Lady Mary Wortley. *The Complete Letters*, ed. Robert Halsband. 3 vols. Oxford, 1965–7

Moody, T. W. and Vaughan, W. E., (ed.). *A New History of Ireland*. Vol. IV. Oxford, 1986

(Mount-Edgecumbe, Lord Richard). *Musical Reminiscences of an Old Amateur*. 2nd edn. 1827

Myers, Robert Manson. *Handel's Messiah, a Touchstone of Taste*. New York, 1948

Handel, Dryden and Milton. 1956

Nalbach, Daniel. *The King's Theatre 1794–1867*. 1972

Nash, Mary. *The Provoked Wife: the Life and Times of Susannah Cibber*. 1977

Newton, John. *Messiah: Fifty Expository Discourses* . . . 1786

Paulson, Ronald. *Hogarth's Graphic Works*. 2 vols. 1965

Pelikan, Jaroslav. *Bach among the Theologians*. Philadelphia, 1986

Petzoldt, Richard. *Georg Friedrich Händel: sein Leben in Bildern*. Leipzig, 1955

Georg Philipp Telemann, trans. Horace Fitzpatrick. 1974

Piggott, Patrick. *The Innocent Diversion: Music in the Life and Writings of Jane Austen*. 1979

Pilkington, Letitia. *Memoirs* . . . *1712–1750 written by Herself*. 1928

Piozzi, Hesther Lynch. *Anecdotes of Samuel Johnson*, ed. S. C. Roberts. Cambridge, 1932

Pool, Robert and Cash, John. *Views of the most remarkable Public Buildings* . . . *in the City of Dublin*. Dublin, 1780

Pope, Alexander. *The Poems*, ed. John Butt. 1963

Pound, Ezra. *Ezra Pound and Music: the Complete Criticism*, ed. R. Murray Schafer. 1978

Prout, Ebenezer. 'Handel's *Messiah*: Preface to the New Edition'. *Musical Times*, xliii (1902), 311 *et seq*.

Ramsay, E. B. *Two Lectures on the Genius of Handel*. 1862

Ring, John. *The Commemoration of Handel: A Poem*. 1786

Robinson, Percy. *Handel and his Orbit*. 1908

Rochlitz, J. F. *Für Freunde der Tonkunst*. Leipzig, 1824

Rockstro, W. S. *The Life of George Frederick Handel*. 1883

Rolland, Romain. *Haendel*. Paris, 1906

Sadie, Stanley. *Handel*. 1962

Sadie, Stanley and Hicks, Anthony (eds.). *Handel Tercentenary Collection*. 1987

Samuel, Harold E. 'John Sigismund Cousser in London and Dublin'. ML, lxi (1980), 158

Sands, Mollie. *Invitation to Ranelagh 1742–1803*. 1946

Schering, Arnold. 'Händel und der protestantische Choral'. *Händel-Jahrbuch I*. Leipzig, 1928, 27

Schoelcher, Victor. *The Life of Handel*. 1857
Scholes, Percy A. *The Great Dr. Burney*. 2 vols. 1948
Shaw, George Bernard. *Music in London 1890–1894*. 3 vols. 1932
Shaw, H. Watkins. *The Story of Handel's Messiah 1741–1784*. 1963
A *Textual and Historical Companion to Handel's 'Messiah'* (1965). 1982
Shenstone, William. *The Works*. 4th edn. 3 vols. 1773
Sheppard, Elizabeth Sara. *Charles Auchester: A Memorial*, introd. Jessie A. Middleton. 1911
Smith, Ruth. 'The Achievements of Charles Jennens, 1700–1773'. ML, lxx (1989), 161
Smith, W. C. 'George III, Handel and Mainwaring'. *Musical Times*, lxv (1924), 789
Concerning Handel, his Life and Work. 1948
A *Handelian's Notebook*. 1965
Handel; a Descriptive Catalogue of the Early Editions. 2nd edn. Oxford, 1970
Smither, Howard E. *A History of the Oratorio*. 3 vols. 1977–87
'Oratorio and Sacred Opera, 1700–1825: Terminology and Genre Distinction'. PRMA, cvi (1979–80), 88
'*Messiah* and Progress in Victorian England'. *Early Music*, xii (1985), 339
Sonneck, Oscar G. T. *Early Concert-Life in America*. Leipzig, 1907
Steglich, Rudolf. 'Betrachtung des Händelschen Messias'. *Händel-Jahrbuch*. IV. Leipzig, 1931, 15
(Stendhal). *The Lives of Haydn and Mozart, with Observations on Metastasio*. 2nd edn. London, 1818
Stendhal. *Life of Rossini*, trans. Richard N. Coe. 1956
Sternfeld, F. W. *Goethe and Music*. New York, 1954
Stockholme, Johanne M. *Garrick's Folly*. 1664
Stockwell, La Tourette. *Dublin Theatres and Theatre Customs*. Kingsport, 1938
Swanston, Hamish. *Handel* (Outstanding Christian Thinkers). 1990
Swift, Jonathan. *Poems*, ed. H. Williams. 3 vols. Oxford, 1937
Prose Writings, ed. H. Davis. 14 vols. Oxford, 1939–69
Talbot, Michael. *Vivaldi*. 1978
'Jennens and Vivaldi'. *Vivaldi Veneziano Europeo*. Firenze, 1980, 73
Taylor, Sedley. *The indebtedness of Handel to Works by other Composers*. Cambridge, 1906
Temperley, Nicholas. 'The Limits of Authenticity: a discussion'. *Early Music*, xii (1984), 16
Terry, C. S. *John Christian Bach*. 2nd edn, rev. H. C. R. Landon. 1967
Thompson, Francis. *A History of Chatsworth*. 1949
Tickell, R. E. *Thomas Tickell and the Eighteenth Century Poets*. 1931
Tobin, John. *Handel's Messiah; A Critical Account of the Manuscript Sources and Printed Editions*. 1969

Townsend, Horatio. *An Account of the Visit of Handel to Dublin.* Dublin, 1852
(—) *The Tryall of a Cause for Criminal Conversation, between Theophilus Cibber,
    Gent., Plaintiff, and William Sloper, Esq., Defendant.* 1739
Turnor, Reginald. *James Wyatt 1746–1813.* 1950
Walker, Ernest. *A History of Music in England.* 1907
Walpole, Horace. *Letters,* ed. Mrs. Paget Toynbee. 16 vols. Oxford,
    1903–5
Walsh, T. J. *Opera in Dublin 1705–1797.* Dublin, 1973
Weber, William. 'Intellectual Bases of the Handelian Tradition, 1759–
    1800'. PRMA, cviii (1981–2), 100
White, Eric Walter. *A History of English Opera.* 1983
White, Harry. 'Handel in Dublin: a note'. *Eighteenth-century Ireland.* ii
    (1987), 182
Wilkinson, Tate. *Memoirs.* 4 vols. York, 1790
Young, Percy. *Handel.* 3rd edn. 1975
Zelter, Carl Friedrich. *Darstellungen seines Lebens,* ed. J.-W. Schottländer.
    Weimar, 1931

GENERAL WORKS OF REFERENCE

The Dictionary of National Biography, ed. Sir Sidney Lee
The New Grove Dictionary of Music and Musicians, ed. Stanley Sadie
*Händel-Handbuch, herausgegeben vom Kuratorium der Georg-Friedrich-Händel-
    Stiftung von Dr. Walter Eisen und Dr. Margaret Eisen.* 4 vols. Leipzig,
    1978–86

EDITIONS

Full scores:
Friedrich Chrysander and Max Seiffert (eds). *Händelgesellschaft.* Vol. 45.
    Berlin, 1902
John Tobin (ed.). *Hallischen Händel-Ausgabe* (Bärenreiter). Kassel, 1981

Vocal scores:
Watkins Shaw (ed.) (Novello). 1959
Donald Burrows (ed.) (Peters). Frankfurt, 1987

FACSIMILES

The autograph has been published in facsimile by the Sacred Harmonic
Society (London, 1868) and the Händelgesellschaft (Hamburg, 1892;
reprinted New York, 1969); the conducting (Tenbury) score has been
published by the Royal Musical Association (London, 1974).

Index

Page numbers in italic type refer to illustrations.